W9-CHZ-115

STATES OF NEGLECT

*How Red-State Leaders Have Failed Their
Citizens and Undermined America*

* * * *

WILLIAM KLEINKNECHT

THE
NEW
PRESS

NEW YORK
LONDON

© 2023 by William Kleinknecht
All rights reserved.
No part of this book may be reproduced, in any form, without written permission from the publisher.

Requests for permission to reproduce selections from this book should be made through our
website: https://thenewpress.com/contact.

Published in the United States by The New Press, New York, 2023
Distributed by Two Rivers Distribution

ISBN 978-1-62097-641-8 (hc)
ISBN 978-1-62097-642-5 (ebook)
CIP data is available

The New Press publishes books that promote and enrich public discussion and understanding of the issues
vital to our democracy and to a more equitable world. These books are made possible by the enthusiasm of
our readers; the support of a committed group of donors, large and small; the collaboration of our many
partners in the independent media and the not-for-profit sector; booksellers, who often hand-sell New Press
books; librarians; and above all by our authors.

www.thenewpress.com

Composition by Westchester Publishing Services
This book was set in Garamond Premier Pro

Printed in the United States of America

10 9 8 7 6 5 4 3 2 1

For my children, Christopher and Danica

Contents

Part III—The Road Ahead

Introduction

FOR A NATION WHOSE GOVERNANCE IS SCATTERED across fifty states—what de Tocqueville called our "assemblage of confederated republics"—America has a strange way of acting as if the only political culture that matters is the one in its capital city. There has been a lurch to the right in Republican-controlled statehouses across the country that has had dire results for ordinary citizens but, until very recently, has largely escaped the lens of the national media. Major news outlets came to this story late and with blinders on. They have tended to pay attention to manifest injustices in GOP states, such as the attack on voting rights, only to the degree that they impinge on the balance of power in Washington. They lionized Georgia's election officials in 2020 for facing down Trump's attempt at election fraud, then switched to vilifying the state's GOP for its new Jim Crow–style election law, and yet throughout ignored the state's perennial mistreatment of its most vulnerable citizens in almost every other sector of society. Mississippi Governor Tate Reeves was condemned during the COVID-19 pandemic because he defied federal guidelines relating to mask mandates—a topic de jour for the national media—not because his state had spent years slashing funds for rural hospitals, education, and infrastructure to free up money for corporate tax cuts. Florida Governor Ron DeSantis is pilloried by liberals and

celebrated by conservatives for the thumb he places in the eye of
Joe Biden, but media on both sides otherwise ignore his far-right
agenda, such as his studied refusal to collect taxes owed by major
corporations in his state. What affects the lives of politicos, pun-
dits, lobbyists, and journalists inside the Beltway has blared from
the cable news shows. What has really been going on in the lives of
working people in Mississippi, West Virginia, or North Carolina is
rarely heard above a whisper.

Only when Republican states began walking in lockstep with
Trump's authoritarianism, truly imperiling our democracy for the
first time since the Civil War, did most Americans in the blue states
take full notice that something dangerous was happening in the rest
of the country. How they could have missed it is a question that
will animate future historians. The corporate money that flooded
into state elections after the Supreme Court's *Citizens United* decision in 2010 brought to power a new generation of far-right governors and legislators—Tea Party zealots far more radical than the
Reagan Republicans who preceded them. The names of governors
elected in the class of 2010 are synonymous with government breakdown and attacks on workers' rights: Sam Brownback, whose "Kansas experiment" decimated his state's public sector and ended his
political career; Rick Scott, the scandal-scarred businessman whose
environmental deregulation in Florida exposed the Gulf Coast to ru-
inous algae blooms; Rick Snyder of Michigan, architect of a forced
state takeover of Democrat-controlled cities that resulted in the
Flint water crisis; New Jersey's Chris Christie, disgraced by the
Bridgegate affair and the successive downgrade of the state's bond
rating; and Scott Walker, who crippled collective bargaining rights
in Wisconsin, a state that was once a labor stronghold.

This new generation of state Republicans and their corporate
allies not only cut deeply into the public services crucial to the
lives of the poor and working class in regions decimated by global-
ization and deindustrialization; they enacted their anti-worker
agenda by filling the public sphere with political propaganda that

stoked fear and anger among the white working class. They have used billboards, TV and radio ads, and social media to demonize Democrats and provoke hysteria over divisive issues such as immigration, abortion, gun rights, teachers' unions, and the "socialism" of the moderate who became the nation's first Black president. They have left no semblance of civility in the conduct of our public affairs. The anger and cynicism that they injected into Republican state politics shook loose an avalanche of popular disaffection that came crashing down on American democracy in the Trump years, culminating in the January 6 assault on the Capitol and widespread support within the GOP for "stop the steal" and the election-sabotage movement. Republicans accelerated their efforts to disenfranchise Black voters at the very time that protesters were driven into the streets in revulsion over the killing of George Floyd, setting up a dangerous divide in American politics.

But the stampede to the far right in Republican states has trampled on the interests of working people across a far broader range of issues than just voting rights and police reform. Since *Citizens United* opened the floodgates of corporate political spending, the states sprawled across the Old Confederacy and the American Heartland have sought to return to a Gilded Age relationship with their citizens, slashing already meager budgets, cutting taxes for the wealthy, curtailing workers' rights, scaling back regulation, and entrusting the people's welfare to the free market. As a result, their working-class citizens have become poorer, sicker, less educated, and otherwise ill-equipped to compete in the postindustrial economy when compared with their counterparts in the blue states. This long neglect of public investment has helped create a bifurcated society in which the blue states enjoy a socio-economic status comparable to the rest of the developed world while the red states slip into the ranks of developing nations like those in Latin America or Eastern Europe.

Progressives were lulled into complacency by Joe Biden's victory in 2020 and his embrace of big-government solutions to the nation's mounting inequality. The election results even set off speculation among political commentators that America was poised for a realignment as momentous as the New Deal or the Reagan Revolution. The media spent less time dwelling on an ominous portent for Democrats—the Republican Party had actually tightened its grip on state governments. How much of a realignment was it when Republicans were left with governing trifectas or control of legislatures in twenty-eight states and attorney general offices in twenty-six states? To put it another way, 55 percent of the nation's population and two-thirds of its contiguous square mileage were in states whose legislative leaders were implacably opposed to the goals of the national government and openly disdainful of democracy. Heading into the 2022 elections, with partisan gerrymandering at a fevered pace across the country and inflation depressing Biden's approval ratings, it appeared the balance would shift even more toward the Republicans' favor.

The left tends to be reassured when progressive regimes are in control of the federal government, with its awesome powers to intervene in the social welfare of Americans. But in previous eras of federal activism, most notably in the Roosevelt and Johnson administrations, Washington was not contending with unified and even militant opposition to its goals in more than half the states. It is easy to forget how much of the country's governmental apparatus is controlled by the states and how much federal policy depends on state cooperation. The actions of state leaders can make the difference between an enlightened society and a political backwater. State and local governments are not only responsible for the nation's entire system of elections; they also control the police and most civil and criminal courts, virtually all of public education, and the lion's share of public health. They collect billions in taxes, handle most health and safety regulations, and control a huge share of the federal money that flows to their states for everything from flood control and highway construction to high-speed rail and unemployment insurance. All that federal funding has little meaning if states refuse to accept it, as grandstanding Republican governors and legislatures have begun to do with some regularity.

In 2010, New Jersey Governor Christie turned away $3 billion in federal funding for a commuter rail tunnel under the Hudson River—a move that the state's senior U.S. senator, Frank Lautenberg, called "one of the biggest policy blunders in New Jersey history." But he was hardly the first Republican governor to cheat his or her citizens in the name of short-term political gain or service to corporate contributors. Former Texas governor Rick Perry and other Republicans rejected billions in unemployment benefits contained in the Obama administration's stimulus package in 2009. Three other Republican governors, Rick Scott of Florida, Scott Walker of Wisconsin, and John Kasich of Ohio, turned down federal money for high-speed rail projects in their states in 2011, despite their obvious economic and environmental benefits. A more recent example was the decision by twenty-five Republican governors in the spring of 2021 to order an early termination of unemployment benefits for more than four million of their citizens, claiming the money—part of the Biden administration's response to the pandemic—was keeping people from going back to work. In fact, numerous studies found that states that stopped the benefits early saw no greater job growth than those that continued the checks until the expiration of the federal program in September 2021. Meanwhile, the congressional Joint Economic Committee found in June 2021 that the early cutoff would cost red-state economies more than $12 billion. As of this writing, twelve states have frustrated one of the key elements of Obamacare by refusing to expand Medicaid, even though that decision has cost thousands of lives and meant rejecting billions in federal funds.

Turning away money is not the only way red states have successfully thwarted the federal government. They also have done so by defying the mandates of federal agencies and simply not participating in enforcement. Missouri Governor Mike Parson signed a law in June 2021 that barred state and local authorities from cooperating with any federal investigation that impinges on Second Amendment rights, which, according to a legal brief by the Justice Department, essentially nullified federal firearms laws in the state and impeded joint federal-state cases against gun and drug traffickers. Missouri's was the most of extreme of nine laws adopted in Republican states that had in some form prohibited local cooperation in federal gun cases. They were part of a trend toward a relaxation of state gun laws aimed at countering Biden's plan to strengthen such laws at the federal level. Montana Governor Greg Gianforte even signed legislation to allow citizens to carry guns into the state Capitol and on university campuses.

The Environmental Protection Agency is another agency whose mission can be undermined by state resistance. The EPA was designed to set national policy, establish legal mandates for pollution control, and disburse funding, but it relies on the states for most enforcement and has no easy remedy if state officials, such as those in Texas, refuse to do the job. In the Obama years, Texas Governor Perry defied EPA permitting requirements for polluting industries and called on the president to "rein in this rogue agency." His successor, Greg Abbott, likewise announced during an appearance in the West Texas oilfields in January 2021 that his administration was launching a broad legal assault on President Biden's clean air initiatives. Abbott said he wanted to "make clear that Texas is going to protect the oil and gas industry from any type of hostile attack from Washington, D.C." This was from the same public official who, while serving as his state's attorney general, had sued the Obama administration forty-four times, once summing up his job this way: "I go into the office in the morning, I sue Barack Obama, and then I go home." Indeed, Republican state attorneys general have used lawsuits to delay or defeat federal initiatives on a wide range of issues, including the Affordable Care Act, immigration reform, criminal justice oversight, same-sex marriage, abortion, and gun control. It's the reality under our system of federalism: Washington set aside money for your unemployment benefits, but can't prevent your Republican governor from turning away the funds. It can enact criminal justice reform, but can't stop state authorities from kicking in your door.

* * * *

THE DEFIANCE of our national government became truly dangerous in the post-Trump era as Republican state leaders took aim at democracy itself. In the last months of 2021, there was a storm of activity in virtually all the Republican states that appeared designed to counter any Democratic victories by engineering the kind of electoral coup that Trump failed to carry out in the 2020 elections. It is ironic that in drafting the Constitution, the Founders worried about overweening power in the states for the threat it might pose to owners of property and businesses. More than a few members of the Continental Congress feared that the state legislatures, if they came under the sway of the unwashed masses, would take actions to jeopardize the interests of the wealthy. "The mutability of the laws of the States is found to be a serious evil," Madison wrote to Jefferson in October 1787. "The injustice of them has been so frequent and so flagrant as to alarm the most steadfast friends of Republicanism. . . . A reform, therefore, which does not *make provision for private rights* must be materially defective." But the electoral despotism at the state level that concerned the Founders has not come in the form of a threat against the propertied interests, but rather as an attempted coup *by* the propertied interests.

For years the Republican assault on democracy was limited to voter suppression and gerrymandering—corrosive enough in themselves—but blossomed after the 2020 election into an attack on the election machinery at the very heart of our system of government. Trump's false claim that there was widespread voting fraud in the election hit home with the rank and file of his party, despite the failure of his campaign to present compelling evidence in dozens of unsuccessful state and federal lawsuits that any such thing had happened. An ABC News / Ipsos poll found in January 2022 that more than 70 percent of Republicans believed the election was stolen. Between January 1 and December 7, 2021, nineteen Republican-led states had passed thirty-four laws that made it harder to vote, either by curtailing mail-in or early voting, imposing harsher voter ID laws, or enabling purges of voting rolls.

More worrisome, Republican lawmakers filed ten bills in seven states that would have directly empowered partisan officials to overturn election results. None of those bills passed, but the mere fact that they were proposed and taken seriously—and were expected to be reintroduced in 2022—was enough to keep defenders of democracy awake at night. As the nonprofit Brennan Center for Justice put it: "While none of these bills have become law, they expose the antidemocratic motivation behind the larger election sabotage movement and provide a worrying marker of how far voting rights opponents want to go. Their widespread introduction is an urgent warning sign for the health of our democracy."

The enemies of free and fair elections have moved against democratic institutions on a dizzying number of fronts. Republican legislatures in three battleground states, Wisconsin, Pennsylvania, and Texas, have followed Arizona in launching groundless audits of their 2020 election results, without any chance that they could convince federal courts to overturn the election. Michael Gableman, a former state supreme court justice overseeing the Republican audit in Wisconsin, even threatened to jail the mayors of Madison and Green Bay if they refused to sit for depositions. In what the Associated Press termed a "slow-motion insurrection," Republican states across the country were seeking to remove oversight of elections from nonpartisan agencies and put it in the hands of state legislators, the most publicized example being in Georgia, where Governor Brian Kemp signed a bill that removed Secretary of State Brad Raffensperger as chair of the State Elections Board and gave authority to the legislature to hire and fire members of county elections boards. Armed with this new power, legislators have deputized local GOP officials to purge the boards of Black Democrats.

In state after state, including the battleground of Michigan, Republicans were replacing county elections board members with "stop the steal" zealots, an effort made easier by the resignations of election officials harried by Trump supporters. As of December 2021, Michigan's GOP had replaced members of the county boards in eight of the state's eleven most populous counties. How successful these efforts in Republican states would be in overturning election results in 2022 or 2024 remained to be seen, but they appeared certain to reduce vote counting to chaos and further undermine Americans' faith in democracy. Protect Democracy, a nonpartisan watchdog group made up of former government officials, corporate executives, and academicians, predicted that the new state laws would "make elections more difficult to administer and even unworkable; make it more difficult to finalize election results; allow for election interference and manipulation by hyper-partisan actors; and, in the worst cases, allow state legislatures to overturn the will of the voters and precipitate and democracy crisis."

Much of the ferment in state election law boils down quite simply to an effort to keep racial and ethnic minorities from voting, an issue that was thought to have been settled decades ago but which the far right has resurrected in the last decade. The Voting Rights Act of 1965 had thwarted Jim Crow–era suppression tactics in the South, which Earl Warren, chief justice of the Supreme Court, had described as "an insidious and pervasive evil which had been perpetuated in certain parts of our country through unremitting and ingenious defiance of the Constitution." But in 2013, a narrow conservative majority of the Supreme Court, in *Shelby County v. Holder*, threw out the act's requirement that states with a history of voter suppression obtain pre-clearance from the federal government before making changes to their voting laws. Violations of the act were still illegal, but states wouldn't have the federal government breathing down their necks. The ruling opened a new era of voter suppression not only in the South but in other Republican-controlled states around the county. Within two hours of the court's decision, Greg Abbott, then Texas attorney general, tweeted that the state would immediately reinstate a strict voter ID law that had previously been thrown out as a violation of the Voting Rights Act. The next day, the North Carolina General Assembly set the wheels in motion to do the same thing, ultimately adopting restrictions so severe that a federal appellate court found they had targeted Black voters "with almost surgical precision." Across the country, polling places in minority districts were moved or shuttered entirely. Within five years, twenty-three states had implemented newly restrictive voter ID laws, all of them Republican-controlled. The "insidious and pervasive evil" was back in business.

In addition to Texas and North Carolina, Arizona, Kansas, Mississippi, Tennessee, Indiana, Virginia, and Wisconsin issued particularly strict voter ID laws. But no state moved with greater alacrity to reverse gains in minority voting than Georgia. The U.S. Commission on Civil Rights, a bipartisan federal agency, found in a 2018 report that Georgia was the only state that had deficiencies in every category of voter suppression in the commission's purview—restrictive voter ID laws, proof of citizenship requirement, purges of registration rolls, curtailment of early voting, and closed or relocated polling places.

The 2018 Georgia gubernatorial election, in which Kemp faced Stacey Abrams, a Democratic state representative, was an ugly showcase for the tactics of voter suppression. The fix was in from the beginning, since Kemp, then Georgia secretary of state, was overseeing the election in which he was a contender, as clear a conflict of interest as there ever was. Abrams's campaign was aggressive in its efforts to register Black voters, and polls ahead of the election showed the race was competitive, so Kemp did everything he could to keep Blacks from voting. The Associated Press reported less than a month before the election that his office had frozen 53,000 voter registrations—predominantly those of African Americans—because their registration form was not an exact match to records the state had on file. The way the rules were written, a registration could be thrown out for as little as a missing hyphen in the last name or because the state had entered the information incorrectly. Kemp also pursued a controversial policy of purging the rolls of citizens who had not been active in recent voting. His office had pared 1.4 million voters from the rolls in the previous six years, including 670,000 in 2017 alone. Kemp, who Abrams called "a remarkable architect of voter suppression," won the election by about 55,000 votes.

The pattern continued in the 2020 election, when so many polling places were closed in Black neighborhoods that voters in Atlanta had to wait hours to cast their ballots. One would think that the national adulation showered upon Georgia's Republican officials for facing down Donald Trump might have made the state GOP warm up to the idea of holding honest elections in the future. That was decidedly not the case. Instead, Kemp in March 2021 put his pen to the first major election law to emerge from the "stop the steal" movement, which ironically had made him one of its villains. Besides giving the GOP-dominated state legislature control of the State Election Board, the new law reduced the amount of time voters have to request an absentee ballot, set new ID requirements for absentee ballots, barred officials from mailing out absentee-ballot applications to all voters, banned mobile voting centers, and reduced the number of ballot drop boxes by nearly 75 percent and required they be placed inside government buildings. Kemp and his allies had wanted to get rid of voting by mail almost entirely, but local business leaders who met with them for days over the drafting of the bill, including representatives from Delta Air Lines, prevailed upon them to keep it. The law was enacted to solve a problem that didn't exist, since there were no significant issues of fraud in the election. In reality, the measure was aimed at the same citizens of color that Georgia had sought to disenfranchise since Reconstruction. Kemp signed the law surrounded by six white males in front of a painting of a slave plantation, while a Black female state lawmaker, Representative Park Cannon, who had knocked on his office door seeking to witness the ceremony, was forcibly removed by state troopers and arrested. The symbolism could not have been more powerful. As Aunna Dennis, executive director of Common Cause Georgia, told *Mother Jones*, "This bill is Jim Crow with a suit and tie." The Justice Department filed a lawsuit seeking to overturn the Georgia election law, but the inferno, the battle for American democracy, was already raging out of control.

* * * *

IT WAS SO out of control that the corporate leaders who had spent years bankrolling the very politicians pushing the election-sabotage movement were alarmed at how far toward sedition they were willing to go. Even Charles Koch, the oil billionaire who had been at the forefront of injecting "dark money" into state politics, was startled by the divisiveness he did so much to create. "Boy, did we screw up," he wrote in a memoir. "What a mess!" After Georgia passed its election law, leaders of major corporations in the state, including Delta Air Lines and Coca-Cola, spoke out in opposition, and hundreds across the country joined in a statement condemning the passage of legislation anywhere that made it harder for people to vote. The U.S. Chamber of Commerce, the Business Roundtable, and the National Association of Manufacturers were among the business groups pushing Congress to certify the Electoral College tally that gave Biden victory. This corporate statesmanship, absent so long from this country, did not sit well with the far right. Senator Marco Rubio called Delta Air Lines and Coca-Cola "woke corporate hypocrites" for criticizing the Georgia election law. Senate Minority Leader Mitch McConnell advised corporations to "stay out of politics." But the corporations continued to stick their necks out for fair elections. Overturning democracy, they suddenly realized, would be bad for business. There could be consumer boycotts, shareholder revolts, and a tarnishing of their brands. As it turned out, this moment of corporate of enlightenment was all for naught. Election-sabotage laws were still passed, and plans for throwing out election results were still hatched, in state after state. The "malefactors of great wealth," as Teddy Roosevelt called the business elite, were unable to control the wildfire they had done so much to ignite.

Many of the same corporations and business groups suddenly rallying to the cause of democracy had helped propel the swing to the far right in the red states. Their ability to fund political campaigns and guarantee the passage of pro-business legislation had been severely hampered by the 2002 Bipartisan Campaign Reform Act, better known as McCain-Feingold, which made it illegal for corporations and other organizations to contribute money for the benefit political candidates. The legislation was in response to corporate "soft money" that had come to dominate U.S. politics in the post-Reagan era. But in *Citizens United v. Federal Elections Commission*, the Supreme Court threw out those restrictions, ruling that the First Amendment guaranteed the rights of corporations to give unlimited sums to candidates as long as they were "independent expenditures," not made in concert with any candidate's campaign. The decision wiped out virtually all of the limits on corporate political spending that had been put in place after the Watergate era, and fueled the rise of super PACs, whose donors need not even be disclosed.

Citizens United had a profound impact on state governments. In the fall elections following the court's 2010 decision, eleven states flipped from Democratic or divided government to full Republican control of both the governorships and legislatures, and more dominos would fall in succeeding years. What followed over the next decade was a deluge of legislation in Republican-controlled states geared toward increasing corporate profits and weakening protections for working people—tax cuts, deregulation, and reductions in funding for health care, education, and other public services. "This includes not only restrictions on public- and private-sector unions," writes Gordon Lafer, a University of Oregon professor who studies labor issues, "but also legislation regarding the minimum wage, child labor, wage theft, tipped employees, construction wages, occupational safety, job discrimination, employee misclassification, overtime pay, unemployment insurance, budgetary retrenchment, and privatization of public services."

Within five years of *Citizens United*, fifteen states had passed legislation impinging on public employees' collective bargaining rights, including a law signed by Wisconsin Governor Walker that made one of the nation's traditional labor strongholds a right-to-work state. Michigan, an even bigger citadel of organized labor, became a right-to-work state in 2013 under a law signed by Governor Snyder within a week of its introduction, with no committee debate or public hearing.

The corporate assault on America's public sector has unfolded over decades with great stealth, only coming fully into view with the 2016 publication of *Dark Money*, a book by *New Yorker* writer Jane Mayer. She described the enormous influence on U.S. public policy that has been exerted by misanthropic billionaires and corporately funded foundations whose libertarian pretenses masked their bald quest for bigger profits, a group that included the brothers Charles and David Koch, oil magnates who set up a sprawling political operation, Americans for Prosperity; Richard Mellon Scaife, heir to a Pittsburgh fortune rising from banking, aluminum, and oil; and the Dick and Betsy DeVos Family Foundation, whose seed money came from the Michigan-based Amway empire. Their success at the national level has tended to swing with the political pendulum, but their penetration of state government in the South and large parts of the Sun Belt, the Midwest, and the Great Plains has been breathtaking.

No one has been more responsible for this than Charles Koch, who for decades has used a vast stream of oil money from his Wichita-based Koch Industries to pursue an ultra-conservative vision for America. Americans for Prosperity, the nonprofit that Koch and his late brother David set up to advance their political causes, has held annual meetings at posh resorts where business leaders strategize on how to deflate the public sector and promote corporate interests in states across the country. From these meetings flow millions of dollars to candidates, activists, and disinformation campaigns aimed at achieving the goals of the corporate lobby.

Koch has claimed to be an earnest libertarian who views excessive government as a threat to human freedom and productivity. But his political advocacy has appeared less concerned with the fate of humanity than with influencing government to increase the profits of Koch Industries. One example was the campaign by Americans for Prosperity beginning in 2015 to block the creation of public transit systems in Nashville, Little Rock, Phoenix, and more than a dozen other communities around the country. The group paid foot soldiers to knock on thousands of doors and distribute materials warning that public transit systems produce tax increases and a tide of gentrification that prices longtime residents out of their neighborhoods.

Never mind that public transit is proven to reduce traffic congestion and pollution and promote neighborhood development. The Koch brothers (David was still alive then) were looking after their own interests. Their colossal corporate empire has made billions selling gasoline, asphalt, seat belts, tires, and automotive parts. So while wrapping themselves in the mantle of libertarianism, they were crassly using their wealth to move public policy toward their own ends. In Nashville, a $5.4 billion ballot measure to fund the mass transit plan began in 2018 with wide popular support. But after the Koch brothers were done, it went down in defeat.

In similar fashion, Americans for Prosperity successfully derailed Tennessee's plan for Medicaid expansion under the Affordable Care Act to bring coverage to two hundred thousand low-income residents. The state's popular Republican governor, Bill Haslam, unveiled an expansion plan in 2015 with the backing of legislative leaders and polls showing the public approved of the plan. But the Koch bothers dispatched an army of field operatives to the state and paid for advertising and phony demonstrations depicting the plan as "a vote for Obamacare." As with public transit in Nashville, the proposal was defeated.

In yet another example, the Koch brothers bore a large degree of responsibility for the disaster that Governor Sam Brownback brought to their home state of Kansas. The two brothers had been supporting the deeply conservative Brownback as far back as 1994, when he first ran for Congress, and they were his biggest backers when he was elected Kansas governor with plans to use the state as a laboratory of libertarian government. The state's senate minority leader at the time of Brownback's election, Democrat Anthony Hensley, went so far as to say the Kochs had been "handed the keys to the governor's office."

Brownback's "Kansas experiment," one of the biggest tax reductions in the state's history, included a 30 percent cut in the personal income taxes of the highest earners and the elimination of business income taxes for more than three hundred thousand small business owners. By 2018, six years after the legislation was approved, it had cost the state budget $4.5 billion. In the meantime, Kansas had three credit downgrades and nine votes for budget cuts, including reductions in education, pensions, housing, law enforcement, and fire protection—leaving the state with lagging economic growth and what studies showed were woefully inadequate public services. Between 2012 and 2017, Kansas's 4.2 percent job growth was weaker than all of its neighboring states except Oklahoma, and less than half of the 9.4 percent national average. In 2017, the state's Republican-led legislature defied Brownback and voted to repeal the tax cut. Elected by nearly two-thirds of the vote in 2010, Brownback became so unpopular he never finished his second term. Trump appointed him as U.S. Ambassador-at-Large for International Religious Freedom.

Brownback may be out of mainstream politics, but Charles Koch and his network are still very much in the business of eroding democracy. Koch told the *Wall Street Journal* in November 2020 that he regretted the role he played in polarizing the American electorate and pledged to henceforth proceed in the spirit of bipartisanship. But just months after he made that statement, his network was lobbying to defeat the For the People Act, an election-reform bill that, among other things, would curtail corporate influence on elections and require that the identities of political donors be disclosed to the public. According to an article Jane Mayer wrote for the *New Yorker*, Kyle McKenzie, research director of Stand Together, the mother organization of the Koch network, joined members of other conservative groups in a January 8, 2021, conference call with an adviser to Senate Minority Leader Mitch McConnell. McKenzie told the group the bill would have to be killed by filibuster, rather than through appeals to public opinion, because research had shown that not only liberals were in support. He described a "large, very large, chunk of conservatives who are supportive of these kinds of efforts."

That was hardly the first time that lobbyists kept voters in the dark about how corporations are influencing public policy. The corporate lobby's behind-the-scenes efforts at the state level have largely been engineered by the American Legislative Exchange Council, or ALEC, a corporate-funded advocacy group that has quietly worked with Republican lawmakers to enact prepackaged legislation in states across the country. According to Lafer, more than a hundred ALEC-drafted pieces of legislation—literally written by corporate lobbyists—became law every year in the first decade of this century. As of 2017, ALEC had on its membership rolls some two thousand state legislators—a quarter of the nation's total—and could count as past or present members scores of well-known corporations, including Coca-Cola, Verizon, Walmart, Bank of America, Google, Facebook, Visa, Home Depot, Anheuser-Busch, Ford Motor Company, FedEx, Exxon-Mobil, McDonald's, United Air Lines, UPS, Geico, and General Motors.

Many of those companies have cut ties with ALEC, especially after it became known that the group had drafted model legislation to restrict voting. But they were members in good standing long enough to share blame for the destructive effect of ALEC's work. Douglas Clopp, then deputy program director at Common Cause, told *The Atlantic*: "If it's voter ID, it's ALEC. If it's anti-immigration bills written hand-in-glove with private prison corporations, it's ALEC. If it's working with the NRA on (Stand Your Ground) laws, it's ALEC." ALEC swung into high gear with the election of Barack Obama and the *Citizens United* decision, helping to energize the voter-suppression movement. More than half of the sixty-two voter ID laws proposed in the 2011–12 state legislative elections were sponsored by lawmakers affiliated with ALEC, according to Columbia University researcher Alexander Hertel-Fernandez. ALEC's work at the state level has had a hugely negative impact on American life in the last two decades—on wages, collective bargaining rights, workplace safety, health care, education, and the environment—and yet few members of the public are even aware the group exists. Both the Kansas experiment and the right-to-work legislation in Michigan were based on model legislation from ALEC.

Corporate lobbyists have no bigger priority than tax relief. It is a mantra for the likes of ALEC and Charles Koch, borrowed from Arthur Laffer, the supply-side guru of the Reagan Revolution, that lessening the tax burden on corporations and wealthy individuals promotes economic growth and ends up benefiting everyone. It is a useful way of justifying tax laws that are baldly designed to benefit the highest earners, but it flies in the face of the evidence. The failure of the Kansas experiment to spur job growth may have been the most famous repudiation of supply-side doctrine at the state level, but is hardly the only one. A 2017 study by the Institute on Taxation and Economic Policy found that states with the highest personal income tax rates have greater economic growth, higher wages, and better employment opportunities than the states with no personal income tax.

It is no secret how states pay for those tax cuts—through cuts in government programs that benefit their most vulnerable citizens. Across America, Republican states are freeing up money for tax cuts by cutting funds for infrastructure, public schools, and higher education, despite years of economic expansion that preceded the COVID-19 pandemic. The dismal funding for school buildings and salaries provoked recent teachers' strikes in West Virginia, Kentucky, Oklahoma, and Arizona, where one school reported using broken laptops, books held together with duct tape, and a biology text book that was twenty-five years old. A recent study by the Center on Budget and Policy Priorities in Washington found that nine states—Alabama, Arizona, Louisiana, Mississippi, Missouri, New Mexico, Oklahoma, Pennsylvania, and South Carolina—had cut funding for public colleges by more than 30 percent from 2008 to 2018.

In Republican-led states, it is not the people's interests being served. In West Virginia, important elected officials maintain eye-popping conflicts of interest: the speaker of the House of Delegates is a paid lobbyist for natural gas companies who openly advocates for legislation benefiting that industry. The man who until recently served as state senate president was a cable company executive who pushed state broadband contracts for the two firms that have employed him. And Governor Jim Justice is a coal magnate who never divested from his company and makes no secret of fighting for its interests.

In many cases, the leadership of Republican states have passed measures that by no stretch of the imagination could reflect the popular will. After heavy lobbying from telecommunications giants like Comcast and AT&T, twenty states by 2015 had enacted laws banning or restricting municipalities from setting up their own broadband networks, which would give consumers a greater choice of cable companies instead of one company having a local monopoly. Eight red states have passed laws that enable highly profitable subprime consumer lenders, like OneMain Financial, formerly a division of Citigroup, to increase interest rates they charge low-income borrowers. In North Carolina, the law was passed despite complaints from military commanders that it would gouge active service members. "There was simply no need to change the law," Rick Glazier, a Democratic lawmaker who voted against the measure, told the *New York Times*. "It was one of the most brazen efforts by a special interest group to increase its own profits that I have ever seen."

* * * *

THIS MAD SCRAMBLE for corporate profits, little seen by the public at large, is undermining one of the world's great democracies. We now have a country where tens of millions of people live under state regimes that are gutting budgets for education and health care, empowering polluters, and starving badly needed public infrastructure. The results jump out from any objective assessment of their citizens' well-being. Studies show that on average red states, compared with blue states, have lower per capita economic growth, higher poverty, inferior school performance, higher rates of suicide, greater prevalence of diabetes, higher rates of infant mortality and teen pregnancy, less effective health care systems, and lower health care spending. The blue states have most of the country's top universities, wider broadband coverage, more spending on schools, and cleaner air and water. Studies by the Rockefeller Institute and others show that Republican-led states are more dependent on federal funds than states led by Democrats, despite their leaders' supposed fealty to limited government.

In 2014, public health experts were startled to find that average life expectancy—which was on the rise in many parts of the world—had dropped in the United States for the first time since World War I, a trend driven by skyrocketing drug overdose deaths and a smaller increase in suicides. They were even more alarmed when the increase continued over the next two years. Suicide deaths had been climbing since 1999, and in rural counties were double that of the most urban counties, a disparity that experts blamed on easier access to guns in the countryside. Needless to say, red states were at the forefront of the downward trend in life expectancy. In 2018, the ten states with the highest life expectancy, all above 80 years, were blue; the ten states with the lowest were red, with Mississippi at the bottom with a life expectancy of 74.4.

The citizens of the red states are not just sicker and dying at an earlier age; they lag behind the blue states in almost every measure of well-being. A widely cited American Human Development Index published annually by the CFA Institute, an association of professional investors, uses a measure combining health, education, and income to compare nations and different places in the United States. Using that yardstick, the institute found that the states supporting Hillary Clinton in the 2016 election had a combined human development index comparable to that of the Netherlands, while the Trump states were on a level with Russia. Another revealing measure is a list of the Western world's fifty most important scientists, based on their Twitter following, published by *Science* magazine. The list was dominated by Americans, but only five were clearly identified as working in red states. Likewise with high school science awards: they are mostly won by students from blue states. None of this is a coincidence. It is plainly due to a relative lack of public investment. Statistics on research-and-development expenditures by universities, compiled annually by the nonprofit State Science and Technology Institute, show that on a per capita basis, blue states tend to be clustered toward the top of the list and red states toward the bottom. In 2019, seven of the top ten states were led by Democrats, while eight of the ten states at the bottom were Republican. Texas, Arizona, and Florida, whose Republican leaders portray their states as the future of America, each ranked toward the bottom, with Florida forty-fifth, just above Arkansas and West Virginia.

Statistically, America has poorer health, inferior educational standards, more antiquated infrastructure, and higher rates of disease and suicide than most other places in the developed world. But when individual blue states are measured against those other countries, they fare much better. The 2019 suicide rate per 100,000 people in the United States was 16.1, well above that of the European Union (11.3), but New York's (8.3 percent), New Jersey's (8), and Massachusetts's (8.7) were superior to that of Europe. Every red state had a higher suicide rate than that of the European Union, including Wyoming (29.3), Alaska (28.5), and Montana (26.2), whereas only nine fully blue states were higher. Similarly, Massachusetts's 2017 infant mortality rate of 3.7 percent per 1,000 births or Connecticut's rate of 4.5 were in the same league as the EU's rate of 3.4, while twelve red states had rates higher than 7 percent, comparable to Russia and the Ukraine and higher than Saudi Arabia (6.3).

Over the years, data from the International Telecommunications Union have tended to show that the percentage of Americans with access to the internet is either comparable to or lagging slightly behind that of nations in the European Union. But if the data for the blue states were treated separately, the numbers would tell a different story. The U.S. Census Bureau has found a stark disparity between blue states and red states in their citizens' internet use. In 2018, nineteen of the twenty states with the lowest percentage of wired households were governed by Republicans.

Certainly regional economic disparities also exist in Western Europe, between eastern and western Germany, or between the northeast and the southeast of the United Kingdom, for example. And that raises the question of whether it is misleading to compare the most prosperous regions of the United States with European nations in all of their regions. But it is important to remember that regional disparities in health care and other social indicators are less pronounced in many European countries because of stronger social-welfare policies at the national level. Every citizen of the United Kingdom has access to the National Health Service, whereas more than 29 million people were uninsured in the United States as of 2019, including more than 18 percent of Texans and 13 percent of Floridians.

The statistical disparities between red and blue states would have made perfect sense fifty years ago, when many southern and southwestern states were mostly rural and had lower populations and less development. But there has been a huge shift of population to the Sun Belt over the last few decades. These states' economic and political influence have grown enormously, their sports teams and corporations are household brands, but their contributions to science, medicine, and other academic disciplines—the building blocks of the nation's greatness—have lagged behind. It is not because their people are lacking in intelligence or industry; it is a consequence of political leadership that is loath to invest in the human potential of their states. What this means is that not all of us are living in a declining nation, only half of us. If the United States were thought of as two countries, the Blue Nation would have much more in common with the America of the mid-twentieth century, when we led the world in almost every measure of progress, whereas the Red Nation would be middling and second-rate. But we are not two nations, we are one. The part of America that wants to invest in health, education, infrastructure, and science, that wants to erase the corrosive influence of corporate money on public policy and truly restore America's greatness, must drag along its corrupt and malingering cousin.

This cleavage, running through the heart of America, is surely not what Supreme Court Justice Louis Brandeis envisioned when he spoke of the states as "laboratories of democracy." The Jeffersonian democrats, when they stood up for the right of each state to craft laws "well adapted to its own Genius & Circumstances," in the words of Samuel Adams, could not have imagined that the genius would include undermining the very principles upon which the nation was founded.

How this vast gulf between Republican and Democratic states arose and what the consequences have been for ordinary Americans, those least able to make their voices heard in the halls of government, is the subject of this book. Part I, "Laboratories of Democracy?," looks at the breakdown of ethical norms and sound government in Republican states, with emphasis on West Virginia, Kentucky, and North Carolina. Part II, "Portraits of Failure," examines state policies impacting the environment, health care, and education, with profiles of Texas, Mississippi, and Arizona. Part III looks toward the future, showing how the most active Democrat-led states have shaken off the stasis of Reaganism and begun investing in environmental protection, clean energy, and progressive initiatives in health care and education. This section also asks whether California or Texas is the model for the nation's future, and challenges the blue regions of America, including major cities in Republican states, to use their superior economic and cultural resources to forge new coalitions of good governance. This is not to suggest that blues states have become paragons of progress. The needs of their most vulnerable citizens are still neglected, and corporate money still plays an outsized role in their politics. But, as chapter 7 points out, states such as California and New York have filled the vacuum left by decades of partisan gridlock in Washington with massive new government initiatives in education, health care, and the environment, while Republican-controlled states have herded in the opposite direction.

What follows in these pages is an attempt to direct more attention to the travesty unfolding in huge swaths of America, and not just over the issue of voting rights. Only by fully understanding the trend toward autocracy and corporate domination in the red states, and how abjectly it has undermined the nation, can progressives wrest control of the narrative from the far right and begin to alter the course of American politics.

Part I

Laboratories of Democracy?

1

Dead Last in Everything: Profile of a Failed State

THE DRINKING WATER OF CHARLESTON, WEST Virginia, is born high in the Alleghenies. Streams as fresh as the primordial forest flow together to form the Elk River, which descends from the headwaters teeming with trout and walleye, snakes, muskrats, and even a unique species of fish called the diamond darter. The river follows an arduous path for 172 miles, cascading down ridges and hollows and at times disappearing entirely in underground caverns. It swells in the spring rains and meanders slowly in summer, offering itself to a gauntlet of rural communities for fishing, bathing, and the occasional baptism. Then, in the last miles of its journey, the distinctly green water moves sluggishly through an industrial corridor of Charleston and down the intake pipe of the West Virginia American Water Company.

By that time, the river has lost its innocence. Before it becomes the water supply for nine counties and three hundred thousand people, it flows past abandoned coal mines in the southern part of the state and absorbs their rivulets of acids and metals. The river is an abomination when it reaches the intake, a rancid mixture of sewer runoff and industrial discharge, forcing the water company to resort to the most draconian treatment measures. No one should be surprised, then, in a region once known by the unsavory nickname of "Chemical Valley," that the water doesn't always taste so good. On some days, the water flows crisp and clear, as if it just came out of the mountains; on others, it's like drinking chlorine.

So when residents of that nine-county area began to notice a taste of licorice in their drinking water in January 2014, some just shrugged their shoulders. They'd been through this drill before. In the working-class neighborhoods of the capital, in brick mansions overlooking the Kanawha River, in trailers and shotgun shacks in the countryside, in schools, hospitals and nursing homes, many went ahead and drank—drank, showered, washed their dishes, and bathed their children.

But they would soon wish they hadn't. A few hours before the licorice taste showed up in the water, residents of a ramshackle Charleston neighborhood abutting the Elk River noticed a powerful odor of licorice seeping into their homes. "It was sickeningly sweet," said Jeff Ellis, a man in his thirties living with his mother near the river. "You couldn't get away from it, even in the house or the car. It was making my mom sick."

Denise Witt was overcome by the aroma of licorice as she carried laundry out of her home on Arlington Avenue, and soon noticed something strange. Like a scene from a sci-fi movie, workers in protective suits and trucks from the water company were all over the neighborhood. "I thought they might have been fixing a water main, but it looked a little odd."

American Water knew something that it wouldn't tell the public for seven more hours—the sweet scent in the air was a harbinger of disaster. Floating thickly down the Elk River, heading straight for the intake pipe, was a dangerous slick of chemicals about to create one of the worst cases of contaminated drinking water in American history.

Less than two miles upstream from the water company, an aboveground storage tank containing chemicals strong enough to separate rock from coal had ruptured and begun spilling its contents into the river. Employees of the West Virginia Department of Environmental Protection (DEP) arrived at the site just after eleven o'clock on the morning of January 9 and found chemicals bubbling "fountain-like" from under the storage tank and collecting in a pool four inches deep. The pool was filtering right through a crumbling concrete dike designed to contain leaks. But the dike was meaningless in any case; the chemicals were also draining into a twelve-inch-wide underground culvert that dumped directly into the river.

Freedom Industries, a chemical distributor that maintained a farm of storage tanks at the site, had made no notification to the DEP or the water company about the leak, though there was evidence it had been going on for some time. When the DEP inspectors arrived, they were greeted by a company official who claimed there was no problem at the site. Just a little odor from a heavy schedule of deliveries, he said. But the inspectors asked to be shown around the facility and were led to the ruptured and spewing storage tank.

There they found no sign that the company was doing anything to contain the spillage, other than a lone cinder block and a single bag of absorbent powder placed in the area where the four-foot-wide stream was going through the concrete dike. "This was a Band-Aid approach," a DEP inspector told the *Charleston Gazette*. "It was apparent that this was not an event that had just happened."

Over the next few hours, the magnitude of the disaster came into focus. Hundreds of people reported to emergency rooms or called poison control centers complaining of symptoms ranging from difficulty breathing and skin rashes to nausea and stomach pain. No one knows for sure how much spilled or how long it was leaking. Freedom Industries initially told authorities the leak amounted to a thousand gallons, but later estimates put the spill at more than ten times that amount. The chemicals not only contaminated the regional water system but also flowed from the Elk River into the Kanawha River and then into the Ohio River, polluting water as far as four hundred miles away in Louisville, Kentucky.

After the water company finally issued a "do not use" advisory at six o'clock in the evening, the region came to a standstill. An eerie silence settled over Charleston. Downtown skyscrapers went dark, restaurants and department stores closed, and organizers canceled the Rough N' Rowdy Brawl, an amateur fighting event at the Charleston Civic Center. Even the state legislature stopped doing business. With the National Guard bringing in emergency supplies of water to hospitals and nursing homes, the city looked like a war zone.

The full shutdown lasted for five days—and in some areas, ten—during which time officials seemed at a loss for what to do about the contamination, since they knew little about the properties of the escaped chemicals or the extent of the leak. "We don't know that the water is not safe. But I can't say that it is safe," Jeff McIntyre, president of the water company, told reporters a day after issuing the "do not use" advisory.

In a tragically large number of cases, the warnings against drinking the water were ignored. The poor don't always have the luxury of running to the convenience store for a bottle of water, especially in areas where there are no convenience stores. In the businesses that did carry bottled water, the shelves were wiped clean in a matter of hours and scuffles broke out for what remained. A survey by the federal Centers for Disease Control later found that 37 percent of households continued to drink and bathe in the poisoned water even after the "do not use" advisory was issued.

The grim events of those ten days were presented in the media as another environmental disaster in a state whose forests and rivers have been degraded by coal mining since the nineteenth century. But the implications were far broader. The despoiling of an entire region's water supply could not have happened without the government neglect that has spread like a contagion to almost every one of the Republican-led states—the budget cutting, deregulation, curtailment of labor rights, and crony capitalism that are the proud handiwork of elected officials whose loyalties no longer lay with their citizens but with the corporate elites that keep them in power.

The byproducts of corporate malfeasance and denuded government are everywhere to be found in the Mountain State—ghost towns that were once thriving communities, pristine mountaintops shaved off by coal companies, crumbling and underperforming schools, polluted rivers, rampant opioid deaths, skyrocketing cancer rates, and public health clinics overwhelmed by cases of diabetes and hepatitis, the twin scourges of the poor. While the decline of the coal industry has had a big hand in West Virginia's misfortunes, most of the state's problems are in some way bound up with the failure of its leadership, both the conservative Democrats who reigned for many years, such as U.S. Senator Joe Manchin, and the far-right Republicans who have taken their place.

There is no better state to begin an exploration of the damage that modern conservative politics have done to the lives of ordinary Americans. West Virginia is a place where Republicans have governance virtually to themselves. Besides Manchin, there are no Democrats elected statewide, and the GOP holds more than three-quarters of the seats in the legislature. Unlike in many other red states, there are no big cities with Democratic majorities to provide a progressive counterweight to conservatives in the statehouse. The GOP cannot blame immigrants or other minorities for the state's problems because their numbers are negligible. Republicans pretty much have the state the way they want it. Taxes have been cut to the bone and state government regulators beaten into submission. If America's system of federalism allows states to be "laboratories of democracy," West Virginia is the perfect controlled experiment for unfettered market capitalism.

That it should be so flies in the face of the state's political history. In West Virginia, the Democratic Party was once viewed in the same divine light as church and family. Not only had the New Deal brought rural West Virginians back from the brink of starvation, but the Kennedy and Johnson administrations had given Appalachia a special niche in the War on Poverty. When President Kennedy issued an executive order creating the food stamp program, the first recipients were in the impoverished coal region of McDowell County, West Virginia. "When I grew up, if people had a few pictures up in their house, it was FDR, JFK, and Jesus Christ," said Ted Boettner, a liberal policy advocate in Charleston and lifelong West Virginian. For much of the twentieth century, the United Mine Workers of America was a powerhouse in the state that could make or break political careers.

Labor matters little in Charleston these days. The state's devotion to business values is so complete that its leaders are not just slavish to the corporate interests; they *are* the corporate interests. Governor Jim Justice is a coal-mining magnate who steers the state's policies in a way that directly benefits his business interests. Manchin, who was the state's governor and secretary of state before becoming senator, has watched out for his investments in the coal industry throughout his political career. As one of the key Democratic votes in President Joe Biden's effort to win passage of his Build Back Better legislation, Manchin was fighting in the fall of 2021 to weaken any portion of the bill that would harm West Virginia coal mining. It is certainly not a coincidence that he had earned $4.5 million from his coal investments while serving as a senator, had up to $5 billion in stock options in a coal brokerage firm he founded in 1988, and got more campaign donations from coal, oil, and gas interests in 2021 than any other senator.

It is that kind of crony capitalism, found all across the red states—that is, across more than half of the states in this country—that led to the Elk River disaster. Nothing that came to light in the days following the spill suggested that the state's government or private industry had been in *any way* protective of the public's health. Even after the leak, no one was able to offer frightened residents reliable information about the long-term threat posed by the water or whether it was ever really rendered safe to drink. "There are so many chemicals out there that are not properly characterized," said Kevin Thompson, a lawyer who filed a class-action suit against the companies responsible for the spill. "It's only after they dump it in our water and it smells like licorice that we know about it. If it didn't smell like licorice, we wouldn't even know."

The chemical mixture that escaped from the ruptured tank was mostly composed of crude 4-methylcyclohexanemethanol, better known as MCHM, which is a foaming agent used to separate shale, clay, and other impurities from coal. American Water found that its treatment system was a useless barrier against such toxicity, so the chemical flowed into the water system uninhibited.

In responding to the emergency, the DEP quickly obtained a safety data sheet from the chemical's manufacturer, Eastman Chemical Company, which stated that MCHM can cause eye and skin irritation and is harmful if swallowed. That was pretty much it. As the *Washington Post* later reported, many of the safety form's fields were essentially left blank: "Under the section titled 'most important symptoms and effects, both acute and delayed,' Eastman's form says 'no data available.' Under toxicological effects of inhalation, 'no data available.' It was the same for whether it causes cancer, affects reproduction or affects specific organs."

Freedom Industries was not the kind of company to ask probing questions about the dangers of its chemicals. The company was owned by Cliff Forrest, a Pennsylvania coal baron outspoken in his contempt for environmental regulations. When more responsible corporate leaders put forth a "business case" for supporting the Paris Agreement on climate change, he wrote an opinion piece in the *Wall Street Journal* calling on Donald Trump to ditch the treaty. He was so excited by Trump's promise to lift restrictions on coal mining that he donated $1 million to the president's inauguration.

Nor were West Virginia's officials going to ask too many questions, not when coal company interests were at issue. In his State of the State address delivered a day before the spill was detected, Governor Earl Tomblin said, "I will never back down from the EPA, because of its misguided policies on coal." And those were not just words. His administration had just spent two years cutting the DEP's budget and reducing its staff.

It was hardly a shock, then, when it was disclosed after the disaster that the DEP had not inspected Freedom Industries' storage tanks *for more than ten years* even though there had been previous spills and odor complaints. A number of state and federal laws required inspections, but no one from the DEP or any other state agency ever came to look at the tanks.

Tank 396, the one that ruptured, was seventy-six years old. It was built in 1938 by Elk Refining Company, which originally owned the property. Though its floor had occasionally been reinforced in the intervening years, it eventually rotted away, exposing two holes that allowed the chemicals to escape. Freedom Industries, which had merged with another previous owner, Etowah River Terminal, only days before the rupture, had no evidence on the premises that either company had ever maintained the tank or containment dike.

But perhaps the biggest culprit in the whole affair was the West Virginia American Water Company. The company is a subsidiary of New Jersey–based American Water Works, the largest for-profit supplier of water and sewage treatment in the country and a major force behind efforts to privatize municipal water systems. About 86 percent of consumers still get their water from municipally owned systems, but American Water wants to change that. It spends large sums on political campaigns and engages in aggressive lobbying in an effort to buy up more and more municipally owned systems. It has subsidiaries in fifteen states and has a myriad of other interests in the United States and Canada. In the decade and half before the Elk River spill, the company donated more than $1 million to political candidates and PACs and spent $3.5 million in lobbying, with most of the money going to Republicans. It also maintained strong connections to the American Legislative Exchange Council.

In its annual reports, American Water makes clear that environmental regulations are among the "risk factors" that must be overcome to maintain its steady rise in profits; the net income for the company in the twelve-month period ending on September 30, 2021, was $763 million, up 15 percent from the previous year.

But all that political spending and lobbying has not altered an inconvenient fact: privatizing the water has not been a good deal for the public. American Water has come under attack across the country for charging excessive rates, downsizing and cutting wages in its workforce, providing poor service, and polluting the environment. At least nine counties or municipalities—including Monterey County, California, and Will County, Illinois—have either taken back their water supply from the company or are attempting to do so. Eighteen other jurisdictions have had controversies or lawsuits involving water quality, infrastructure failure, or excessive fees.

In 2006, former Illinois Attorney General Lisa Madigan filed a lawsuit against the state's American Water subsidiary for overcharging Will County customers, including one house in Homer Glen erroneously charged for use of 140,000 gallons in a month, twenty times what an average house would use. "Illinois-American Water mistreated its customers by first allegedly overcharging them and then failing to inform them of their right to dispute their outrageous water bills," Madigan said.

The same allegations of excessive rate hikes and paltry investments in infrastructure have been lodged against West Virginia American Water, which charges its customers considerably more than customers of publicly owned systems in the state. Local officials have complained that the company requests—and receives—rate hikes every two years and turns over millions to its parent company for stockholder dividends, but puts little investment into its aging network of water pipes. The term "water advisories" appeared in the *Charleston Gazette* nearly two thousand times between 2000 and 2018 because of constant pipe breaks that left the water undrinkable. The year of the Elk River spill, the company had 3,752 breaks and leaks, 20 percent more than the year before. Meanwhile, the company supplied data to the West Virginia Public Service Commission showing that, at the rate it was upgrading water lines, the job wouldn't be finished for 384 years.

The company had neither invested in a second intake pipe as backup to the one in Charleston nor installed monitors in the Elk River that could have detected the MCHM before it entered the water system. In the summer of 2015, the same water main in Dunbar, West Virginia, broke three times in less than two weeks, each time leaving twenty-five thousand households without water—and the Dunbar Fire Department with only a fifteen-minute supply of water in the case of a fire. "Our No. 1 resource in West Virginia is not coal or natural gas; it's water," said Charleston Mayor Danny Jones. "We certainly have plenty of it here in the Kanawha Valley and in the entire state of West Virginia . . . the only impediment we have to getting our water . . . is West Virginia American Water Company."

But the complaints about the water company always come from county and municipal officials and advocacy groups, rarely from state legislators, the governor's office, or the Public Service Commission, whose job it is to guard the public against excessive rate hikes. James Van Nostrand, a West Virginia University law professor who studies utility regulation, said the state's public service commission is known to be friendly to private utilities. "These companies usually get what they want from the commission," he said. "They're not hurting."

A June 2018 report by Americans for Tax Reform, a conservative advocacy group, noted that West Virginia and Tennessee were the only two states that did not order private utilities to use part of the money they collected from the 2017 federal tax cut to bring rate relief to its customers. In fact, American Water had asked the Public Service Commission for a rate hike in April 2018 that would have added an average of more than $10 to its customers' monthly bills, despite the fact that the company gained $11.4 million in annual savings from the tax cut. The commission balked at the increase only after being singled out in the report. The water company then put out a press release saying it had decided to earmark $4.6 million of its tax windfall for rate relief, as if it were an act of civic benevolence. The company's statement was issued by Brian Bruce, Jeff McIntyre's successor as company president, since McIntyre had been rewarded for his disservice to the public by being put in charge of American Water's entire mid-Atlantic region.

McIntyre did have one moment of corporate statesmanship during his time in the public spotlight. He told a legislative hearing less than a month after the spill that the company had to "rebuild the public trust" and would not seek its biannual rate hike, even though it was eligible in 2015. "I'm going to do everything I can to protect customers from rate increases," he said.

That statesmanship did not last. In April 2015, West Virginia American Water announced it was seeking a 28 percent rate increase, which a company spokeswoman said was partly due to the cost of responding to the Elk River spill. McIntyre later revised the reason for the rate increase, saying the money from the rate hike would of course be used entirely to offset past investments in the system. But nobody was fooled—that is, nobody except every news organization that reported on the increase. They all missed the most galling story to come out of the Elk River disaster. A wealthy private company had let poison into the water, and now the public was going to pay for it.

* * * *

RARELY IN THE MODERN history of the U.S. has a state been more disdainful of the public's welfare than West Virginia in the last two decades. The Elk River chemical spill was a massive regulatory failure that sickened untold numbers of people and forever destroyed the region's faith in its water supply. But it was hardly an anomaly. The state's frenzy to repeal environmental regulations and otherwise eviscerate government, at the behest of coal and natural gas companies, has made disasters like Elk River all but inevitable.

In 2014, Republicans captured control of the statehouse for the first time in eighty years, and maverick coal baron Jim Justice was elected governor as a Democrat two years later, announcing almost immediately that he was switching parties. It was a double cross that the Democrats richly deserved, after spending their years in power rattling around in the pockets of the coal industry like so much loose change.

The combined effect of the two elections has been an era of conservative scorched-earth politics in Charleston that is astounding even by West Virginia standards. Between January and March of 2015, the Republicans served up a package of bills so geared toward the interests of big business that it could have been designed by the American Legislative Exchange Council, which in large part it was. (West Virginia is among the three states where Republicans have introduced the most ALEC-generated legislation.) The legislature made West Virginia a right-to-work state and repealed the prevailing wage, two gut punches to working people and their ability to earn a living in a state that once had a proud history of supporting labor organizations like the United Mine Workers of America. Another bill approved in that session allowed natural gas companies to seize the mineral rights of a property without the owner's consent. There were also measures to weaken mine safety protections, promote the hiring of non-union teachers, and make it more difficult for injured workers to sue their employers.

But perhaps the biggest affront to West Virginia's citizens was a gutting of the state's Aboveground Storage Tank Act, enacted after the Elk River chemical spill. The law had required state inspections of aboveground tanks for the first time, but the new amendment reduced the number of regulated tanks from fifty thousand to five thousand and curtailed the list of regulated chemicals so drastically it didn't even include the compound that spilled into the Elk River. Natural gas companies were exempted from the rules altogether.

The West Virginia AFL-CIO called the 2015–16 legislative session "the most egregious assault on workers in our state's history," while Norm Steenstra, former executive director of the West Virginia Citizens Action Group, a progressive advocacy group, said, "Almost everything we got done in my career has now been undone."

The same conservative leadership presided over cuts to funding for education, health care, and other essential programs. In early 2021, Governor Justice gave his backing to legislation that would gradually phase out the state's personal income tax, which generates more than $800 million in annual revenue, and replace it with a sales tax increase that would fall hardest on the poor.

It is hard to imagine a state more likely to suffer from further retrenchment of a government already profoundly neglectful of its people's needs. West Virginia's poverty is notorious, a staple of political commentary since the nineteenth century, and it has not budged for decades. In the two-year period between January 2018 and the end of 2019, the state's official poverty rate of 14.9 percent was the fifth-highest in the country, surpassed only by Mississippi, Louisiana, New Mexico, and Arkansas. Owing to the strength of the national economy, that percentage was lower than it had been in any other year of this century, and a far cry from its rate of 34.6 percent in 1959, but it was still double that of blue states like Maryland, Massachusetts, and New Jersey, and several points higher than California, which contends with soaring housing costs and the legacy of enormous immigration.

In recent measures, the state has recorded the nation's highest rate of overdose deaths, third-highest rate of cancer deaths, lowest life expectancy, second-highest rate of obesity, second-highest rate of diabetes, highest rate of hepatitis C, eighth-highest suicide rate, sixth-highest rate of teen pregnancy, sixth-highest infant mortality, and even the highest rate of accidental deaths.

To these add the highest rate of people collecting Supplemental Security Income (payments for the indigent elderly, blind, and disabled), the third-lowest median household income, and the third-highest unemployment rate. If you combine the per capita number of unemployed with those not even looking for work, West Virginia ranked dead last.

West Virginia's poverty in its worst pockets has few counterparts in the developed world. Many rural counties, especially in the regions that have lost coal-mining jobs, have more in common with Third World countries than the rest of the United States. McDowell County, in the southeast corner of the state, has a male life expectancy of sixty-four years, roughly that of Kenya. In 2013, the county was reported to have an infant mortality rate of 16 per 1,000 live births, higher than Libya.

"Dead Last in Everything" could be a sign that greets travelers when they enter the state.

But faced with such daunting challenges, the state's response has been to leave the people to their fate. Elected officials in both parties have been obstinate in refusing to fund programs to foster employment growth and better the lives of the poor and working class. Even before the Republicans took power, each year brought renewed proposals to reduce already paltry sums earmarked for infrastructure, job training, health care, and education.

West Virginia's politicians justify their miserly budgets by noting that the state's population is declining and that the government must live within its means. But studies by the West Virginia Center on Budget and Policy, a progressive advocacy group, show that the state's general fund is shrinking even on a per capita basis. When adjusted for inflation, the general revenue fund appropriation for 2018 was $350 million less than it was five years earlier. "What many of these lawmakers neglected to mention," said Ted Boettner, the group's executive director, "is that our state budget has already been drastically reduced over the last several years and that our tax levels are at an all-time low."

The most glaring example has been the state's failure to better train and educate its workforce, one of the key factors that large companies weigh into their decisions on where to build new facilities. Only 20 percent of West Virginia's citizens have a bachelor's degree, putting it in last place among the fifty states. But despite this obvious need for education funding, the legislature has slashed $70 million from higher education in recent years. Its per-student spending was lower in 2018 than it was in 2008.

As a result, the state's public colleges and universities doubled their tuition between 2002 and 2017, which drove many poorer students out of the system. In 2017, the state's Higher Education Policy Commission reported that enrollment at the eleven four-year institutions in West Virginia had declined for seven consecutive years. West Virginia University, the flagship of the system, has been in such financial turmoil that Moody's Investors Service in August 2017 reduced it to junk bond status.

Previous generations of elected officials in West Virginia, even in the Republican Party, recognized that they could not eradicate their state's poverty and isolation without public investment. In his book *An Appalachian New Deal*, Jerry Bruce Thomas wrote that the state's Republican leadership acted in lockstep with the state's business interests in the 1920s but still found the public resources to help bring West Virginia into the modern era:

> The size and cost of government grew substantially as the pro-business Republican regime of the twenties . . . provided more public services such as building, maintaining, and policing a system of highways; expanding the department of public safety; building up a state agricultural bureaucracy; overseeing a state system of worker's compensation; increasing the functions of

the state auditor; expanding the department of mines; and supporting numerous health and educational institutions. In response to women's suffrage and in acknowledgment of other Republican constituencies, the regime put together the elements of a state welfare system with the establishment of the Bureau of Negro Welfare and Statistics, a Veterans' Service Officer, and the State Board of Children's Guardians. The regime also undertook the building of a costly new capitol on the banks of the Kanawha in east Charleston. Though some of these efforts were sparingly funded, they nevertheless indicate a willingness to expand the power of state government.

That is not the state's Republican Party in the twenty-first century, nor even its Democratic Party. Both have taken the position that the state cannot afford an expansion of its budget or raise additional tax revenues. What, then, is West Virginia's strategy to lift itself out of last place in so many measures of public welfare, if not investing in education, worker re-training, and health care? It has been to follow the dictates of the Koch brothers and other corporate donors—shrink state government, cut corporate taxes, and, above all, do nothing to stand in the way of a resurgence of coal mining.

In 2006, Democratic Governor Joe Manchin became a darling of conservative think tanks when he pushed through a reduction in the state's corporate tax rate from 9 to 6.5 percent, which the right-wing Cato Institute called "the most pro-growth tax reform" in the country. As it turned out, this raid on the state's revenues did nothing to create growth. While states around the country set records for job growth in the succeeding years, West Virginia had 39,000 fewer jobs in 2015 than when the tax cuts began, despite a boom in natural gas drilling in the northern part of the state. In 2016, its corporate tax revenues were lower than they had been in 1990.

"The business tax cuts blew a huge hole in the budget, to the tune of $236 million this year alone," the Center on Budget and Policy wrote in a 2015 report. "Instead of competing better nationally, West Virginia has fallen further behind."

* * * *

WEST VIRGINIA'S POLITICS are rife with conflicts of interest and ethical breaches that would be the stuff of scandal in many other states. The most obvious example is Governor Jim Justice himself. Justice won over the voters with a folksy accent and plainspoken manner that come straight from the hollows. He is six feet seven, weighs nearly four hundred pounds, and is not afraid to dish it out to his opponents. In vetoing a budget sent to him by the legislature, he showed up in the Capitol rotunda with a pile of fresh bull manure on a silver platter and called the spending plan "a bunch of political you-know-what."

As a coal company owner and the state's richest man, Justice argued in his campaign that no one was better equipped to bring back the state's flagging coal industry. But it's to the state's enduring shame that it was willing to overlook his well-publicized disregard for the public's welfare as a businessman.

At the time he was campaigning for governor, Justice's mining companies, including Southern Coal Corporation, owed more than $2 million in federal fines for more than four thousand violations spanning seven years and five states, fifteen hundred of them considered reasonably likely to cause injury or illness. Justice, whose net worth *Forbes* has put at $1.6 billion, also owed mountains of debt for unpaid suppliers and delinquent property taxes, according to various lawsuits. One of his coal companies, Sequoia Energy, was in arrears with Harlan County, Kentucky, for $653,169 in back taxes covering three years. While owing the government money, Justice shelled out $175 million to buy and restore the historic Greenbrier Resort in White Sulphur Springs, West Virginia, a project that included $25 million to build three football fields and a training center for the New Orleans Saints.

U.S. Representative George Miller, then the ranking Democrat on the House Committee on Education and the Workforce, told National Public Radio in 2014 that Justice obviously was wealthy enough to pay off his fines. "He's a major figure within the community, and yet he just simply chooses to ignore this," Miller said. "He's certainly exhibit A of the kind of operator that should not be allowed to continue with reckless disregard of the law."

Justice's priority as governor has been to promote the interests of the coal industry, and thus his own. Shortly after Trump's inauguration, he asked the president to support $4.5 billion in annual subsidies for eastern coal companies, and he vocally supported Trump's reversal of President Obama's Clean Power Plan, the centerpiece of the nation's effort to combat global warming. (The *Washington Post* pointed out that the coal subsidy, which Trump took seriously but was never adopted, would have come to $130,000 for every coal employee in Appalachia.)

Like Trump, Justice failed to divest himself from his complex network of business interests and put no mechanism in place to ensure that they would not conflict with his duties as governor. Quite to the contrary, not long after his election, he made Larry Puccio, who had run his campaign and transition, a registered lobbyist for Greenbrier and his coal interests. His conflict of interest descended to one of its lowest points in March 2019 when he pushed through a reduction in the severance tax for steam coal—used in coal-fired power plants—from 5 to 3 percent, which is projected to cost the state budget $60 million.

Mitch Carmichael, who served as the state senate president before losing his seat in the 2020 election, was another politician with an ethical blind spot. He spent years promoting legislation that benefited Frontier Communications, a large internet provider that also happened to employ him as a sales director. In April 2013, he voted for an amendment to bar other companies from competing with Frontier in offering high-speed internet to areas the company already covered. Frontier had lobbied for the amendment, and Carmichael added his voice in support, saying the state's effort should go toward areas without internet, not where Frontier was already operating. "The Broadband Council should focus on households that don't have broadband right now, not on upgrading homes that already have it," Carmichael said. "It's not speed. It's access."

Frontier had a poor track record in West Virginia. The state hired the company in 2010 to lay fiber-optic cable and extend high-speed internet in rural areas under a $126 million federal grant from the Obama administration's fiscal stimulus plan. At the time, West Virginia ranked forty-seventh among the fifty states in broadband availability, with only 52 percent of households equipped with high-speed internet. Frontier bungled the job. In April 13, a Virginia-based consultant hired by the administration of then governor Tomblin, ICF International, found that the stimulus funds were going to a "fragmented" high-speed network that solely benefited Frontier instead of opening up the territory to competition. State and federal audits later found that Frontier had "padded" hundreds of invoices, inflated the amount of cable installed, and run fiber-optic lines to public facilities where cable already existed. The company only installed a little more than two-thirds of the 915 miles of fiber-optic cables called for in the contract, but was still paid the full $42 million for the project. A report commissioned by Senator Manchin in 2018 found that West Virginia was still forty-seventh in the country in broadband coverage.

But none of this kept Carmichael from advocating for Frontier after the Republicans gained control of the Senate in 2014 and he was promoted to majority leader and then senate president. Frontier lobbied against a proposal in 2015 for the creation of a state-owned fiber-optic network to bring internet services to rural areas that had been ignored by the company. Carmichael told reporters that he would abstain from voting on the measure, but then the powerful senate president made it clear where he stood on the issue. "It takes what is a private enterprise and makes it a public enterprise," he said. "And if you believe that the government runs things better than the private sector then I would say you'd probably be inclined to vote for that."

In 2016, an unseemly bidding war broke out over which internet provider would have the privilege of having Carmichael on its payroll. A smaller firm, Citynet, hired Carmichael away from Frontier. Not to be undone, Frontier hired him back the next week with what embittered Citynet executives said was a doubling of his salary. Was he worth that money merely because of his sales abilities? A possible answer was provided in April 2017 when Carmichael defied the company and supported a bill that would allow nonprofit co-ops to set up high-speed internet in rural communities. Frontier fired him a month later. But the senate president wouldn't be unemployed for long. He had a job waiting for him at Citynet.

And, finally, there is the third pillar of West Virginia's ethically challenged leadership, Roger Hanshaw, speaker of the House of Delegates. Hanshaw, who was elected speaker in August 2018, is a lawyer for natural gas companies who has unashamedly done their bidding on the House floor. In 2017, he was a prime mover of the bill that exempted natural gas companies from the aboveground storage tank law passed after the Elk River chemical spill. On the financial disclosure form he filed with the state's Ethics Commission, he stated that he works for the Charleston firm of Bowles Rice but made no mention of its work for gas companies.

There are more than a dozen other legislators with ties to natural gas concerns. But none of these conflicts need stop the lawmakers from voting on legislation that could affect their interests. Because the rules of the House of Delegates include a provision stating that lawmakers only must recuse themselves if fewer than five people would benefit from the legislation that poses the conflict. In fact, the rule *requires* them to vote if they are in a "class" of five or more people. Since few pieces of legislation benefit fewer than five people, the rule is perfectly designed to ensure corporate influence in the legislature.

* * * *

ON MAY 5, 2016, a billionaire named Donald Trump came to Charleston on his personal 757 to bask in the adulation of the poorest white people in the country. He had clinched the Republican nomination a day earlier, and cheering coal miners in their helmets and coveralls would be the perfect backdrop for his victory lap. They waited outside the Charleston Civic Center for hours in full regalia: blue-and-yellow miner's uniforms, helmets with flashlights affixed on front, boots caked with the black dust of the mines.

Trump lumbered onto the stage with the crowd stamping and singing and waving signs that read "Trump Digs Coal." He put on a miner's helmet for less than ten seconds and told them to not bother voting in the primary, to forget local races, because he had already won. "Save your vote for the general election," he said. "Forget this one." Then he spoke the words that would not come true no matter how many times he said them: "We're going to put the miners back to work. We're going to put the miners back to work."

That the miners of West Virginia would align themselves with a fast-talking New York real estate developer and help elect a corrupt coal baron as governor is more than just a sad irony of twenty-first century American politics. It's like one of the planets veered out of its orbit. Miners struggling against the coal companies was once as much a part of Appalachia as moonshine and bluegrass. It may seem trite in a country where even many liberals have turned against the labor movement, but West Virginia miners once fought and died for a living wage. Labor enthusiasts in West Virginia still commemorate the Battle of Blair Mountain, the 1921 insurrection in which a hundred striking miners were killed battling sheriff's deputies funded and armed by the coal barons. The miners lost that battle, the biggest insurrection since the Civil War, but victory would not be long in coming. After the Wagner Act of 1935 legalized the rights of private-sector unions to bargain collectively, the United Mine Workers of America (UMWA) emerged as a major force in West Virginia politics, secured good wages and benefits for its members, and helped keep the state a Democratic stronghold for decades.

This bears little resemblance to modern-day West Virginia. The UMWA was routed and driven out of most coal operations in the anti-union climate that prevailed after Ronald Reagan's presidency, and now mostly represents retirees trying to hang on to their health benefits. To its shame, the union gave its endorsement to Jim Justice, essentially turning a blind eye to his flagrant violations of mine safety, once one of the focal points of its bargaining. Worse still, the union is now complicit in a political movement that can only mean further misery for the working people of West Virginia. During the overlap of the Trump and Justice administrations, coal companies were once again unbound, free to shave off mountaintops and pollute surrounding communities while providing few of the jobs promised to unemployed miners.

West Virginia's leaders have hoodwinked voters into believing that reviving coal is the key to their state's future, that high-paying jobs can be brought back—but it is really just about maintaining profits in the short term for coal company owners like Jim Justice. As recently as 2011, it was boom times for the U.S. coal industry. Coal consumption had recovered from the Great Recession, and both the prices of coal and the stock of coal companies were at record highs. But then the shale revolution dramatically reduced the price of natural gas, and technological advances had a similar effect on the cost of renewable energy. Almost overnight, coal was no longer competitive in electricity markets. At the same time, a reduction of Chinese demand for metallurgical coal, which had been a major source of income for the industry, depressed coal prices worldwide. By 2015, the coal industry was in virtual collapse. Three of the four biggest coal producers in the United States were in bankruptcy.

The implications of this market Armageddon were obvious. If the environmental devastation wrought by strip mining was once justified by coal's central place in the world's supply of electricity, why was it needed now that cleaner and cheaper sources were available? Is it still worth the destruction of coalfield communities, the poisoning of human beings, and the destruction of ecosystems? Is preserving a stream of profits for a small, politically influential coterie of coal company executives a sufficient reason to preserve coal mining?

Certainly it could not be justified on the basis of jobs. The coal industry had stopped being an engine of job creation many years ago, in part because the advent of mountaintop removal and decades of automation in underground mining had dramatically reduced coal companies' manpower needs. West Virginia's coal-mining employment peaked at 130,000 people in 1940 and has been in steady decline ever since. By 2016, only eleven thousand people were mining coal in the state. When Donald Trump appeared at the Charleston Civic Center in May 2016 and proclaimed that a revival of coal mining was going to bring better times to West Virginia, he was talking about an industry that employed only 1.4 percent of the state's workers that year. After Trump took a wrecking ball to almost all of the environmental regulations that Obama had placed on the coal industry, and Justice pushed as hard as he could for his industry, the number of mining jobs rebounded to nearly fourteen thousand in 2019, still a fraction of the state's total employment.

* * * *

A HANDFUL OF JOBS that will go to someone else mean little to the rural poor of West Virginia, who only get misery from the coal industry. There are still people in the southern counties of the state who remember the horrendous mining disasters of the past and know how easily they could happen again. The most shameful episode came after a coal slurry impoundment dam maintained by the Pittston Coal Company in Buffalo Creek, West Virginia, collapsed in 1972, wiping out four thousand homes and drowning 125 people in a tsunami of toxic sludge. In April 2010, an underground explosion at Massey Energy's Upper Big Branch mine in Montcoal, West Virginia, killed twenty-nine miners, the worst U.S. mining disaster in forty years. The federal Mine Safety and Health Administration slapped the company with a record $10.8 million fine after concluding that Massey's corporate culture had led directly to the accident.

Even without outright disasters, the rural communities of West Virginia pay a huge price for mountaintop removal. This most destructive form of strip mining is home grown, first introduced to the world in 1970 in Fayette County, West Virginia. Ironically, it turned into a broad assault on the Appalachian landscape only after environmentally friendly amendments to the Clean Air Act were enacted in 1990. In an effort to curtail the production of acid rain, the new provisions required power companies to burn cleaner, low-sulfur coal, the kind that is predominant in the mountains of southern West Virginia. Just as timber companies once leveled all of the Appalachia forest, industry now was going after the mountains themselves, which do not grow back. The area covered by blasting permits, which amounted to less than ten thousand acres in the entirety of the 1980s, exceeded twelve thousand acres in 2002 alone. By 2009, Appalachian Voices, a nonprofit group that fights mountaintop removal, calculated that five hundred mountains had been blown apart in Appalachia and 1.2 million acres flattened, an area the size of Delaware. Duke University researchers published topographical imagery in 2016 showing that parts of Appalachia were 40 percent flatter than before the advent of mountaintop removal.

Communities in the pathway of this destruction have been treated as collateral damage. In the early 2000s, Shirley Stewart Burns, a doctoral candidate at West Virginia University, set out to document the human cost of mountaintop removal. Property owners told her the blasting had ruined their wells, put cracks in their foundations, separated walls from floors, knocked windows out of their framing, and hurled boulders the size of softballs into their yards. "If a rock this big hits you or your car or your house, you're going to have more than a headache," one property owner told her. "It's going to ruin your whole week, because there's going to be a funeral." Even under the coal-friendly regime of President George W. Bush, the U.S. Environmental Protection Agency found in a 2003 draft environmental impact statement that the dumping of blasting debris into "valley fills" had smothered more than seven hundred headwater streams across Appalachia, which other studies said had allowed arsenic and heavy metal contamination into groundwater.

It's not hard to find people in the state's coal regions whose families have been shattered by the coal mining that the state's leadership is so eager to preserve. Junior Walk, a bearded man in his twenties who works as an anti-coal activist, grew up in an old company shack wedged in the hollows of a place called Coal River Valley, which is surrounded by the gouged peaks of Coal River Mountain. From the time he was a small boy, a mining company, Massey Energy, had been blowing the tops off those peaks, sending clouds of dust and debris and chemicals raining down onto his community. "There was blasting dust being peppered down on us all the time," Walk said. "Our well water came out blood red, because they did underground slurry injection on those hillsides. You wouldn't let your dog drink it."

Researchers have documented a bleak pattern of ill health in the regions around the coalfields. Indiana University professor Michael Hendryx has published numerous studies showing higher rates of cancer, kidney disease, and other ailments, even after adjusting for age, poverty, smoking, obesity, and cultural factors. The studies are consistent with the commonsense observations of people in the coal regions, where everyone knows someone who died before their time. "When twenty-year-old nonsmokers start coming down with lung cancer, something is wrong," said Debbie Jarrell, co-director of Coal River Mountain Watch, a group that opposes mountaintop removal in the southern part of the state.

* * * *

WHAT HAPPENS TO THE state's business while its elected officials are busy influence peddling, promoting coal and natural gas, and slashing departmental budgets? The answer is simple. It doesn't get done, and the results are often tragic.

There could be no more distressing example than the state's handling of the opioid epidemic, which in recent years has killed a higher percentage of people in West Virginia than any other state. Between 2014 and 2018, overdose deaths claimed 4,066 people in the state, the vast majority of which involved heroin, fentanyl, and other opioids. As in many other states, the social and economic effects of the pandemic made the problem worse. The state saw a spike in deaths, from 878 in 2019 to 1,275 in 2020.

For more than two decades, crooked pharmacies known as "pill mills" were flooding West Virginia, especially in depressed coal regions in the southern part of the state, with highly addictive opioids like OxyContin and Vicodin. Addiction to prescription drugs was causing such devastation in rural areas that state Attorney General Darrell McGraw filed two lawsuits in 2012 that accused fourteen national drug wholesalers of turning a blind eye to the suspiciously large orders of painkillers from small-town pharmacies. According to the lawsuit, H.D. Smith Wholesale Drug Co. shipped 39,000 pain pills over a two-day period to two small pharmacies in Mingo County. Over four years, Top Rx sold more than 300,000 tablets of hydrocodone to a pharmacy in the town of War, with a population of 808 people. Tug Valley Pharmacy in Mingo County ordered 820,000 hydrocodone pills in 2007, a number that increased to three million in 2009. Mingo County has 24,000 people. "The distribution of vast amounts of narcotic medications to some of the smallest towns and unincorporated rural areas of our state should have set off more red flags than a school of sharks at a crowded beach," said a member of the state's House of Delegates, Don Perdue.

It was not just the pharmaceutical companies that should have noticed something was wrong. After the lawsuits were filed, the drug companies, concerned about their continuing liability, began obeying a state law requiring them to report suspicious levels of prescriptions to the West Virginia Board of Pharmacy. Between June 2012 and December 2016, the companies sent more than 7,200 reports to the board. But the board did nothing with the reports. It made no contact with pharmacies and no referrals to law enforcement agencies. When Eric Eyre, a reporter for the *Charleston Gazette-Mail*, asked to review the records at the board's offices in 2016, he found them stuffed into two banker's boxes, uncounted and filed in no meaningful order. At the same time that West Virginia taxpayers were paying for a lawsuit against companies, their state government was not lifting a finger to stop crooked pharmacies from flooding the state with opioids. As is now well known, the nation's failure to prevent pharmaceutical companies from aggressively pushing prescriptions drugs on the populace led to the heroin and fentanyl epidemic, which has cost so many lives that the life expectancy of the United States went down in 2014 for the first time since World War I.

One of the lobbyists who worked feverishly to prevent government from interfering with the pharmaceutical trade was Patrick Morrisey, a conservative Republican who defeated McGraw in the 2012 election to become West Virginia's new attorney general. Morrisey had previously been a lobbyist for a pharmaceutical trade group, Health Care Distribution Management Association, that represented ten of the companies named in McGraw's suits. What's more, Morrisey's wife, Denise Henry, remained a lobbyist for one defendant, Cardinal Health, the nation's second largest drug distributor, even after her husband took office. Between 2013 and late 2015, Morrisey's first two years as attorney general, Cardinal Health had paid $1.47 million to his wife's Washington lobbying firm. Cardinal Health and its employees donated $5,000 to Morrisey's campaign, and a lawyer for the pharmaceutical company, Mark Carter, served as co-chair of his campaign transition team.

If it was not enough of a conflict that Cardinal's lawyer was serving on Morrisey's transition team at the same time his office was suing the company, it only got worse. Morrisey claimed that he recused himself from any role in the case shortly after taking office in January 2013. But the *Gazette-Mail* obtained documents showing otherwise, including a May 2013 email that Morrisey's chief deputy, Dan Greear, sent to Jim Cagle, an outside counsel the AG's office had hired to work on the case. In the email, Greear wrote that he had discussed the case with Carter and that Morrisey had been looped into the conversation. "I have discussed this with the AG and he has given me specific instructions," Greear told Cagle. The newspaper also reported that Morrisey met with Carter in March of 2013 and with Cardinal Health executives in May of that year.

There is no way of knowing whether Morrisey's intervention caused his office to ease up on Cardinal Health. In 2017, Cardinal Health and another company announced that they had jointly settled the lawsuit for a combined $36 million, just a cost of doing business for a company with a 2016 net income of $1.4 billion.

Federal funds to provide treatment for opioid addiction made their way to West Virginia in the last years of the Obama administration, but very little has come from the state's own resources. Cabell County, West Virginia, set up a pathbreaking program for treating addicts after its emergency medical service provider responded to twenty-six overdoses in a single day in August 2016, an outbreak that drew international attention. The county's EMS created a quick response team that follows up with offers of treatment to overdose victims. But the effort had to rely on two federal grants after the state refused to provide any funding. "If we hadn't found federal grants, this program would not exist," said Connie Priddy, coordinator of the quick response team. To Justice's credit he later earmarked money to replicate the program in a handful of other counties.

The governor also took advantage of a provision in the Affordable Care Act that allows states to obtain a waiver so that Medicaid can used for drug treatment. Prior to the ACA becoming law, low-income adults without physical or mental disabilities were generally denied coverage for substance abuse disorders. The ACA's passage vastly expanded drug users' access to treatment and also prevented private insurers from denying coverage based on preexisting drug addiction. According to data released by the federal Agency for Healthcare Research and Quality, the number of West Virginians showing up for drug-related hospitalization without coverage dropped by 86 percent after the ACA became law, the third largest decrease in the nation. While the number of overdose deaths in the state increased by 25 percent between 2015 and 2016, the increase dropped to 11 percent the following year. West Virginia's overdose deaths in 2017 still gave it the highest per capita rate in the country, but the epidemic was slowing. Lives were being saved.

But in January 2018, Morrisey joined seventeen others state attorneys general in a federal lawsuit that sought to have the ACA ruled unconstitutional. After a Texas federal judge ruled in favor of the plaintiffs in December of that year, Morrisey justified his participation by claiming that the ACA had driven up health premiums in West Virginia by 160 percent. There was, in fact, an average 30 percent increase that year in the lowest marketplace premiums offered in each region, although the premiums later stabilized and even declined in 2021. But Morrisey conveniently left out the reason for the short-term increase. It is well established by nonpartisan experts that Donald Trump's public vow to destroy the law created such uncertainty in the insurance industry that companies increased premiums to hedge their bets. Trump's administration cut funding for insurance industry subsidies designed to stabilize premiums, and the 2017 tax cut law repealed the requirement that every American have insurance, ensuring an exodus of younger and healthier people from the insurance rolls and further upward pressure on premiums. The ACA was hacked nearly to death by the same people who expressed shock that it was not working as intended.

Morrisey wasn't marshaling real facts. He was acting as an apparatchik of the corporate right wing, which is determined to repudiate the success of any government program that benefits the working people of America, lest they are awakened to how badly they've been deceived. The misplaced anger of the white working class is the logjam holding back real progress in America, and that's why a place like West Virginia, with fewer than two million people, is so important symbolically. Its citizens, sidelined by globalism and a postindustrial economy, are the exact constituency the Democratic Party needs to bring back into the fold. Call them rednecks and racists, picture them on the barstool with their cigarettes and painkillers and disability checks, but never forget that they are victims, not executioners, and the fate of our democracy rests in their hands.

2

"A Good, Honest, Christian Man": The Decline of Ethical Norms and the Erosion of Democracy

It wasn't much of a milestone, but it was his first. Dequante Hobbs, a playful child with a smile that lit up a room, was to graduate from the first grade in his elementary school in Louisville's west end, and he was wild with excitement. He planned to wear his red, white, and black sneakers, a shirt with a denim collar, and his favorite blue cap, a little boy's proud regalia, which the seven-year-old insisted on choosing himself and was already laid out days in advance. On May 22, 2017, as Dequante sat alone at his kitchen table eating a piece of white sheet cake, the innocence of childhood was entirely his.

The bullet that took that innocence away—which was fired in a dispute over a dice game in the rear yard next door, smashed through the kitchen window, and struck the little boy in the head—would reverberate across Kentucky and provide a ripe political opportunity for Matt Bevin, the brash Republican serving as governor. Bevin denounced the tragedy as "unacceptable" and said he shortly would unveil a plan for tamping down Louisville's escalating gang violence.

Bevin refused to provide details of the plan in advance, but some of the possibilities were obvious, such as augmenting Louisville Metro police patrols with state troopers or funding outreach programs to dissuade young men from joining gangs. That and more would be justified. Homicides recorded by the metro police had jumped from 56 in 2014 to 117 in 2016, and were headed for another record-breaking year when Dequante was killed. No one had come up with a real explanation for the rising tide of violence. It was natural, then, that there was some suspense over the governor's plans. The dead boy's mother, Micheshia Norment, asked that she be allowed to attend when the governor presented his new initiative to a meeting of clergy in the largely Black neighborhood.

On the day of the meeting, more than four hundred people packed the auditorium of Western Middle School. Bevin stepped to the podium with a black sports coat and an open-collar shirt, a surprisingly casual ensemble for such a somber occasion. To his left were three easels supporting large black maps with orange circles around the violence-ridden areas of the west end. It was evident that there had been preparation. The governor, a former military officer, appeared ready to announce a surgical strike on the neighborhood's crime. Bevin had wanted the event closed to the media, but his staff were told there had been a misunderstanding. The school's rules dictated that any assemblage on its premises be open to the public. Anyone who wanted came that day. They came to hear how Bevin was going to marshal the resources of the state to avenge Dequante's death.

And then the plan was unveiled. *Prayer.* The gangsters and drug dealers were going to be dispersed with prayer, like a Chinese lion dance scaring away evil spirits. With a straight face, Bevin told the clergy and residents that he recommended they walk through the neighborhood two to three times a week and stop on every corner for prayer. He said the beauty of the plan was that it would cost the state nothing, not even personnel costs because his administration would not be involved. "I'm not going to have a commissioner of prayer walks," he told the press later in the day. "We're not going to have 1-800 numbers and websites. . . . You don't need permission from me on how to do it."

Bevin's political stunt outraged the ministers in the room. One of them, the Rev. Clay Calloway, an associate pastor of

St. Stephen Baptist Church, said afterward he needed a "barf bag" to contain his revulsion. They were angry because they knew Bevin's plan was not directed at them or street crime in Louisville, but rather at white evangelicals who form a powerful political bloc in Kentucky. He was speaking right over the heads of those clergy, as if they and their grieving community didn't even exist, to send a message to a distant constituency more crucial to his political advancement. For the rest of Bevin's term, there would be no real initiative targeting urban crime. The governor was candid about regarding such violence as a cultural deficiency in the Black community that neighborhood leaders should deal with themselves, as if the previous three decades had not offered myriad examples of public policy driving down crime rates, such as CompStat in New York and Boston's Ten-Point Coalition, the latter involving clergy, but not clergy standing on street corners praying.

The bodies continued piling up in Louisville—173 dead in 2020. On any given week in the west end of Louisville, you can look up in the sky and see multicolored balloons wafting heavenward, as if there were a grand celebration every few days. But there is no celebration. It's become a tradition in the city's Black community, the release of balloons on the days they bury their young.

* * * *

BEVIN'S CYNICAL ATTEMPT to exploit a little boy's murder was just another day in the hard right's takeover of Republican state politics. It hardly stands out at all, and that is part of the tragedy of our times. Republicans governors and legislators seem to be in competition for how low they are willing to go to maintain their grip on power. No tragedy, not even a child's death, is too sensitive to use as political fodder. No amount of cynicism or demagoguery in how a politician exploits wedge issues like religion, abortion, guns, and immigration is out of bounds in the new political landscape of the red states. Republicans will champion the rights of citizens to carry guns right into our state legislatures, they will openly conspire to deny Black people the right to vote, they will demonize Syrian refugees, they will pass laws that allow motorists to plow into crowds of protesters—if that's what it takes to excite their core supporters and hold on to power.

What was once an indelible part of our country is slipping away. You can call it democracy, or just plain decency, the belief that here, more than anywhere else in the world, the majority's will prevails and leaders in the end strive for the common good. Herbert Croly, the Progressive-era journalist, once wrote, "We may distrust and dislike much that is done in the name of our country by our fellow-countrymen; but our country itself, its democratic system, and its prosperous future are above suspicion." A disturbing number of Republican state leaders now regard our democratic system not just with suspicion, but outright disdain. The day seventeen Republican states attorney general joined in an amicus brief arguing for overturning the results of the 2020 presidential election, that ideal was no longer the American consensus.

But it had been a long time since it was. While the Trump-inspired assault on voting rights and fair elections has rightfully generated national attention, the erosion of democratic norms in Republican states has been mounting for years with less publicity. The things we have come to associate with Trumpism—political cynicism, norm shattering, vilification of the media, voter suppression, the unseemly exploitation of God and Guns, the gushing of lies—were the predominant ethos in many Republican statehouses well before the 2016 election. The die was already cast when Michigan Governor Rick Snyder won passage of a law in 2012 that allowed him to usurp the power of local elected officials in Detroit and other cities across the state; when Republican legislatures in North Carolina and Wisconsin stripped their governorships of much of their authority so they could hamstring incoming Democrats; when Jim Justice, a billionaire coal magnate and resort owner, was elected governor of West Virginia, refused to release his tax returns, cut taxes on coal operations, and allowed state money to flow into his resort business; when thirty-four states, almost all Republican, passed new voter ID laws between 2000 and 2016 designed to impede minority voters; and when the Texas legislature in 2003 approved an unprecedented mid-decade redistricting plan that gerrymandered formerly Democratic districts and disenfranchised Blacks and Hispanics.

Most of the outrages emanating from red-state legislatures are about pure political opportunism rather than sincerely held beliefs—the use of wedge issues to stoke the passions of working-class voters and distract them from the corporate agenda that is the real business of many Republican lawmakers. This is an age-old strategy employed by Republicans and Democrats alike. As H.L. Mencken once observed, "The whole aim of practical politics is to keep the populace alarmed (and hence clamorous to be led to safety) by an endless series of hobgoblins, most of them imaginary." But in the modern era, Republican use of wedge issues has been in a class by itself. It was the philosophy behind Richard's Nixon's "Southern strategy," aimed at drawing votes in the South away from the Democratic Party with the use of racist dog whistles. It also inspired the highly deceptive Willie Horton ad that the campaign of George H.W. Bush used in 1988 to tar Michael Dukakis as soft on crime, part of Bush strategist Lee Atwater's promise to "strip the bark off the little bastard."

In the age of Trump, divisiveness as a political weapon has broken through all moral boundaries, and Republican states are the arena where the affronts to civility have been the most extreme. Florida Governor Ron DeSantis has shown that he will stop at nothing to inflame the prejudices of his base as he eyes the 2024 presidential election. DeSantis has played a bigger role than any other governor in the hysteria over critical race theory and LGBTQ issues in the public schools. He has fueled fears that critical race theory has infected public schools with the teachings that white people are racists, when all it really does is draw attention to the legacy of oppression in American institutions, a historical fact that few people in the political mainstream would have contested a few years ago. The very existence of a federal holiday honoring Martin Luther King Jr. is an acknowledgment of the country's racist past.

As Brookings researchers Rashawn Ray and Aleandra Gibbons wrote toward the end of 2021, "People who discuss CRT are not arguing that white people living today are responsible for what people did in the past. They are saying that white people living now have a moral responsibility to do something about how racism still impacts all of our lives today." But DeSantis has portrayed critical race theory as a "Marxist" ideology that is exposing schoolchildren to irreparable harm. "In Florida we are taking a stand against the state-sanctioned racism that is critical race theory," he said in announcing proposed legislation to bar such teaching in his state's schools. "We won't allow Florida's tax dollars to be spent teaching kids to hate our country or to hate each other."

DeSantis has been just as passionate in denouncing tolerance for LGBTQ rights in the schools. He generated international outrage when he signed legislation in 2022 that prohibited public school teachers from making any mention of sexual orientation or gender identity among children in the third grade or younger and limited such discussion in older grades. People may disagree on the merits of such legislation. But when Disney's chief executive, Bob Chapek, offered tepid criticism of the law at the company's annual shareholder meeting in March 2022, DeSantis saw a rare opportunity to win points with the Trump base. He declared war on Disney, his state's largest private employer and the linchpin of its tourism industry, backing legislation to eliminate the special tax district that for fifty-five years allowed the company to self-govern its 25,000-acre theme park. "If Disney wants to pick a fight, they chose the wrong guy," he said. "I will not allow a woke corporation based in California to run our state."

Texas Governor Greg Abbott is another presidential aspirant who has been shameless in seeking to inflame his citizens rather than appeal to their better instincts. When Abbott ran for governor in 2014, he came off as a moderate, business-oriented Republican, but in the Trump era he responded to the political climate by embracing far-right shibboleths that had little to do with sound governance and in some cases engendered criticism from his state's corporations. He has committed state funds to helping complete Trump's border wall, signed legislation outlawing the teaching of critical race theory in schools, banned municipal mask mandates, and heartily supported Texas's draconian abortion law. In April 2022, his effort to boost his support among far-right voters became even more divorced from sound government policy. He caused huge backups of commercial traffic at Mexican border crossings, threatening the nation's food supply, after he ordered state authorities to implement "enhanced safety inspections" on the Texas side of the border. He also began spending taxpayers' money to bus and fly migrants from Texas to Washington in an effort to embarrass the Biden administration. "Greg is an arch, arch far-right conservative, which remains a shock to me," Pearson Grimes, a former colleague of his at a Texas law firm, told the *New York Times*. "When I knew him long ago, I never dreamed this would be his politics." In the red states, it is hard to divine elected officials' personal beliefs, so eager are they to dangle shiny objects in front of voters to maintain their grip on power. This explains the unconscionable proposals for legislation to actually *loosen* arms restrictions within days of mass shootings in Texas and Georgia—which the sponsors knew would be the perfect time to appeal to the ugliest elements of their constituencies.

A number of blue states, including Massachusetts, Illinois, Rhode Island, New Jersey, and New York, were once notorious for the swaggering corruption and contempt for democracy on the part of their elected officials. It is hard to forget the Mafia's penetration of New Jersey state government in the 1960s or, more recently, the Big Dig scandals in Massachusetts, Bridgegate in New Jersey, the Governor Rod Blagojevich affair in Illinois, and legendary corruption in the New York State legislature.

But while such outright corruption is on the wane in those states, a studied contempt for good government has intensified in the red states. There is no Democratic counterpart to Texas Attorney General Ken Paxton, who has faced so many corruption allegations, including bribery and abuse of office, that the local media can hardly keep track, and yet he's not been condemned by his party's leadership. Compare that to the decisive role Democrats played in forcing New York Governor Andrew Cuomo from office. There is nothing in the Democratic states like the appalling conflicts of interest at the top of West Virginia government. Blue states don't allow ALEC to draft anti-worker legislation in statehouses across the country.

The GOP's corruption is different from that of the Democratic scoundrels of old. Democratic politicians would occasionally get caught stealing and then be shunned. The Republicans corrupt democracy itself, they do it out in the open, and are lionized by their party for it. As George Packer wrote recently, Republican corruption has "less to do with individual perfidy than institutional depravity. It isn't an occasional failure to uphold norms, but a consistent repudiation of them. It isn't about dirty money so much as the pursuit and abuse of power, power as an end in itself, justifying almost any means."

* * * *

MATT BEVIN MAY have been a one-term governor in a very small state. But his tenure was instructive. It perfectly encapsulated the modern era of Republican politics. He was one of a new breed: hard-right governors who came to power in reaction to the Obama presidency and blazed a trail of cynicism and malfeasance. It was not just their retrograde policies that cost their states so dearly, but the shambles they made of democratic traditions, of decency.

Like Trump, Bevin was once considered too extreme and too obviously self-serving to be elected, and yet Kentuckians woke up one morning with him as their governor. He employed all of the anti-democratic facets of Trumpism before there was even such a thing as Trumpism. He attacked the press, investigated his political enemies, demonized immigrants, gave sweetheart deals to cronies, attacked teachers and other public servants, and made unconscionable use of religion and the abortion issue in an attempt to solidify his base. Some of his stunts went too far even by the standards of his fellow Republicans. He fueled the dangerous anti-vaccine movement by making a show of purposely exposing his children to chicken pox. He dispatched the Kentucky State Police to arrest a retirement board chairman who refused—rightfully, as it turned out—to recognize Bevin's authority to fire him. He was caught on video telling preachers to ignore IRS regulations governing political endorsements from the pulpit. He invited Kentuckians to his Facebook and Twitter accounts, and then blocked six hundred of them because of their views. He sought to burnish his credentials with hillbillies by speaking at a rally for the legalization of cockfighting.

Some in Kentucky's Republican establishment were convinced that his conservatism was a put on, that the New Hampshire-raised Bevin was masquerading as a Tea Partier out of sheer opportunism. "If Matt Bevin had moved to a state where he had a better shot at being elected to office as a Democrat, he would articulate the values of liberalism with the same conviction he now talks about conservatism," said Josh Holmes, former campaign chair to Senator Mitch McConnell. "It's abundantly clear that his guiding light is to embrace whatever gets himself a little further down the road."

Bevin bounded onto the stage of Kentucky politics when he took up the banner of the Tea Party and launched a bid to take down McConnell in the 2014 Republican primary. He had never held elective office and was little known in the state. But he had much to recommend him to conservatives. He was the father of nine children—four of them adopted—and paraded them all to church on Sundays. Handsome and quick-witted, the former army captain and hedge fund entrepreneur had the polish and oratorical skills of a political star. (Later, as governor, he delivered the green flag to a Quaker State 400 racing event while dangling from a Black Hawk helicopter over Kentucky Speedway, prompting NBC auto racing analyst Rutledge Wood to dub him "the coolest governor in the world.") He also had the off-putting arrogance of the far right, but that was seen as a plus: he would not let niceties get in the way of his stated plan to slash big government and put Christianity at the center of public life. Though he had endorsed Bevin's opponent, Kentucky Senator Rand Paul called him "a good, honest, Christian man."

McConnell was considered vulnerable in the primary. Despite his leadership in the Senate and legendary political acumen, McConnell is unpopular in his home state. One poll in 2016 showed him with a 51 percent disapproval rating, the highest of any senator (though he was later edged out by Maine Senator Susan Collins). McConnell had angered Tea Partiers when, as Senate minority leader, he went along with a deal in 2013 to end a sixteen-day government shutdown, a blow to Senator Ted Cruz's effort to use the standoff to force the defunding of Obamacare. It was a bum rap against a leader who arguably had done more for conservatives than any other figure in the Senate, and it ignored the realities of Washington politics. The Democrats at the time controlled the presidency and the Senate, and were not going to accede to the destruction of Obama's signature achievement, shutdown or no shutdown. Meanwhile, more than two million federal employees were going without paychecks, and polls showed a majority of Americans were holding Republicans responsible.

But Bevin made McConnell's deal to end the shutdown the centerpiece of his campaign, and baited his opponent at every turn for what Tea Party groups, in an open letter, called his "progressive liberal voting record" and "willingness to roll over and cede power to President Obama and the liberals in Washington." It didn't matter that McConnell had earned the nickname "the Grim Reaper" for his success at consigning almost every Obama initiative to the graveyard; Bevin hammered away at the glaringly false narrative. Sharing the stage with McConnell at the annual Fancy Farm Picnic in rural southwestern Kentucky, Bevin taunted his state's longest-serving senator, calling him "mud-slinging Mitch" and saying "the only thing he has to run on is destroying other people." He also mocked McConnell for leaving the stage before his challenger spoke. "Be a man, stand up and put your money where your mouth is." The candidate made enough noise to pick up key endorsements and campaign funding from FreedomWorks and the Senate Conservatives Fund, two powerful supporters of far-right causes across the country.

Unfortunately for Bevin, McConnell was a pretty good political brawler himself and went after Bevin in similar fashion, labeling him an "East Coast con man" and "Bailout Bevin" because his family-owned bell factory in Connecticut accepted a $200,000 government check after being destroyed in a fire. It was a scurrilous and truth-challenged campaign on both sides, even by Kentucky standards, and Bevin ended up being trounced by twenty-five points in the primary. He emerged bitter, refusing to endorse McConnell in the general election. "You can't punch people in the face, punch people in the face, punch people in the face, and ask them to have tea and crumpets with you and think it's all good," he said. "Life doesn't work that way."

But when Bevin decided to run for governor the following year, he had second thoughts about being on the outs with a man he had described as having "a Machiavellian death grip" on Kentucky politics. The state's popular Democratic governor, Steve Beshear, was leaving office due to term limits. Bevin entered the race as a dark horse, but he emerged with a narrow victory in a four-way Republican primary after benefiting from an ugly dispute between two of his opponents, Hal Heiner and James Comer. Heiner was forced to apologize in April 2015 after his campaign was linked to a Lexington blogger who had been promoting allegations that Comer had physically abused a former girlfriend in 1991 and accompanied her to an abortion clinic. Bevin eagerly took advantage of the feud, saying in a radio debate with the other candidates that he had personally heard Heiner talking about the allegations for months. "You told me that yourself, Hal," he said. "You told me in your office to my face." He later released a televised campaign ad that depicted Heiner and Comer in a food fight at a children's table and promised Bevin would bring "grown-up leadership" to the table.

After edging out Comer in the primary by a mere eighty-three votes, Bevin reached out to McConnell for his support in the general election, in which he faced the state's Democratic attorney general, Jack Conway. There was lingering animosity between McConnell and Bevin, but the two needed each other. McConnell was in possession of a formidable fundraising apparatus and a database of 1.2 million voters across the state, while Bevin had put the GOP within reach of winning Kentucky's governorship for only the third time since World War II. It didn't hurt that Bevin said he would fight to end Kentucky's distinction as the only state in the South that had not passed a right-to-work statute, a key issue for conservative patrons like the Koch brothers.

In his campaign, Bevin hit all the hot buttons of the far right. He attacked unions and Obamacare. He promised tax cuts and school vouchers and immediate right-to-work legislation. He was particularly animated in his denunciation of a 2015 Supreme Court decision, *Obergefell v. Hodges*, that legalized same-sex marriage, blaming Conway for failing to appeal a 2014 federal court decision that found Kentucky's defense of marriage amendment unconstitutional. He also stood behind Kim Davis, the Rowan County clerk who defied court orders that she issue marriage licenses to gay couples, and said he would defund Planned Parenthood in Kentucky by appropriating the group's federal funding, which goes through the governor's office. "As governor," he said, "I will prevent those dollars from being distributed, and order them returned to the federal government."

It was shameless pandering to evangelical Christians, but it worked. Conway had been ahead in the polls throughout the race, one survey showing him with a five-point lead over Bevin a week before the election. As it turned out, the polls were way off. Bevin ended up with 53 percent of the vote to Conway's 44 percent, a rout that political observers largely attributed to the Kim Davis controversy and Bevin's criticism of Conway for not fighting the legalization of same-sex marriage. Kentucky is close to the bottom in almost any measure of socioeconomic well-being, but Matt Bevin won the governorship by championing a law-breaking and bigoted county clerk.

A realignment of Kentucky politics was in the making. The Democrats who had traditionally held power in the state's government had long been as conservative as their Republican counterparts on many issues, and that had been enough to keep them in power. But that was before the Tea Party and the state Republican Party's plunge into arch-conservatism in the Obama years. Bevin was now the perfect governor for the times. Two years after his election, Republicans captured a majority in the state House for the first time since 1920, giving them full control of the statehouse. The last Democratic fortification standing in the way of the GOP's complete domination of the South had been wiped off the political map.

* * * *

BEVIN MOVED QUICKLY to upend Kentucky's political norms. Most notoriously, he dragged the state's politics into the sewer with his bitter attacks on political enemies, especially his predecessor, Steve Beshear, and his son, Andy Beshear, a Democrat like his father who was elected as attorney general in 2016.

The new governor ignited such an ugly feud with the Beshear family that it mired the state Capitol in litigation for years and, along with his attacks on teachers, probably helped make the difference when the younger Beshear narrowly defeated Bevin in the 2019 gubernatorial election.

The opening salvo in that feud was Bevin's decision to hire an Indianapolis law firm to investigate allegations that members of Steve Beshear's administration had been pressured to give donations to Democratic candidates for various state offices. His move came after federal authorities announced in March 2016 that Beshear's former Personnel Cabinet secretary, Tim Longmeyer, had been charged with accepting more than $200,000 in kickbacks in the awarding of a state contract. Federal investigators told the Louisville *Courier-Journal* that there was no evidence either Steve or Andy Beshear knew about the kickback scheme, but Bevin called reporters to his office and claimed that he had uncovered a mother lode of "greed and oftentimes corruption" in the previous administration and that he was going to root it out.

Such allegations would customarily be referred to the state's Executive Branch Ethics Commission, the Attorney General's Office, or federal authorities. However, none of those agencies would answer to Bevin, so he put the inquiry in the hands of an out-of-state law firm, Taft Stettinius & Hollister, which would naturally shape its conclusions to the interests of its client. The administration paid Taft Stettinius more than $600,000 over the next three years. All it got for its money were three reports and a handful of state ethics violations, but no criminal charges and no evidence of wrongdoing by the Beshears.

Peaceful transfers of power and the civility that political opponents extend to one another are among the hallmarks of democracy. Harvard professors Steven Levitsky and Daniel Ziblatt, in their book *How Democracies Die*, claim that one of the surest signs a country is sliding into authoritarianism is the erosion of "mutual toleration" between political rivals:

Mutual toleration refers to the idea that as long as our rivals play by constitutional rules, we accept that they have an equal right to exist. We may disagree with, and even strongly dislike, our rivals, but we nonetheless accept them as legitimate. This means recognizing that our political rivals are decent, patriotic, law-abiding citizens—that they love our country and respect the Constitution just as we do. It means that even if we believe our opponents' ideas to be foolish or wrong-headed, we do not view them as an existential threat.

Bevin failed that test miserably. His feud with the Beshear family, which consumed the four years of his governorship, was marked by the kind of invective more suited to a barroom than a modern political campaign. In Bevin's estimation, Steve Beshear was an "embarrassment to the state" whose administration engaged in "corruption, self-dealing, embezzlement and bribery." His son was "idiotic," "incompetent," and a "fraud." At a debate a week before the 2019 election, Bevin told the younger Beshear: "You've never created a job in your entire life—ever. You're the Hunter Biden of Kentucky. Everything you've gotten your father has handed to you." In the same vein, Democrats were "whiny liberals." The former head of the state employees' retirement system "should be in jail and that's a fact." A respected reporter for the *Courier-Journal* was "pathetic" and "a sick man." The list goes on. Joe Gerth, a columnist at the same paper, captured it perfectly two days after the 2019 election. "There will be plenty of time to dance on the grave of the nastiest man ever to hold the governor's office in Kentucky.... Matt Bevin didn't lose because his policies are out of step with Kentucky voters. He didn't lose because in his four years, he didn't govern as he promised when elected in 2015. He didn't lose because of scandal. Matt Bevin lost because he is a jerk."

There was an element of hypocrisy to Bevin's attacks on the Beshear administration for petty ethical lapses that did not rise to the level of criminal wrongdoing, because Bevin was guilty of breaching the public trust himself, including one scandal in which he derived personal financial benefit, something that was never the case with the Beshears. In March 2017, a company owned by Bevin purchased a gabled mansion in Anchorage, Kentucky, from another company belonging to fellow hedge fund investor Neil Ramsey. The very fact that Bevin was using a company to purchase his personal residence should raise eyebrows. It suggests he hoped to gain a tax advantage that is not available to the average Kentuckian. But there was a much bigger problem. Ramsey was a Bevin campaign contributor, a state contractor, and one of the governor's appointees to the state pension board, and he sold the mansion to Bevin for a price less than two-thirds of its value. The sale price was $1.6 million, but Jefferson County had assessed the house and ten adjoining acres at $2.57 million. Bevin hired his own appraiser in an unsuccessful effort to knock down the assessment and quell the controversy, and he later gave the appraiser's wife a $90,000-a-year state job. And it didn't stop there. He sought to have the state's taxpayers cover his legal fees during the tax appeal and initially barred the county's assessors from the second and third floors of the house. All this from a "good, honest, Christian man."

It wasn't just nasty words and hypocrisy that constituted Bevin's affront to Kentucky's democratic traditions. It was also his affront to another indispensable feature of democracy described by Levitsky and Ziblatt, and that is forbearance, "the idea that politicians should exercise restraint in deploying their institutional prerogatives." In other words, don't slash and burn your way through the halls of government just because you can. Give proper respect to precedent. Bevin failed that test as well. Because the Democrats still controlled the House of Representatives in his first two years, the new governor sought to go around the state's legislature, the General Assembly, and impose his will through executive actions, some of them legal and some not, but almost all of them defying the norms of the state's politics.

In his first year in office Bevin sought the abolishment or reorganization of seventy-six public boards governing higher education, medicine, public pensions, and of a host of professions. The professional boards oversaw the employment of more than a hundred thousand Kentuckians. Bevin made the boards a weapon in his crusade for deregulation. His goal was simple and brazen: to replace the boards' Democratic appointees with his own and restructure the institutions to give more power to the executive branch. Although many of the boards were creatures of the legislature, Bevin cited a state law that allowed governors to restructure boards when the General Assembly was not in session. His office claimed other governors had exploited that law in some fashion, including Steve Beshear, but clearly none in the modern history of Kentucky politics had ever taken such draconian action to consolidate power.

His most controversial move came in June 2016 when he signed an executive order dismissing the entire board of the University of Louisville so he could stack it with people more amenable to his plan for deep cuts to all of the state's colleges and universities. Bevin made no secret of his enmity toward the traditional mission of higher education. He regarded liberal arts courses as particularly expendable because they didn't prepare students for careers in business. "Find entire parts of your campus . . . that don't need to be there," he said in a speech to educators. Kentucky had been cutting higher education funds since 2008, but that was not enough for Bevin. Two months before taking his action against the Louisville board, he ordered a 4.5 percent budget reduction in the state's colleges and universities, again without authorization from the legislature. The unilateral budget cuts were a blatant violation of the separation of powers, and the Kentucky Supreme Court overturned his action later that year.

Another one of his power grabs involved the Kentucky Retirement Systems board, which Bevin wanted to control as part of his plan to cut back on retirement benefits for teachers and other public employees. Kentucky's public-employee retirement systems, which were fully funded as recently as 2001, had one of the biggest shortfalls in the nation a decade later. By the time Bevin took office in 2015, the systems were dangerously close to defaulting on their obligations. But the reason behind the shortfall was not that the state was being too generous to its retirees. Rather, the cause of the crisis was Kentucky lawmakers' failure to fund the systems, mismanagement on the part of the pension boards, and the fact that the system's administrators were duped by hedge funds into making risky investments. Desperate for a quick windfall to close the deficits they had been hiding from the public, the funds' administrators were easy marks for the hustlers on Wall Street. A 2018 investigative documentary by PBS's *Frontline* put it this way: "Starting in the fall of 2009, Kentucky's public pensions decided that to dig out from under, they would invest a portion of their portfolio in some of Wall Street's more exotic and risky investment vehicles, like hedge funds. . . . Wall Street was more than happy to answer Kentucky's call."

Bevin's fix for the shortfall was to put more hedge fund entrepreneurs on the board, such as his buddy Neil Ramsey, and make teachers, firefighters, police officers, and sanitation workers sacrifice benefits for others' mistakes. But first he had to take over the board. On the same day he revamped the university board, he issued an executive order that abolished the retirement board. He then established a new board with the same members, but added four new appointees, giving him effective control over the body. Before the restructuring, he fired board chair Thomas Elliott, prompting a legal opinion from Andy Beshear, then attorney general, stating that the move was illegal. Bevin showed what he thought of Beshear's opinion by dispatching state troopers to the next board meeting with orders to arrest Elliott if he tried to chair the meeting. By the time Beshear's lawsuit over the dismissal reached Franklin County Circuit Court, Judge Phillip Shepherd ruled that it was moot, because the legislature was by then fully controlled by Republicans who had upheld the governor's action. But the judge made no secret of his disgust with Bevin's tactics, saying from the bench, "The Commonwealth of Kentucky is not a police state."

* * * *

ONE OF THE OFT-STATED priorities of Matt Bevin was to make Kentucky more business friendly. He issued one press release after another boasting of the latest corporation that had agreed to put a factory or distribution center in the Bluegrass State. His goal of job creation justified other policies that might not seem so helpful to his working-class base, such as corporate tax cuts, the rollback of health and safety regulations, curtailment of public pension benefits, and the damage to unions produced by his right-to-work legislation. Getting rid of workplace safety regulations makes a coal miner's job more hazardous. Busting a union means lower wages and fewer benefits for a factory worker. These moves are very pleasing to the Republican Party's corporate benefactors. But how do you sell them to working Kentuckians? Matt Bevin knew the answer very well. You don't. Instead, you whip up the electorate's anger with wedge issues like the Second Amendment, abortion, school prayer, Obamacare, and immigration. Republican state leaders knew this long before Donald Trump came around. They learned the modern form of the art at the knee of Ronald Reagan. Bevin was an eager student of the discipline, so much that he'd still be in office if he hadn't overplayed his hand.

He wielded the politics of fear throughout his campaign and his governorship. He joined two dozen other Republican governors in pledging to block any Syrian refugees from coming into their states, even though refugees had almost never been tied to terrorist activity in this country. He said blood might be shed if Hillary Clinton were elected president and suggested her immediate impeachment if she were. He labeled Mitch McConnell soft on gun rights not long after the senator had won the NRA's

"Defender of Freedom" award. He promised to resist any cooperation with Obamacare even though his predecessor's acceptance
of one of the law's key measures, Medicaid expansion, had made
Kentucky a national leader in reducing its uninsured rate.

But there is one issue that Bevin exploited above all the others,
and that is religion. And he had good reason for doing so. According to the Pew Research Center, 49 percent of Kentuckians are
evangelical Protestants, and 75 percent of the state's residents believe in God, a higher rate than any other state outside the Deep
South except for neighboring West Virginia. The same research
found that roughly half of all Christians in Kentucky have no college and earn less than $30,000 a year. Republicans bank on the
assumption that they don't have the worldliness or intellectual
wherewithal to know when they're being had. Biven pounded
home the message that he was a "good, honest, Christian man,"
over and over. He signed a bill in 2017 that gave public high
schools the option of offering Bible literacy courses. He encouraged the student-led "Bring Your Bible to School Day." He went to
prayer breakfasts and declared a "Year of the Bible" in Kentucky
two years in a row. He lauded a Supreme Court decision upholding the right to prayer at public meetings, warning that religious
values are "under assault." He gave millions in state tax breaks to a
Noah's Ark theme park, which restricted its hiring to Christians.

In 2017, Bevin signed a religious freedom bill that prohibited
colleges, universities, and high schools from interfering in the
policy decisions of student groups, raising concerns among
human rights activists that it was green-lighting discrimination
against LGBTQ rights. The law prompted California to ban its
employees from making non-essential visits to Kentucky on state
time and led to the cancelation of two conventions in Louisville.

Bevin nearly succeeded in making Kentucky the first state in
the union to completely rid its territory of legal abortion. The
Pew Research Center found that 57 percent of Kentuckians be-

lieve abortion should be illegal in all cases, but no one really needed a pollster to tell them that. As Kentucky radio host Matt Jones put it, "For many in Kentucky, the issue of abortion isn't just an important issue, it's the only issue. . . . You can agree with them on every issue ranging from health care, to unions, to education. But if you are pro-choice, for some that is a level too far." It took political courage for the Beshears to support abortion rights, because it could only cost them votes. But Bevin was more about pandering. When Planned Parenthood of Kentucky and Indiana was about to open a new facility for abortions in downtown Louisville, having gotten clearance from the Beshear administration, Bevin blocked its license, setting off a federal court battle that was still pending when he left office. He almost harassed the state's other abortion provider, EMW Women's Surgical Center of Louisville, out of existence with prohibitive licensing requirements until a judge stepped in. In his 2019 campaign against Andy Beshear, he was over the top on the issue, saying his opponent would "always stand for death over life" and blasting him again and again for taking contributions from abortion providers. "He has accepted blood money time and again," he said, "and he continues to proudly do so."

No one has ever tallied the legal bill for Bevin's endless court battles over executive actions that were either illegal or irrelevant to the real needs of his state. Nor would it be possible to quantify the waste of political energy expended in his reckless attempt to tear down the pillars of Kentucky government, when his time could have been used improving education, health care, and infrastructure, the building blocks of a successful economy. Like Trump, Bevin thrived on divisiveness and chaos, no matter how it interfered with the state's business.

What is clear is that after four years of Matt Bevin, Kentucky's democracy was poorer and its social and economic life had deteriorated. Bevin often bragged about his administration setting new records for business investment, that his policy of corporate tax cuts and deregulation was paying off. In May 2017, Bevin told a news conference that in the first five months of the year, the state had attracted new business investment valued at $5.8 billion, surpassing the previous year's record of $5.1 billion. At that point in his tenure, he had announced 9,500 new jobs and promised many more. He had convinced the legislature to earmark $15 million to help a company called Braidy Industries build a $1.5 billion aluminum rolling mill in Ashland, Kentucky, a project that was to create 550 jobs at the plant and thousands more in spin-off industries. Bevin said it would be "as significant as any economic deal ever made in the history of Kentucky."

But as of late 2020, the plant had not been built and the company had run into trouble. In January 2020, the company's investors ousted its CEO, Craig Bouchard, paying him a settlement of $6 million, and changed Braidy's name to Unity Aluminum. A few months later, it was disclosed that the company had gotten a $200 million investment from a Russian company, United Co. Rusal, partly owned by Oleg Deripaska, an oligarch who is close to Vladimir Putin and is suspected by U.S. officials of having ties to organized crime. Governor Andy Beshear said if the company did not soon make good on its promises, he would ask for the state's money back.

More to the point, Bevin's claims of record job growth turned out to be a mirage. Numbers from the U.S. Bureau of Labor Statistics show that the pace of job growth shrank in the Bevin years. In 2015, the state had added 29,000 jobs, ranking it twenty-fifth in the nation. In 2018, after Bevin was in office for two full years, that number had decreased to 6,500 new jobs and Kentucky ranked forty-seventh in the country. In 2019, his final year in office, when the economy was still raging, the state actually lost 5,300 jobs. When pressed on Bevin's claim in October 2019 that his administration had created 57,000 new jobs, his spokesman told the *Courier-Journal* that the number referred to companies' commitments and would not come to fruition for several years, a qualifier that the paper said was rarely mentioned in the governor's public statements and campaign ads. Other economic measures showed similar backsliding. In 2016, Kentucky's official poverty rate was the ninth highest in the nation. In 2019, it was the seventh highest. Kentucky went from being tied for twenty-third highest in unemployment in 2015 to eleventh highest in 2019. The "coolest governor in the world" put a lot of money in the pockets of business leaders with his tax cuts, but he didn't do anything for the average citizen.

Nor did Bevin solve the state's pension mess, despite the ordeal he inflicted on Kentuckians—the questionable executive actions and resulting legal battles, the attacks on teachers, and the constant turmoil in the state Capitol. Part of Bevin's proposal for pension reform envisioned putting teachers hired after January 2019 into a hybrid retirement plan similar to a 401(k), instead of traditional pensions, requiring them to contribute more from their paycheck than existing teachers. It also would have ended the option for existing teachers to cash out accrued sick time and limited the cost-of-living increases for retired teachers, although the latter provision was eliminated in a later version of the bill. Kentucky's teachers, who cannot collect Social Security, were already angry about low pay and budget cuts, and Bevin's plan sent them into the streets for protest rallies. But those initial actions were nothing compared to what happened after Bevin and his Republican colleagues in the General Assembly resorted to an underhanded and patently illegal strategy to get the bill passed. The GOP had told the Democrats the bill was dead and then, on March 29, 2018, shoehorned it into a piece of legislation dealing with sewer issues. Democrats were blindsided, along with the press and the public. Nine hours after the 291-page measure was amended to the sewer bill, it was passed by both houses of the General Assembly and signed by the governor, with no hearings, no public comment, and no actuarial review, as required by law.

The teachers' anger boiled over. More than twenty-five schools around the state were closed as outraged teachers staged a sickout and converged on Frankfort in protest. Bevin, of course, was bristling and brought his continuing insults of teachers to a new low. When a reporter asked him on April 13 about the work stoppage, he gave the wrong answer: "I guarantee you somewhere in Kentucky today a child was sexually assaulted that was left at home because there was nobody to watch them."

Attorney General Beshear filed a lawsuit challenging the legality of the bill's passage, and a judge tossed out the legislation. Bevin left office without obtaining pension reform and no doubt harboring deep regrets about what he had said about the teachers. This was one group that knew it was being had. No one among the state's punditry had any doubts that his sexual assault remark and other rudeness toward teachers had cost him the election. And that is a disheartening reality: Matt Bevin was tossed out of office not because of his policies, not because he betrayed working people and undermined democracy, but because of his big mouth. The far right was still in control of Kentucky politics, the GOP having captured every other statewide office. Andy Beshear might have been elected governor, but he had little room to maneuver with Republican supermajorities in control of the General Assembly. This, of course, raised the prospects of a kinder, gentler Matt Bevin making a comeback. In early 2021, his website still contained the verbiage of a politician on the make; it still boasted of those 57,000 phantom jobs, the ones that may never appear, and it included a phrase that should give progressives a chill: "We're just getting started."

3

The Mirage of Success: Sun Belt States and the Future of America

HICKORY, NORTH CAROLINA, IS A CITY IN THE foothills of the Blue Ridge Mountains that to outward appearances is emblematic of the state's "economic miracle." Its historic downtown and neighborhoods of stately Victorian homes, oak-shaded streets, and big stone churches are part of what prompted *Reader's Digest* to name the city one of the country's ten best places to "live and raise a family." The city's low real-estate costs and pro-business posture have won plaudits from *Forbes* and *Money*. With museums, outdoor cafés, brewpubs, universities, and a twice-a-week farmers market in quaint Union Square, Hickory has seemingly earned its moniker of "All-American City."

It's a startling turnabout for a town that a little more than a decade ago was written off as one of the nation's biggest losers to global competition. Hickory and other communities in western North Carolina were once home to thriving furniture manufacturers. It is almost unimaginable today, but in 1961 the city of forty thousand people had forty-six furniture makers, eighty-nine hosiery mills, and twenty-seven other factories. The state as a whole was the national leader in the production of upholstery and wooden household furniture for much of the twentieth century, in part because its companies undercut their northern competitors with the help of low wages and anti-union militancy. By the end of the twentieth century, however, cheaper workers could be found in China and other Asian countries, and many of North Carolina's furniture makers said goodbye to their local employees and their vaunted reputations for craftmanship and moved operations offshore. Between 1999 and 2009, North Carolina lost half of its jobs in furniture manufacturing, an economic catastrophe that followed the loss of some 170,000 jobs in the state's textile and apparel industries in the five years following the passage of the North American Free Trade Agreement in 1996. Hickory, whose prosperity was built on both industries, textiles and furniture, saw the loss of 45,000 jobs between 2000 and 2013, and its unemployment rate skyrocketed from 2.8 percent to 15.5 percent in roughly the same period. The city entered the new century on the verge of becoming one of those rusted and listless old mill towns that dot the landscape of former industrial regions in the Northeast and Midwest.

That's where the "miracle" comes in. Beginning around 2010, technology companies recognized the region around Hickory as the perfect place for vast campuses that centralize the storage, processing, and dissemination of data. Catawba and Caldwell counties were already hubs for the production of fiber-optic cable and were eager to form a technology corridor along the lines of the Research Triangle that had long existed in the Raleigh-Durham area. They were able to offer huge tracts of inexpensive land for plants ten times the size of football fields, cheap electricity, and a moderate climate to accommodate the facilities' huge air-cooling systems. The shortage of skilled labor was not a problem, because the "data centers," as they are known, are essentially run by computers, requiring a relatively small number of employees, and those can be brought in from elsewhere. It also helped that state and local authorities, despite the limited potential for job creation, offered the companies generous tax breaks.

Google came first, opening a data center in 2008 in the Caldwell County seat, Lenoir, a half-hour drive from Hickory.

Apple came a year later, opening a similar facility in the Catawba County town of Maiden, twenty minutes from Hickory, that has blossomed into a $5 billion investment. Others followed, including Facebook in Forest City, Bed Bath & Beyond in Claremont, and AT&T in Kings Mountain, which together have formed what is now dubbed the North Carolina Data Corridor.

None of these new tech hubs brought more than a few hundred jobs to the region, but there has been enough economic spin-off to spur a building boom in downtown Hickory and return the aura of affluence to its streets. With the spate of technology investment have come high earners eager to restore those old Victorian homes, treat themselves to $35 entrées at Boca and $12 classic cocktails at Notions, and drive gleaming luxury automobiles off the lot of the Porsche dealership on South Center Street.

It is places like Hickory that former governor Pat McCrory had in mind in 2015 when he began trumpeting the "Carolina Comeback," the explosion of job creation and business investment that he attributed to the Republican takeover of the state's government in 2010 and the successive rounds of tax cutting, budget slashing, and deregulation that the new majority rammed through the legislature. He made it sound very simple. All it takes is for government to get out of the way and trust the state's fortunes to the wiles of big corporations. In North Carolina, that's how you get a miracle.

The problem is this: for quite a lot of people in Hickory, the real miracle would simply be a roof over their heads. Tucked in little patches of woods on the fringes of Hickory are hundreds of homeless people whose daily round is a struggle for survival. They are the detritus left by the region's shift from plentiful jobs in manufacturing to vast data campuses run by machines. Clustered in encampments in the weeds behind chain restaurants or abandoned furniture warehouses, they are largely invisible until they wander raggedly into intersections to beg. This is a new problem for Hickory, arising in the last decade, and it has flummoxed city officials. They initially treated it as a law enforcement issue, dispatching police into the woods to clear out the homeless for violating an ordinance against urban camping. But the city has of late adopted a more compassionate and proactive approach, hiring a former director of the local Salvation Army to spearhead an effort to help people get housing. The program can only get so far because it relies almost entirely on donations and nonprofit agencies to meet its goals. At the state level, the homeless issue is met with silence.

Gene Nichol, a law professor at the University of North Carolina at Chapel Hill who has long studied poverty in his state, has chronicled deplorable conditions in the town's homeless camps—people dying of hypothermia, women pregnant or huddled with small children, women raped, men beaten and robbed. He found that many of the homeless suffered from drug addiction and mental health issues, but a significant number were once employed and had just fallen through society's cracks. Just like everywhere else in the South, there has always been entrenched poverty in North Carolina, part of the legacy of slavery and segregation. It might not surprise anyone to find that it endures in relatively undeveloped states like Mississippi or Alabama, but it is far less excusable in an economic powerhouse like North Carolina. In his book *The Faces of Poverty in North Carolina*, Nichol called the issue of poverty "North Carolina's most potent problem, its greatest sin against defining democratic promise." He wrote that the hard right's takeover of state politics in 2010 had made the lives of the poor even more desperate:

> Legislative decisions since 2010—restricting Medicaid and other healthcare services, dramatically cutting unemployment benefits, eliminating the state earned-income tax credit, turning back proffered federal funding for poverty programs, restricting traditional access to food stamps and legal services, pairing back housing and daycare subsidies for low-income residents, eliminating pre-K prospects for at-risk children, while raising the tax burden on poorer residents to dramatically reduce the tax rates of wealthier

ones—have had a *profound impact on impoverished North Carolinians.*

Hickory's story resonates well beyond the foothills of the Piedmont. It is part of a broad pattern of societal failure that has resulted from the flawed assumption on the part of Republican state leaders that they can lift their states out of mediocrity without investing in their citizens. Resilient and equitable societies have never emerged that way. Luring corporations with the promise of tax giveaways and see-no-evil regulatory regimes may bring short-term prosperity to the few, but if it means depressing working people's wages and slashing funds for education, scientific research, health care, infrastructure, and job training, which has happened in one Republican state after another, it will stifle each of those states' greatest asset: a healthy, educated, and financially secure populace. When elected officials are primarily serving their wealthy campaign donors while claiming to be fostering prosperity, it must be asked who the supposed miracle of a state like North Carolina actually benefits.

* * * *

REPUBLICAN LEADERS OF high-growth states like North Carolina, Florida, Texas, Arizona, and Georgia are fond of bragging about their economic prowess and ridiculing blue states they claim are driving away businesses with onerous taxes and regulation. They see themselves as the future of America, and in many respects, they are right. Those five states in recent years have experienced stupendous growth in population and economic output. Barely a week goes by without a press release from one of them announcing the latest local investment by a major corporation. A Houston business consultant tallied more than a hundred big companies that relocated to or opened major offices in Texas between 2018 and June 2021, including Tesla, Hewlett-Packard, Oracle, and Charles Schwab. After the financial firms Elliott

Management and Blackstone bolted New York for South Florida during the pandemic, there was speculation that Wall Street as a whole was ready to bid farewell to Gotham. "Are Texas and Florida the new California and New York?" asked *Business Insider* in late 2020. Charlotte has become the nation's second largest banking center after Manhattan, and Arizona is a leader in aerospace and defense manufacturing, and mines two-thirds of the nation's copper.

The 2020 census brought into stark relief where population trends are headed. Over the previous decade, Texas's population had grown by 16 percent, nearly four million people, while Florida saw an increase of 15 percent, and North Carolina, Arizona, and Georgia posted gains in the neighborhood of 10 percent, about twice the growth of states like New York (4 percent) and New Jersey (6 percent). The media was abuzz when census figures showed that California actually lost population in the year 2020, the first time that had happened in at least a century. Meanwhile, Texas was reported in 2019 to be gaining a thousand people a day. Figures on economic growth are just as dramatic. For the five-year period between 2015 and 2019, Florida posted a real GDP growth rate of 14 percent and Texas 11 percent, compared with less than 1 percent in New York and Connecticut.

It is easy to fall into the trap of equating population gains, economic growth, and business investment with successful governance, or of viewing low taxes and spending as surefire engines of progress, since the mainstream media have trained us to see it that way. Media accounts of growth in Texas or Florida, and the supposed decline of New York and California, abound with superlatives. "13 Mind-Blowing Facts About Florida's Economy," blared a *Markets Insider* headline in 2019. Describing the "Texas miracle," the *Washington Post* recently lauded the state's "business-friendly" policies and lax regulations. "Why is Texas's population skyrocketing while other big states—notably, New York, Illinois, and California—are languishing? The answer: Texas built a sturdy economic growth engine, and it drives population growth." In June 2021, CNN's Fareed Zakaria marveled at the exodus of businesses from New York, New Jersey, and California and stated without evidence that high taxes and out-of-control spending were to blame. Indignant that Florida's state budget is roughly half of New York's, even though their populations are comparable, Zakaria said, "Put bluntly, too many Democratic states have gotten bloated, mismanaged, and corrupt."

And that is the supposedly liberal media. Right-leaning publications are even harder on the governance of the blue states. "Major cities, such as New York, Los Angeles and San Francisco, have punishingly high tax rates and lack business-friendly policies," wrote Jack Kelly in *Forbes*. "With pushes to defund the police and cutting down on prosecutions, cities have been plagued by crime, violence, looting and disorder." Kelly stated gleefully that hedge fund billionaires Carl Icahn, Paul Singer, and Leon Cooperman had moved their businesses to Florida, which he attributed to New York's high taxes, "ever-increasing crime," and "poor governance on the part of New York City Mayor Bill de Blasio."

The problem is that almost nothing in that thesis holds up to scrutiny. The idea that red states like Texas, Florida, and North Carolina have superior governance, and that this explains the southward migration of businesses and people, is Republican wish fulfillment, and it eschews even the most basic facts. There are complex factors behind the decades-long population shift from the North to the Sun Belt, and they became even more complex in the wake of the pandemic. The competence of individual state governments has never been prominent among them. If it had been, a historically corrupt and mismanaged state like Arizona would still be a sparsely populated desert. Rather, what is at play here is an attempt to score cheap political points with the immense social and economic upheavals unleashed by the pandemic, which happens to have hit hardest in New York and California, through no fault of their public officials.

Take the claim that the post-pandemic crime wave in New York City, Los Angeles, and San Francisco was due to "poor governance." The fact is that crime rates exploded in cities across the country in 2020, including in Texas, Florida, Arizona, and North Carolina, the destinations for people that Kelly would have you believe are fleeing in fear from New York and California. Five major cities in Texas had bigger spikes in homicide than New York City. Kelly must have a willful case of amnesia to forget that New York, Los Angeles, and San Francisco were among the safest big cities in America prior to the pandemic, with homicide rates in 2019 that were well below those of most big cities in Texas, Florida, and Arizona. New York City's murder rate that year was 3.8 per 100,000 people, just a little more than a quarter of Dallas's rate of 14.5. The number of murders in New York peaked at 2,245 in 1990 and had been reduced to 332 by the end of Mayor Mike Bloomberg's tenure in 2013. That historic reduction continued in the de Blasio years, reaching 289 in his fifth year in office, even though his administration discontinued harsh stop-and-frisk policies in minority neighborhoods. Now we are to believe that his mismanagement produced rising crime after the pandemic, even though worse happened in others part of the country?

Two of the biggest reasons for the growth of the Sun Belt have not changed over the decades: sunny weather and cheap real estate. Florida in particular is a prime destination for retirees eager to trade their high-priced homes in the Northeast or Midwest for a place in the sun, a trend that has accelerated as baby boomers reach retirement age. When the Pew Charitable Trusts asked a Florida demographer about his state's growth in 2016, he stated the obvious. "The state continues to attract retiring baby boomers because of our climate and the relatively low costs of living," said the demographer, Richard Doty of the University of Florida's Bureau of Business and Economic Research. "You can sell a home in New York or Ohio or Michigan for substantially more than you would spend in Florida, so it's still relatively attractive." As Bloomberg was fond of pointing out, New York's high real-estate prices were a result of its *success* in attracting businesses and high-earning residents from around the world. The same could be said for California. But the elevated prices create a natural incentive for businesses to move some of their offices to less expensive markets, where they can both save money on real estate and lure employees with the promise of a more affordable cost of living. It was that consideration that drove an assortment of finance and technology companies to set up offices in the Phoenix area in recent years, including American Express, J.P. Morgan, and Yelp. In many cases these companies were moving lower-paying jobs to Arizona, the kinds of positions that do not pay enough for employees to live in places like the Bay Area. Yelp's headquarters is in San Francisco, but it moved hundreds of lower-paying sales and customer services jobs to the Phoenix area. In early 2020, tech jobs on average paid $80,000 to $85,000 in Phoenix, compared with $110,000 to $115,000 nationally.

This was nothing but the churn of the marketplace, not the shrewdness of Arizona state officials. When the pandemic spurred thousands of corporations to allow employees to work from home, those market forces came crashing down on New York and California. Remote work dramatically accelerated the migration of white-collar workers to places less expensive than Manhattan or San Francisco. Those cities were left with the task of recreating themselves, and that process began right away. New York came out of the pandemic with 100 million square feet of vacant office space and five hundred thousand fewer jobs. But, as the *New York Times* reported, about the same time some financial firms were bolting from the city, "Amazon, Apple, Facebook, and Google swooped in and expanded their footprint." The city and state in 2020 were planning to expand affordable high-speed internet, 5G technology, and solar capacity, while seeking to turn the city into a technology hub with clusters like Hudson Research Center in Manhattan and the so-called Brooklyn research triangle, home to companies pioneering investment in blockchains and artificial intelligence. "What ghost town?" the *Times* wrote. "Robot town is more like it." The *Times* reported in July 2021 that tech workers who left San Francisco in droves in the middle of the pandemic were starting to trickle back. "Bumper-to-bumper traffic has returned to the region's bridges and freeways. Tech commuter buses are reappearing on the roads. Rents are spiking, especially in San Francisco neighborhoods where tech employees often live."

Sun Belt leaders who boast about their booming economies and credit the policies of laissez-faire forget that it was an activist federal government that brought about their tremendous growth in the first place. In the 1930s, President Roosevelt called the South the nation's "No. 1 economic problem" and launched New Deal programs, like the Rural Electrification Administration, to foster the region's development. The Pentagon poured defense dollars into the South and West during World War II, and not only because the regions' warm climate, cheap land, and inaccessibility to foreign attack made them perfect for military bases. The government was also interested in fostering economic growth in what were then seen as depressed areas. Keith Orejel, a history professor at Wilmington College in Ohio, wrote in an essay for the *Washington Post* that the government helped create a "booster class of bankers, retailers, insurance executives, real estate agents" and other businesses executives that sought to "pirate manufacturing plants from Northern industrial centers, using the lures of cheap labor, low taxes, lax regulations and weak unions." Orejel wrote that the government unwittingly hastened the decline of industrial states in the North "by giving Sun Belt state governments the money to resurface highways, construct airports and upgrade utilities. Yet, not all communities benefited equally. Sun Belt spending favored metropolitan boomtowns—Atlanta, Charlotte, Dallas, Denver, Houston, Los Angeles, Miami, Oklahoma City and Phoenix—over poor, rural agricultural areas."

Another major element of growth that Republicans don't like to talk about is immigration. Texas, Arizona, and Florida have all experienced mass migrations from Latin America in the last four decades. In each of those states, about one in three people is an immigrant or the child of an immigrant. In Texas, immigration has accounted for more of its recent growth than migration from other states. It is a cruel irony that at the same time Texas Governor Greg Abbott committed state funds to complete Donald Trump's border wall and asked other Republican states to dispatch National Guard troops to the border in the summer of 2021, businesses in his state were relying on foreign-born workers to cope with a labor shortage. In 2018, immigrants made up 42 percent of the state's construction and extraction jobs, which includes the oil industry. Hispanic immigrants tend to be younger and have a higher birth rate than non-Hispanics, which further spurs population growth in those states.

The point is that a constellation of forces has driven the population surge in the Sun Belt, most of them involving market forces or federal action rather than public policy at the state level. And when there is population growth, GDP naturally follows. In August 2020, when *USA Today* published a ranking of the best state economies, using data from 24/7 Wall Street, Arizona, Texas, Florida, and North Carolina were all in the top twenty, and most blue states ranked toward the bottom. But that is because the ranking's main criteria for assessing the states' economies was the five-year annualized growth in GDP. It was a flawed system of rankings, as the paper's "best of" features often are. If a state experiences rapid growth in population, naturally it has an effect on the level of economic activity. It should not be a cause for bragging that Texas is the nation's third fastest growing state by population and yet, according to the *USA Today* rankings, had only the twelfth highest growth in five-year GDP. A better measure of a state's economic performance is GDP per capita. When the states were ranked by per capita GDP in 2019, Massachusetts was No. 1, New York No. 2, and California No. 5. Texas was ranked thirteenth, North Carolina thirty-fifth, Florida fortieth, and Arizona forty-first. Pound for pound, the blue states remain the country's centers of economic activity.

That is not to say that there hasn't been prodigious growth in some business sectors in Texas and North Carolina arising from local investment and innovation, not just poaching from other states. But there is a degree of luck there as well. Texas is an economic powerhouse primarily because it happens to sit on top of huge reserves of crude oil, particularly in the Permian Basin in the western part of the state and the Eagle Ford Shale in the east. When a plucky oil man named George Mitchell perfected hydraulic fracturing near Fort Worth in 1998, he not only paved the way for America's energy independence, but guaranteed an economic boom in his state for many years to come, even within the confines of the boom-and-bust cycles of the oil industry. The author Daniel Yergin has calculated that the oil and gas sectors accounted for two-thirds of U.S. net industrial development between 2009 and 2019, much of it taking place in Texas. From oil has flowed so much of Texas's fortune, including the rise of other sectors, such as finance and manufacturing. After the passage of the North American Free Trade Agreement, Texas also benefited enormously from its 1,200-mile frontier with Mexico and the network of highways and rail lines that pass through the state on the way to the border. Texas's exports to Mexico more than doubled between 1993 and 2000, with the trade deal accounting for 25 percent of that increase, according to the Federal Reserve Bank of Dallas.

Texas and North Carolina are also home to thriving technology sectors, but those sectors are not the result of the policy decisions and fiscal conservatism of their current crop of leaders. Rather, the leading-edge research centers in both states grew from public-private partnerships set up in the middle of the twentieth century. Research Triangle Park, a major center of technological research named for its proximity to Raleigh, Durham, and Chapel Hill, was established in the late 1950s when the president of Wachovia Bank, Robert Hanes, and Greensboro developer Romeo Guest convinced Democratic Governor Luther Hodges to secure state funding for the project. The idea was that the University of North Carolina, North Carolina State, and Duke University would supply enough research heft to attract tech companies to the non-profit facility, a strategy that paid off when IBM set up shop there in 1965. Hodges and his partners had the foresight to recognize that North Carolina's reliance on three industries—tobacco, textiles, and furniture—did not bode well for the state's future.

In Texas, a similar concern about the state's reliance on a single industry, in this case oil, lay behind a decision by public and private leaders in 1957 to launch the Austin Area Economic Development Foundation, which set out to attract technology companies by offering as inducements the research infrastructure of the University of Texas and the city's low cost of living. IBM moved its Selectric typewriter plant to Austin in 1963, and both Texas Instruments and Motorola had opened plants there within a decade. With the oil slump in the 1980s, Austin intensified its efforts to become a "technopolis" along the lines of Silicon Valley. In 1984, a University of Texas student started what would become the state's first homegrown computer giant, Dell Technologies. Now, Austin is considered the nation's capital of startups. In both North Carolina and Texas, the research infrastructure was sustained with a steady growth of funding for the states' public universities. But in the last decade, those universities have watched the growth of their funding dwindle at the hands of the anti-government zealots who now run the two states' governments. Between 2008 and 2018, Texas reduced its inflation-adjusted spending per pupil at public universities by 23 percent, and North Carolina reduced it by 17 percent. Whatever impact the shortchanging of higher education has on Austin and Research Triangle Park, it is clear that neither would have emerged as world-renowned centers of research and innovation under the small-government ethos that now predominates in the two states.

* * * *

"BUSINESS FRIENDLY" IS THE MANTRA of leadership in the high-growth Republican states. What they generally mean by that phrase is low taxes, generous tax incentives, and lax regulations. If Republican state leaders can lay claim to any special genius in the fostering of economic activity, this would be the logical place to look for it, since their governing philosophies amount to little else. But suspicions always arise about whether they are really striving for anything like genius in their fiscal policies, since this is also the realm where wealthy campaign donors exert their greatest influence. These elected officials may talk a lot about gun rights, immigration, abortion, election fraud, or critical race theory, but most of that is in service to whipping up their base to support the fiscal policies that matter to their wealthy benefactors. This is where the hoodwinking of their white working-class constituencies is the most glaring and the most abject.

Texas Governor Abbott blasted out a tweet in 2018 that gloated over the pipeline of Californians flowing toward his state: "If you are abandoning California for Texas, just remember the reason you are escaping, high taxes and burdensome regulations. We plan to KEEP Texas, Texas." Florida Governor DeSantis told a news conference that he had a message for New York State. "You are driving them away and we are simply opening our arms," he said. "I've been able to be very clear that Florida will always remain a low-tax state." Florida's chief financial officer, Jimmy Patronis, went even further. He told Fox News in May 2021 that nine hundred people a day were moving to his state, many of them fleeing the "tax hell" and "financial train wrecks" of New York and New Jersey.

It is true that Florida places a low tax burden on businesses and wealthy individuals, especially when lax enforcement and exemptions are taken into account. Florida is one of eight states, like Texas, that have no personal income tax. Its corporate income tax is one of the lowest rates in the country at 5.5 percent, compared with 7.25 percent in New York, 8 percent in Massachusetts, 8.8 percent in California, and 11.5 percent in New Jersey, the highest in the country. But the low rates don't tell the whole story. DeSantis and his predecessor, Rick Scott, have conspired with Republican majorities in the state legislature to make sure few corporations even pay any income taxes, no matter how high their profits. In November 2019, the *Orlando Sentinel* reported that an estimated 99 percent of corporations pay no tax at all. The number of state tax auditors had been cut by nearly a third over the previous twenty-five years, and the tax avoidance the state allows borders on the criminal. In one example, eBay, which made $34 million in profits in Florida in 2014, should have paid $1.8 million in taxes. Instead, it paid $18,810. "The Florida corporate income tax leaks like a sieve," Richard Pomp, a University of Connecticut law professor who studies state taxes, told the *Sentinel*. "Business has it pretty much the way they want it."

So if Florida doesn't fund its budget through personal or corporate income taxes, who pays the bill? That is the question that media outlets, particular the financial press, rarely ask when celebrating the state's low taxes. The answer is that the state raises the vast majority of its revenue from sales taxes, which fall much harder on the poor and middle class than the wealthy. Watchdog groups cite Florida as having one of the most inequitable tax systems in the country. An October 2018 study by the Institute on Taxation and Economic Policy found that Florida had the third most inequitable tax system in the country. The poorest 20 percent of taxpayers in Florida pay 12.7 percent of their income in state taxes, the middle 60 percent pay 8.1 percent, and the top 1 percent pay 2.3 percent. By contrast, the poorest fifth in California pay 10.5 percent, while the top earners pay 12.4 percent. In an opinion piece for the *Tampa Bay Times*, Esteban Leonardo

Santis, an analyst for the left-leaning Florida Policy Institute, de-cried the heavy load his state's tax system places on low-earning residents: "While the Sunshine State has a reputation as being 'low tax,' the truth is that Florida has one of the most upside-down tax systems in the nation due to its overdependence on sales taxes. In our state, a worker making minimum wage spends a greater share of their hard-earned cash paying state and local sales taxes than a millionaire."

According to the Institute on Taxation and Economic Policy, Texas's tax system is even more inequitable than Florida's, ranking second worst. (Democratic-led Washington State was ranked as having the most inequitable system, though seven of the ten most inequitable states had Republican-controlled legislatures.) The poorest fifth in Texas pay 13 percent of their income, compared with top earners, who pay 3.1 percent. Texas has no income tax; it collects revenue from corporations through gross receipts taxes, which even the conservative Tax Foundation says have been aban-doned in most developed nations because they lack transparency and tend to "forward shift" costs on to consumers. The foundation concluded in one study that as gross receipts taxes are "pyramided into the final household price, the households that consume a large percent of their income will bear more of the burden and the gross receipts tax will be an even more regressive version of a sales tax."

Texans may be spared an income tax, but the state's homeowners pay a larger share of their income in property taxes than those in almost any other state. In 2017, property taxes accounted for 45 percent of what Texans paid in state and local taxes, third high-est in the nation. In New Jersey, where high property taxes have long been a source of controversy, the rate was only slightly higher, 46.4 percent. California's percentage was 26 percent. There is no consensus among economists on the question of whether property taxes are regressive or progressive, but a University of Chicago re-searcher tossed a bomb in the middle of the debate when he released a major study in early 2021 that showed how unfairly they are applied in poor neighborhoods. Christopher Berry's study of 26 million properties sold between 2006 and 2016 found that owners in low-income neighborhoods effectively paid property taxes double those of wealthy neighborhoods because of skewed assessments of property values. In a state like Texas, where government services are funded disproportionately through local property taxes, the people of the most modest means take the biggest hit.

* * * *

REPUBLICAN ELECTED OFFICIALS measure success by the number of corporate headquarters sprouting in their newly fashionable cities, not on the quality of life enjoyed by ordinary citizens, who often live well outside those cities. Few of the media gushing over low taxes and slim budgets in the Sun Belt ask what price is paid for that fiscal austerity and who pays it. All five of the states often celebrated for their growth—Texas, Florida, Arizona, North Carolina, and Georgia—rank toward the bottom in their per capita outlays for health care, education, infrastructure, job training, environmental protection, and just about any other public program that makes a difference in people's lives. They tend to have lower-quality education, shoddier health care, unchecked pollution, meager unemployment benefits, low median wages, and poorly trained workforces. None of this is of concern if you're a banking executive in Charlotte or a tech worker in Phoenix and you live in an exclusive suburb, have good health benefits from your employer, and send your children to private school. But it matters to millions of people who are poor or lower-middle class— that is, a huge slice of the population.

To understand how right-wing sensibilities seep into the mainstream media's treatment of states like Texas and Florida, it is instructive to return to the piece that CNN's Fareed Zakaria aired on June 27, 2021, based on his *Washington Post* column entitled

"Democrats Need to Show They Can Be Trusted with Power." Zakaria is widely respected for his evenhandedness on most issues, but in this report, he threw in his lot with free-market propagandists. His piece was based almost entirely on a flawed guest editorial in the *New York Post* and an article in *City Journal*, which is published by the Manhattan Institute, a conservative think tank that has been heavily funded by Fortune 500 companies, including Big Pharma, Big Tobacco, and the Koch brothers. The argument of both articles was that blue states like New York and California have much bigger budgets per capita than Texas or Florida and end up with worse outcomes. "Neither blue state has shown any clear ability to improve the academic outcomes of their kids, alleviate poverty for those in need, or provide good roads and bridges for their people," freelance writer Ryan Fazio wrote in the *Post*. "While Texas and Florida have their share of problems, they seem to foster more upward mobility and trust in government, which partly explains why 6.4 million people have moved to those states since 2010."

It is hard to know where to start in deconstructing such a sweeping and inaccurate statement. As one of his examples, Fazio pointed to National Assessment of Educational Progress (NAEP) scores for fourth and eighth graders in 2017 that were no higher in New York and California than in Florida and Texas. Not much to argue with there, right? Wrong. No legitimate organization that ranks the quality of schools state by state—those most often cited are *Education Week*, WalletHub, and *USA Today*—ever base their rankings solely on NAEP scores. They use a wide range of metrics, including dropout rates, recognizing in part that states with vast inner-city neighborhoods and masses of low-income students must be rated according to how well they meet those challenges. All three of those organizations invariably rate the quality of schools in Florida and Texas well below the blue states of the Northeast. In its 2020 rankings, *Education Week* gave the four top places to New Jersey, Massachusetts, Connecticut, and Maryland, while putting New York at No. 8, California at No. 22, Florida at No. 23, and Texas at No. 41. WalletHub's 2021 rankings (which even *Forbes* published) put Florida at No. 22 and Texas at No. 28, with New York at No. 12. Massachusetts, Connecticut, and New Jersey were given the top spots. The *City Journal* article, written by Steven Malanga, a fellow at the Manhattan Institute, at least acknowledged the superiority of schools in New York and New Jersey, but said they come at the price of "dizzying property taxes." And yet WalletHub ranked Texas as having the nation's seventh highest property taxes and New York as having the ninth highest. The only thing dizzying is the flimsiness of Malanga's argument.

Comparing the condition of infrastructure in old industrial states with those of the Sun Belt, as Fazio did, is highly misleading. In both Florida and Texas, more than half of the population arose in the last forty years. With that surge in population came new roads, new highways, and new bridges. One study found that failing concrete bridges in New Jersey were on average eighty-four years old and in New York seventy-seven years old, whereas in Florida and Texas they were fifty-six and sixty-four years old, respectively. The infrastructure in the North undergoes harsh subfreezing temperatures and higher volumes of traffic. Texas boasts about having the lowest percentage of deficient bridges in the country. It also has a population density of 105 people per square mile, compared with 1,208 in New Jersey and 421 in New York. There are 303 registered vehicles per square mile in New Jersey and 81 in New York. In Texas, there are 31.

Anyone looking to fault New Jersey, New York, California, or other blue states for their poor infrastructure might consider what would have happened if Republicans were in control, which in some cases was not too long ago. In 2010, former New Jersey governor Chris Christie infamously blocked an $8.7 billion commuter rail tunnel linking his state to Manhattan under the Hudson River. Transportation experts long considered a third rail tunnel—the first two were dilapidated, built when Theodore Roosevelt was president—crucial to the region's economic growth. Christie's decision to pull out of the nation's largest transportation project, which Senator Frank Lautenberg called "one of the biggest policy blunders in New Jersey history," meant turning away $3 billion in federal funding and forgoing an estimated six thousand construction jobs. Why did Christie do it? Because he was planning to run for president and wanted to bolster his credentials as a small-government Republican. But he had to wipe prodigious amounts of egg from his face when Hurricane Sandy flooded the existing tunnels and thousands of commuters had to cope with years of train delays. In California, Republicans have steadfastly opposed a high-speed rail link between San Francisco and Los Angeles, even though it would reduce freeway congestion and tailpipe emissions. Republicans across the country are notorious for their opposition to mass transit despite its obvious societal benefits.

More importantly, the cost of upgrading infrastructure in this country is borne largely by the federal government. The widely reported neglect of infrastructure is a result of austerity at the federal level that began in the Reagan years and has been maintained by Republican obstruction ever since. It is obvious that these federal policies have wreaked the most damage in the infrastructure of older and more densely populated states like New York, New Jersey, and Massachusetts. Seeing this as a vindication of the low taxes and austere budgets of Texas and Florida is utter nonsense. Aging infrastructure in this country should be seen as a *repudiation* of that philosophy of government.

The grim consequences of government austerity in the Republican states of the Sun Belt are everywhere to be found. Health care and environmental protection are two obvious examples. The Commonwealth Fund, a New York nonprofit whose board is made up of internationally recognized experts, releases a scorecard every year on the quality of state health care systems. In its 2020 report, Texas was rated as having the ninth-worst health care system and Florida as having the eleventh worst. Georgia and Arizona were in the bottom ten and North Carolina was sixteenth worst. Eight of the top ten were blue states, including New York. The closings of rural hospitals due to lack of funding is a crisis across the South and Midwest, especially in states—such as Texas, Florida, Georgia, and North Carolina—that in late 2021 had still refused to accept federal funding under the Affordable Care Act to expand their Medicaid systems. Texas, which ranked fortieth out of the fifty states in 2019 in the amount per capita it spent from its own budget on health care, has had more hospital closings than any other state, twenty as of this writing and seventy-seven more at risk of closing. Thirty-five Texas counties had no physician, and 147 had no obstetrician/gynecologist—a situation found in none of the Democratic states that Zakaria claimed are bloated and mismanaged.

Partly as a result of meager health care budgets, Florida, Texas, and Georgia rank well below most of the northern blue states in the provision of mental health services. They also have higher rates of suicide, teenage pregnancy, and infant mortality, and have lower life expectancy. And they have higher crime rates, higher rates of incarceration, and even higher rates of accidental death.

For all the talk of economic miracles in the Sun Belt, their citizens on average are poorer. New York's real median household income in 2019 was about $72,000, while New Jersey's and Massachusetts's was $87,000, and California's was $78,000. Compare that to Florida, $58,000; Texas, $67,000; and Georgia, $57,000. More importantly, median household income in all of the Sun Belt states grew at a slower pace than New York and New Jersey over the previous five years. New Jersey's growth rate was 24 percent, New York's 22 percent, and California's 19 percent, while Florida's was only 17 percent, Texas's 15 percent, and Georgia's 5 percent. Somehow that was not included in the "13 Mind-Blowing Facts About Florida's Economy." Poverty is also higher in the Sun Belt. The Census Bureau's supplemental poverty measure is considered by most experts to be a superior gauge than the official poverty measure because it takes into account state-by-state variables such as cost of living and level of public assistance. For the three-year period between 2017 and 2019, the supplemental poverty rates for Texas (12.7), Florida (12.9), Georgia (13.3), and North Carolina (13.6) exceeded those of New Jersey (8.2), Massachusetts (9.2), Connecticut (9.7), California (11.4), and New York (12.1). Florida was also tied with Tennessee and Alabama in 2021 in offering the nation's fourth worst unemployment benefits—a maximum of $275 a week—surpassed only by Mississippi, Louisiana, and Arizona. Massachusetts was the highest at $823 for up to thirty weeks.

As for the claim that low state taxes provide a powerful lure for business investment, that is just another canard put forward by Republican politicians to please their wealthy patrons. Numerous studies have shown that a low tax rate is not the dominant factor that businesses take into account when choosing locations. Real estate prices and the quality of the local workforce play a greater role. It was no accident that Amazon initially chose New York as the place for its second headquarters, before withdrawing because elected officials objected to its demands for corporate subsidies. A 2017 study by the Institute on Taxation and Economic Policy found that states with the highest personal income tax rates have greater economic growth, higher wages, and better employment opportunities than the states with no personal income tax.

Governor Abbott's 2018 tweet about Californians fleeing their state's excessive regulation took on a bitter irony in February 2021 when it was revealed that the gutting of state regulations contributed to the failure of Texas's power grid during that month's winter storm. At least 210 people died, mostly by freezing to death, when hundreds of thousands lost electricity. After subfreezing temperatures caused a similar, though less deadly, breakdown of the system a decade earlier, the enforcement division of the state's

Public Utilities Commission contracted with a nonprofit organization to help with action against power companies for failing to weatherproof their systems. But in 2020, Abbott's appointees to the commission quietly dismissed the nonprofit, Texas Reliability Entity, and disbanded the entire enforcement division. The deregulation yielded cheaper electricity and new investment, but at a terrible cost to society. Senator Ted Cruz may have had the resources to flee with his family to Cancún during the outage, but untold numbers of his low-income constituents were left to freeze in their homes. This was hardly the first time the state's zeal for deregulation had endangered its citizens, especially those who live near oil and petrochemical facilities. In the span of twenty months between 2018 and 2020, Texas had six major chemical accidents that included six deaths, multiple injuries, and the contamination of wide areas.

Florida's cuts in environmental enforcement under Governor Rick Scott have been blamed for contributing to the algae bloom in late 2017 that fouled 150 miles of beaches on the Gulf Coast, killed millions of fish, and cost the state huge amounts in tourist dollars. After a Miami condominium complex collapsed in 2021, killing nearly a hundred people, it was revealed that inspections of Florida's vulnerable, weather-ravaged coastal buildings had been left to local authorities, some of whom did a poor job of it. State regulators were nowhere in the equation.

In his CNN piece, Zakaria asked this question about New York State: "It has a budget nearly twice the size of Florida's, though it has roughly the same population. . . . Can anyone explain why?" Actually, the answer is pretty clear. New York's voters and elected officials, like those in New Jersey or Massachusetts, have chosen a more equitable and sustainable society, where children are better educated, people have greater access to health care, the environment is cleaner, and crime is lower, even if it comes with a higher tax burden. The voters of the blue states are savvy enough to know that when leaders in Texas or Florida use the term "business friendly," what they really mean is "worker unfriendly." In June 2021, when WalletHub issued a ranking of the best states to live in, did it give the top positions to Texas, Florida, Arizona, or North Carolina? No. All of those states were well down the list. Its findings were this: New Jersey, No. 1; Massachusetts, No. 2; New York, No. 3.

* * * *

NORTH CAROLINA DESERVES a special place in the discussion of Sun Belt conservatism because it once was regarded as the most progressive state in the South, and the right-wing takeover of its government in 2010 was so blatantly orchestrated by wealthy ideologues, most notably the discount-store magnate Art Pope.

V.O. Key, in his landmark 1949 study, *Southern Politics in State and Nation*, called North Carolina a "progressive plutocracy" that was not as mired in the "Lost Cause" ethos as the rest of the region. "It enjoys a reputation for progressive outlook and action in many phases of life," Key wrote, "especially industrial development, education, and race relations."

> Its governmental processes have been scrupulously orderly. For half a century no scandals have marred the state administration. No band of highwaymen posing as public officials has raided the public treasury. No clowns have held important office . . . and there have been no violent outbursts by citizens repressed beyond endurance. The state university has pioneered in regional self-examination; it has become famed for academic freedom and for tolerance.

Modern progressives might take issue with Key's assessment of the state's race relations. North Carolina, after all, passed the same Jim Crow laws as the rest of the South at the turn of the twentieth century. There was a white backlash against the state's tepid liberalism after the Supreme Court's *Brown v. Board of Education* decision in 1954. The homes of civil rights leaders were bombed and young Black protesters sitting at white lunch counters in Raleigh and High Point were hit with eggs or bricks just as they were in Mississippi or Alabama.

The state's politics for decades had been a tug-of-war between liberal reformers and the most recalcitrant conservatives. As the *New Yorker* writer Jane Mayer put it, "It was both the face of the New South and the stomping ground of [U.S. Senator] Jesse Helms's race-baiting National Congressional Club." But there is no doubt that North Carolina has had periods of liberalism that set it apart from every other southern state. There was not only the state support for technology research provided by Luther Hodges, a governor otherwise known for his conservatism. In the early 1960s, Democratic Governor Terry Sanford, who had actually campaigned in support of segregation, became a convert to the civil rights movement. Despite attacks from the likes of Helms, then an archconservative TV personality in Raleigh, Sanford raised taxes and poured money into badly underfunded schools, raising teachers' pay by 22 percent and doubling funds for school libraries. He also partnered with the Ford Foundation in setting up the North Carolina Fund, an anti-poverty program aimed at young schoolchildren that was the inspiration for the Johnson administration's Head Start program. "In many ways, North Carolina in the early 1960s was a small-scale laboratory for programs later tried nationally," writes Rob Christensen in his book *The Paradox of Tar Heel Politics*. The state's Democratic Party, which by the late 1960s had overcome its shameful support for white supremacy, dominated North Carolina politics long after it had been wiped off the map in most of the South.

But the wheels came off in 2010. Republicans captured both houses of the legislature for the first time in more than a century. That year's ascendance of far-right conservatives in red states across the country was in part the product of the *Citizens United* decision, which allowed wealthy conservatives like the Koch brothers to donate unlimited funds to independent groups to influence elections at the federal and local level. Nowhere were those tactics more effective than in North Carolina. Art Pope, a key ally of the Koch brothers who was the multimillionaire chairman and CEO of Variety Wholesalers, a discount-store chain in states throughout the southern and mid-Atlantic states, arranged $2 million in donations aimed at twenty-two legislative races. It began as an uphill battle. Democrats could count on riding the coattails of Obama, who remained popular after winning the state narrowly in 2008. But then misleading attack ads against Democratic legislators began appearing around the state, paid for by anonymous donors. In her book *Dark Money*, Mayer wrote about the experience of John Snow, a conservative Democratic senator from the western part of the state. Snow, a retired judge and former college football star whose Tea Party–supported opponent, Jim Davis, had little political experience, was expected to cruise to reelection. But then, wrote Mayer, came one attack ad after another.

> Snow recalls, "I voted to help build a pier with an aquarium on the coast, as did every other member of the North Carolina House and Senate who voted." But a television attack ad presented the "luxury pier" as Snow's wasteful scheme. "We've lost jobs," an actress said in the ad. "John Snow's solution for our economy? 'Go fish.'" A mass mailing, decorated with a cartoon pig, denounced the pier as one of Snow's "pork projects."

Snow was also the subject of two dozen mass mailings, and ended up losing by a few hundred votes. He wasn't alone. Such attacks were made on Democrats around the state, and they hit their mark. Republicans picked up 11 seats in the state senate, giving them a 31–19 majority. They also ended up with a 67–52 majority in the House. Pope and allied groups had targeted twenty-two races and ended up winning eighteen of them. When conservative Republican Pat McCrory, a former mayor of Charlotte, defeated

moderate Democrat Bev Perdue in the 2012 gubernatorial election, the GOP was able to unleash a radically anti-worker agenda
on the state. The results have hardly been a vindication of the media narrative proclaiming Sun Belt conservatism as a model for the
nation.

The new Republican supermajority adopted a tax-reform
package that slashed corporate and individual tax rates and ended
the earned-income tax credit for the poor. The Republicans cut
unemployment benefits from $506 to $350 a week and reduced
the number of weeks it could be collected to as few as ten. They
enacted a law barring municipalities from raising the minimum
wage above the statewide minimum of $7.25. They also enacted a
raft of conservative social legislation, such as the controversial bill
repealing a Charlotte ordinance that protected the right of trans-
gender people to use the public bathrooms of their choice. But it is
the economic legislation that historians will use to judge whether
GOP leaders in the state made good on their claim to be better
at serving the bread-and-butter needs of their constituents.

The Institute on Tax and Economic Policy calculated that the
new tax system had cost the state $2.8 billion in revenue between
2013 and 2019, money that could have been used to better educate
its workforce. "They've prioritized these corporate tax giveaways at
the expense of public education," Morgan Jackson, a senior adviser
to the state's current Democratic governor, Roy Cooper, told the
Raleigh News and Observer. "When the governor talks to CEOs
about coming to North Carolina, the first question they ask is not
about what the corporate tax rate is, it's about the workforce." The
North Carolina Justice Center, a local advocacy group, issued a report concluding that the 2013 tax package amounted to a tax *increase* for low- and middle-income residents—80 percent of the
state's population—while costing them in benefits that would have
gone to education, social services, and unemployment benefits.

For Americans who judge the country by the growth of its corporations, North Carolina did very well in the decade after 2010.

Businesses have flooded into cities like Charlotte and Raleigh, setting up headquarters in gleaming new office towers and bringing with them cadres of young professionals. Charlotte's population of nearly nine hundred thousand people has more than doubled since 1990. The city now has more U.S. banking than any place outside of New York, and Raleigh is flush with technology companies. But all those business-friendly policies have provided little benefit to most of the state's citizens. For the period 2017 to 2019, North Carolina's supplemental poverty rate of 13.6 was ninth highest in the nation. In 2005, its official poverty rate had ranked twenty-sixth. The number of concentrated poverty neighborhoods in the state had tripled between 2000 and 2016. In 2019, North Carolina was thirty-ninth among U.S. states in per capita personal income. State scorecards maintained by the Center for American Progress recently ranked North Carolina forty-second in "hunger and food insecurity" and forty-fifth in health insurance coverage. In the summer of 2018, Michael Walden, a University of North Carolina economist highly respected by legislators in both parties, issued a report noting that the state's recovery from 2010 to 2017 was the weakest of the six recovery periods since 1988 and fell short of both the nation as a whole and other states in the Southeast. "The study throws a wet blanket over the 'Carolina Comeback,'" reported the *News and Observer*, noting that North Carolina had only the fifteenth-highest growth in real GDP in the country in 2016. Among the states with the highest growth was the "tax hell" of California.

The Justice Center issued a report at the end of 2019 that concluded "the 2010s were actually a lost decade where we made little or no progress in solving North Carolina's real economic challenges. At the same time, tax cuts for wealthy individuals and big corporations have undermined our ability to build for the future. We have pulled back from investing in the foundations of a healthy economy, and a whole generation of school children have only known a public education system undercut by austerity policies."

Among the loudest voices protesting the abandonment of the state's poor was UNC law professor Gene Nichol, whose leadership of the Center on Poverty at the Chapel Hill campus had brought him to the homeless in the woods outside Hickory. In 2013, he wrote op-ed pieces in the *News and Observer* accusing the state GOP of an "unforgiving war on poor people." His views exposed him to attack by the network of think tanks run by Art Pope, one of which obtained Nichol's emails as public records, an outrageous affront to academic freedom. Rooting out what he sees as left-wing politics at UNC at Chapel Hill is one of Pope's priorities, and his generous donations to his alma mater make sure his voice gets heard. The university's Board of Governors first warned Nichol to get clearance for his columns. But Nichol refused to relent in his advocacy for the state's poor. In 2015, the university closed the Center of Poverty. Five years later, the legislature appointed Pope to the school's Board of Governors.

Part II

Portraits of Failure

4

The Dead Zones: Surrendering to Polluters in Texas

In November 2019, Bill and Shelby Jane Boudreaux turned off the lights in their cozy ranch home in Port Neches, Texas, and went to sleep untroubled for the last time. Thanksgiving Eve was the next day, and Shelby Jane had already done most of the preparations for the holiday. She had sliced and dressed the smoked turkey and crumbled the cornbread for the stuffing. The potato casserole was in the dish and ready for the oven. After all that work, her back ached so much in the middle of the night that she left her husband in the bedroom and moved to the den, settling on the dark-blue sofa with the southwest pattern they'd had for more years than she could remember.

The Boudreauxs had bought their home in 1967, and with his own two hands Bill had turned it into one of the nicest houses on Merriman Street. He added handsome cedar siding, a porch, another bedroom, and a garage and adjoining workshop. The house sits across the road from the Little League field and the high school stadium, the civic gems of Port Neches and places where the couple had memories of their own children playing. In most small towns, those fields would be the picture of serenity on a moonless night in late autumn.

But not in Port Neches. Just beyond the ballfield is the TPC Group's chemical plant, a sprawling complex of smokestacks, storage tanks, high-tension wires, and concrete buildings that hisses and rumbles and blares its loud speakers at all hours of the day. The hundreds of smokestacks form a great metallic skyline that stretches across the town, breathing fire into the night sky and giving off chemical vapors that befoul the entire region. The Boudreauxs are used to drifting off to sleep with what sounds like a torrential downpour right outside their windows, a noxious by-product of the refining process. "It's terrible," said Shelby Jane. "It just sounds like a hard, hard rain. If you're in the yard and you're trying to talk to someone, you have to come in the house. They can't hear you."

Bill and Shelby Jane Boudreaux are like most people in Port Neches. They're not complainers, not when it comes to the petrochemical industry that has provided so many of them jobs and is the very reason the community arose in the first place.

The plant currently owned by the TPC Group was part of a synthetic rubber manufacturing complex the federal government set up in Port Neches during World War II after Japan gained control of 90 percent of the world's supply of natural rubber. With Washington's sponsorship, a consortium of oil companies set up the Neches Butane Products Company, the plant's first operator, to manufacture butadiene, a colorless gas that is a crucial component of synthetic rubber. Neches Butane in turn supplied the compound to B.F. Goodrich and U.S. Rubber, which the government contracted to operate rubber plants in Port Neches.

Bill Boudreaux, who grew up in Port Neches with seven brothers and sisters, went to work for a successor to U.S. Rubber in 1966 at the age of twenty-seven. Within a year he bought his first house. He bought vehicles and took vacations. He and his wife raised four children and sent them all to college. He retired with no regrets, even after he was diagnosed with bladder cancer a decade ago and began an odyssey of a medical treatments that continues to this day. "The first two things they say to you when you find out you've got bladder cancer is, 'Did you ever smoke?' and

'Did you ever work in a rubber plant?'" he said. "Well, I never smoked."

It's not the bladder cancer that angered him in the spring of 2020. Nor was it his family's years in the shadow of a massive petrochemical plant—the hours spent power-washing the black soot off the front of the house or trying to save the dying shrubbery in the backyard. It's what happened just before Thanksgiving and what has come to light about how the State of Texas could have prevented it.

The butadiene plant has been a dirty operation since the government first set it up eighty years ago. Whether run by Neches Butane or any of its subsequent owners—Texaco, the Huntsman Corporation, Texas Petrochemicals LLC, Texas Petroleum Chemicals, and now the TPC Group—the plant has been polluting Port Neches's air and water for generations. Butadiene may be the magical ingredient of synthetic rubber, but it's also dangerously flammable and a proven carcinogen, linked to stomach, blood, and lymphatic system cancers.

Media outlets, federal regulators, and environmental groups made enough noise about elevated cancer rates in Port Neches in the 1990s and early 2000s that Texas environmental officials began to reconsider their hands-off approach to the state's politically powerful petrochemical industry. In 1993, Democratic Governor Ann Richards, together with the Democrat-controlled legislature, established a powerful new environmental agency, the Texas Natural Resource Conservation Commission, which placed the state's most flagrant chemical polluters in its crosshairs. Under Richards and her successor, Republican George W. Bush, the agency documented dozens of illegal chemical releases at the Huntsman Corporation plants in Port Neches and neighboring Port Arthur and slapped the company with record fines totaling nearly $10 million. In the midst of its investigation, members of the agency's mobile air-monitoring teams were themselves sickened just from driving by the plant with their windows closed. According to an internal memo, the staff members experienced "eye, nose, and throat irritation, coughing, headaches, and nausea, as well as strong odors." The *Houston Chronicle* posted its own air monitors in Port Neches in 2005 and found levels of benzene high enough that one scientist said living in the town would be "like sitting in traffic 24-7."

But Texas government is a different animal these days. In 2000, the state's voters elected Governor Rick Perry, a far-right Republican who made no secret of his hostility to environmental enforcement. Under Perry and his successor, Greg Abbott, funding for enforcement has been sharply reduced at the state environmental agency, renamed the Texas Commission on Environmental Quality, and penalties against polluters have dwindled. Environment Texas, an advocacy group based in Austin, issued a report in December 2019 that found illegal chemical releases in Texas had doubled in 2018 and that the TPC Group's plant in Port Neches was still a major source of illegal butadiene emissions. But the report found that Texas was barely lifting a finger to stop it, issuing penalties in only 3 percent of the 24,839 incidents of illegal emissions statewide between 2011 and 2016.

With Trump's EPA having been similarly decimated after 2016, Bill and Shelby Jane Boudreaux, like millions of other people whose homes are near refineries and chemical plants on the Gulf Coast, were caught in the middle of an environmental free-fire zone. But unless they spent their days poring over EPA documents online, there was no way they could have known it. The EPA records show that TPC's toxic releases, made up largely of butadiene, had reached a low in 2016 of just under 48,000 pounds. But by 2018, that number had spiked to 74,500 pounds. And the plant was awash in illegality, having failed to address "high priority violations" of the Clean Air Act—leaking butadiene—for twelve consecutive quarters.

After Trump's election, the EPA's presence at the plant essentially disappeared. There was a consent decree reached between the EPA and TPC in 2017 that stemmed from action taken during the Obama administration. TPC agreed to implement fence-line monitoring for released butadiene and report any toxic emissions on its website. The EPA fined the company $72,000, and that was it. The agency packed its bags. The last federal inspection was in January 2016, the very month of Trump's inauguration. Between then and Thanksgiving 2019, there were twelve state inspections, but the high-priority violations were allowed to go unaddressed and the state only assessed $51,000 in fines, a pittance for a company that reports annual revenues exceeding a billion dollars.

TPC's website showed a surge of butadiene releases in the fall of 2019, numbers that kept going up even as the company reported efforts to bring them under control. "Clearly there had been mechanical failure after mechanical failure after mechanical failure," Jim Tarr, a California-based air quality consultant, later told the *Texas Tribune*, "which suggests that either, one, they're not paying any attention to what's going on in the processing unit or, two, it's an old facility that's wearing out." Throughout the spring, summer, and fall of 2019, despite TPC's website reporting these alarming levels of butadiene release, there were no inspections at the plant. The hissing mass of steel, gas, and fire a few hundred yards from the Boudreauxs' home had become a ticking time bomb. But no one from the EPA or the Texas Commission on Environmental Quality showed up to investigate the mounting hazard to health and safety that was staring both agencies in the face.

Just after one o'clock in the morning of November 27, 2019, as the Boudreauxs slumbered peacefully in their home, the bill for that neglect came due. This time, butadiene leaking from a damaged storage tank didn't just expose the community to a cancer risk. It formed a highly flammable cloud of vapors that enveloped the plant. When something or someone provided the spark, the bomb went off.

That's what Bill and Shelby Jane first thought—that a bomb had hit their home. The percussion blew out their windows and tore exterior and even interior doors off their hinges. The house was bathed in orange as an intense wave of heat and flame rushed into the house. Just as quickly it was sucked back out, taking the draperies with it.

All along Merriman Street, people emerged from their shattered homes into clouds of butadiene. The plant itself was a glowing orange inferno beneath towering columns of black smoke that blotted out the sky. Homes were blackened with soot, yards and porches littered with debris, including hazardous asbestos. Investigators later found asbestos as far away as Bridge City, ten miles from Port Neches.

That afternoon there was a second explosion at the plant, which showered the neighborhood with a white chalky substance and sent one of the towering steel smokestacks shooting in the air, like a spaceship lifting off. One of the Boudreauxs' neighbors, Fred Vernon, grabbed his four-year-old daughter from her baby swing and ran outside, only to be overcome by fumes so strong his child began vomiting. As he tightened a blanket over her head, he himself vomited. Not long after, police evacuated some fifty thousand people in a four-mile radius of the plant.

Shelby Jane was lucky she had moved to the den, but her husband's head was less than two feet from one of the blown-out windows. His eardrums were shattered and his throat burned. Doctors told him he will require hearing aids for the rest of his life and his voice may never return to normal. "The more I talk, the lower I get," he said. "It bothers me to keep talking. My wife likes that part of it."

Like everyone else in Port Neches, particularly the parents of small children, the couple worry about the health effects of such massive exposure to butadiene. According to EPA records, the 74,500 pounds of toxic chemicals the plant had spewed in all of 2018 had skyrocketed to 316,000 the following year because of the explosion. But those numbers are self-reported by the company and are just estimates in the best of circumstances. The challenges of gauging how much butadiene escaped during a series of explosions and an ensuing inferno are obvious. The actual amount that was released and spread across the region will never be known.

Bill and Shelby Jane are bitter for the first time in their lives. In the summer of 2020, Bill was repairing his home, but doing it without joy and, at eighty-three, without the same energy he'd put to the task as a younger man. He'd grown tired, tired of fighting with the company to make good on its settlement offer, tired of not hearing well, and tired of struggling to talk with a damaged throat.

Shelby Jane was just as exhausted. "If my husband would move, I'd move," she said. "But he won't move. He grew up here. I told him that if it really does blow up to where those chemicals come over here, I hope it's instant. *I hope it takes us with it.*"

* * * *

THE DESPAIR OF PEOPLE like the Boudreauxs is replicated across the map of the United States, but mostly in those parts that are shaded red. Chemical accidents, evacuation orders, poisoned drinking water, red tides, beaches with no-swimming signs, bays with fishing bans, cancer hotspots—these have either disappeared or become rarities in the blue states. But in the "sacrifice zones" of the red states, amid the ruination of fracking fields and oil wells, refineries and chemical plants, factory farms and coal mines, they are what people wake up to every day. The damage visited upon families and communities is only occasionally seen in the daylight. When it results in an explosion or a tainted water system, it ends up on the nightly news. But it otherwise remains quite literally the dirty secret of officialdom, and of environmental activists who struggle to rouse the indignation of the wider public. The victims tend to be poor and powerless. The loss of clean air and clean water in their communities does not resonate politically the way it would in an affluent suburb. It is collateral damage in the quest for economic growth and corporate profits.

In the last decade, leaders of the biggest red states have presided over an enormous rollback in environmental enforcement—when combined with the devastation Donald Trump left at the EPA, perhaps the biggest rollback since the federal government became guardian of the country's natural resources in the early 1970s. Most of the highest-polluting red states have decimated their programs for environmental enforcement while overseeing an expansion of their most toxic industries and thumbing their noses at the specter of climate change. Former Florida governor Rick Scott went so far as to ban the terms "global warming," "climate change," and "sustainability" from his administration's official correspondence. Former Louisiana governor Bobby Jindal called climate science a "Trojan horse" for liberals, "an excuse for government to come in and try to tell us what kind of homes we live in, what kind of cars we drive, what kind of lifestyles we can enjoy."

According to a study by the Environmental Integrity Project, the five states whose industries release the highest amounts of toxic chemicals, all of them led by Republicans, each cut their pollution-control budgets by 20 to 35 percent between 2008 and 2018. This came during a period of strong economic growth and an overall increase in the states' budgets. By some twisted logic, the more polluted they were, the more vexing their environmental challenges, the more they cut their enforcement budgets. At a time when Texas was seeing a huge expansion of oil and gas infrastructure, it cut its pollution-control funding by 35 percent. Louisiana, a close second to Texas in the race for new oil refineries and chemical plants, also cut its pollution control by 35 percent. Illinois, under Republican control until 2019, slashed its funding by 25 percent. And North Carolina, with thousands of hog farm factories whose manure leaches into rivers and streams, reduced funding by 33 percent. By contrast, California increased its pollution-control budget by 75 percent and Connecticut by 117 percent. The study found that some blue states, like New York and Massachusetts, also sharply reduced their enforcement budgets. But those two states have small amounts of toxic releases—in 2018, there were 20.4 million pounds released in New York and 3.4 million in Massachusetts, compared with 222.2 million in Texas—and both are spending money on ambitious plans to reduce their states' reliance on carbon fuels.

The map of environmental carnage in this country shows a stark political divide. Red states are bigger culprits than blue states in virtually any measure of humanity's degradation of the planet. They release more toxic chemicals into the air and water. They generate the highest amounts of carbon dioxide and methane, the two biggest contributors to climate change. They rank highest in the increase in auto emissions. They burn more coal, allow more fracking, and have more oil and gas pipelines. They have more contaminated waterways and more closed beaches. In the last two decades, chemical accidents have occurred far more frequently in red states than in blue. Around the same time as the TPC plant explosion, Texas saw five other major chemical accidents, including an explosion at the KMCO chemical plant in Crosby that killed one worker and injured thirty and a blast at the ExxonMobil refinery in Baytown that injured twenty-two employees. Both facilities, like the TPC plant, had been allowed to operate despite major ongoing violations of the Clean Air Act. Indeed, the most polluted red states are filled with industries that report serious violations of environmental laws quarter after quarter without incurring serious penalties. "When you look at all these facilities and their compliance histories, it's like a rap sheet," Elena Craft, senior director for climate and health at the Environmental Defense Fund, said of the Texas petrochemical industry.

The red states' neglect of environmental enforcement inflicts damage far beyond their borders. While red-state industries on average emit higher amounts of carbon dioxide and methane, not one of the Republican-led states, as of this writing, has adopted a comprehensive plan to combat climate change by reducing reliance on fossil fuels. All twelve states that have adopted 100 percent clean energy goals statewide were blue, according to a 2020 study by the

Center for American Progress. Of the fourteen states where not even local or county governments have set clean energy goals, twelve of them were red.

Red states are largely responsible for fertilizer runoff in the Mississippi River, which has produced harmful algae blooms and caused huge increases in the cost of treating drinking water. The nutrient pollution has afflicted such damage to the Gulf of Mexico, where the Mississippi empties, that it has developed vast "dead zones"—areas with oxygen levels so low that fish and other marine life cannot survive. In June 2019, the National Oceanic and Atmospheric Administration forecast a dead zone of 7,829 square miles, roughly the size of Massachusetts.

Governmental inaction on the nutrient pollution has been glaring. In the ten states whose agriculture abuts the river, eight of them red states, elected officials have been notoriously lax in mandating that politically powerful meat producers and agribusiness concerns control the runoff of phosphorous and nitrogen, the most harmful nutrients. In 2016, a study by the nonprofit Mississippi River Collaborative found that nearly two decades after the EPA called on the ten states to develop nutrient criteria, only two had done so. Minnesota and Wisconsin had developed criteria for phosphorous, but not for nitrogen. Those two states and three others in the upper Mississippi region, Iowa, Missouri, and Illinois, had done some surveying of lakes and rivers for phosphorous and algae, but five deeply red states—Arkansas, Kentucky, Louisiana, Mississippi, and Tennessee—had done no assessments. None of the ten states has enacted laws to regulate nutrient pollution, relying instead on voluntary efforts by agricultural concerns.

The consequences of nutrient pollution can be devastating to entire regions, and not just along the Mississippi. In late 2017, the red tide that occurs periodically on Florida's west coast "bloomed" into a state emergency. Nearly 150 miles of beaches were inundated with a foul-smelling slime that killed millions of fish and cost the state huge amounts in tourist dollars. The plague went on for more than a year. Red tide is an algae bloom that occurs naturally in the Gulf of Mexico and intensifies when it mixes with nutrients near shore. Most scientists agree that red tide has become a monstrous problem in recent years because of increased pollutants in Florida's lakes, rivers, and coastal waters. The red tide became a state emergency under the watch of Rick Scott, who had presided over the decimation of what were once the state's progressive environmental laws, including a deep reduction in agencies that control water quality. He prevented the state from even investigating the role of industrial pollutants in the algae blooms. "He's got to own this slimy mess," wrote Lauren Ritchie, a longtime columnist for the *Orlando Sentinel*. "What Scott failed to do was fight algae, and the result is not only unpleasant but has cost tourism dollars. Enforcement of environmental laws has all but disappeared since Scott first was elected governor in 2010."

Republican states have also been slow to take action to prevent the depletion of the Ogallala Aquifer, which is the only source of water for residents, industries, and agriculture in an eight-state region that stretches across the High Plains from South Dakota to northern Texas. Crops from the region supply a sixth of the world's grain produce, but farmers are pumping water from the aquifer faster than it can be recharged by rainwater and melting snow. Water drawn from the aquifer accounts for a third of all irrigation in the nation. "Long-term unsustainable use of the aquifer is forcing states in the region to face the prospect of a regional economic disaster," wrote Jeremy Frankel, an editor at the *University of Denver Water Law Review*. A study by researchers at the University of Kansas found that the aquifer would be 70 percent empty by 2060 at current irrigation levels, but would last for a hundred years if farmers cut back their water use by a mere 20 percent.

The solution would seem obvious: regulations that force farmers to limit their irrigation, which is exactly what are now in place in

Nebraska. But Kansas and other states have been reluctant to impose regulations on their farmers. "We think it's a harsh method," said Tracy Streeter, director of the Kansas Water Office. "We would like to see groups of irrigators come together and work out a solution." The only problem is that only one group of farmers, whose lands only covered ninety-nine square miles, have agreed to voluntary limits. And that group found it was able to cut back 20 percent without sacrificing profits.

One of the newest red-state affronts to nature is the looming destruction of hardwood forests in the southeastern United States. Low-lying wetland forests, known as bottomland hardwood forests, have been decimated since the settlement of North America, but of those that remain, 65 percent of the acreage is found in eight southern states: Alabama, Florida, Georgia, Louisiana, Mississippi, North Carolina, South Carolina, and Virginia. Conservationists have long battled against their destruction, but now they face a new threat. The trees that grow in those forests—such as bald cypress, swamp tupelo, red maple, green ash, American elm, and black gum—are perfect for the manufacture of wood pellets used as an energy source. Woody biomass, as it is known, is under heavy demand by European energy companies as an alternative to fossil fuels. The only problem is that Europe takes care of its forests. They are highly regulated, which limits the supply of woody biomass.

But that's not an issue in the American red states. As of late 2015, there were twenty woody biomass mills operating in the Southeast and twenty-seven more planned, according to a study by the Natural Resources Defense Council. And there was little standing in the way of their buzzsaws. More than 90 percent of the 26 million acres of bottomland hardwood forest in the eight states were unprotected and ripe for harvest. Saving those forests is not just about scenery. They are the habitat for thousands of species of wildlife, many of them endangered, and are also buffers against pollutants that are contaminating drinking water, including the nitrogen that the same southern states are otherwise doing nothing to control.

* * * *

THERE IS NO MORAL high ground from which the red states can justify their failure to protect their natural resources and the health and safety of their citizens, even in the context of traditional conservativism. The founding myths of the conservative movement revolve around God, family, rural folkways, small-town values. They are about communities adopting their own modes of existence without interference from distant bureaucrats. But what about the interference that comes when a distant corporation contaminates the local stream or fills the community with noxious fumes? Aren't conservative values violated when a region is forced to watch as a mining company shears off its mountaintops or a timber company clear-cuts its forests?

Russell Kirk, a leading light of the conservative movement in midcentury America, was no friend of industrial polluters. From his ancestral home in rural Mecosta County, Michigan, which he called "stump country" because the forests had been so denuded by timber companies, he decried man's "deadly and persistent" assault on nature. In a 1968 essay, "Man, Enemy of Nature," he wrote:

Lake Michigan is being poisoned by man's industrial and domestic wastes, so that within this century it may "die," its fish destroyed by a human upsetting of the natural balance. It may become a vast sewer in which no one can swim: that has already happened to Lake Erie. . . . We poison, too, the air—at even greater risk to our own survival. At Lake Arrowhead, in California's high sierras, certain species of evergreen are said to be dying, afflicted by the man-created smog of the coast which now drifts upward even to such heights. Probably, we will do nothing effective about smog until some dreadful day when a city's air is so polluted that hundreds of people with pulmonary trouble perish within 24 hours.

In propounding his pro-environment thesis, Russell quoted Edmund Burke, the nineteenth-century Irish statesman and critic of the French Revolution, who alluded to "earth, the kind and equal of mother and all." Burke urged his contemporaries not to "commit waste" on their inheritance, lest they bequeath to future generations "a ruin instead of a habitation." Roger Scruton, the conservative British philosopher most noted for the underground academic networks he set up in the Soviet bloc during the Cold War, did not understand the clash between environmentalism and conservatism. "The real evil against which both sides should be united," he wrote, "is the habit of treating the earth as a thing to be used but not revered."

The person most responsible for the federal government's role in protecting the environment was a conservative Republican, President Richard Nixon, who created the EPA and signed the Clean Water Act and the National Environmental Policy Act, two landmark pieces of legislation that have made a huge difference in the nation's quality of life. Ronald Reagan was no friend of environmentalism, but even he signed the Emergency Planning and Community Right-to-Know Act, which required industrial facilities to publicly disclose the chemicals they store in and release from their plants.

The red-state leaders who walk in lockstep with polluters are not standing up for a conservative tradition. They are looking after the economic interests of their corporate backers. And those interests are not those of the public. It is well documented that industrial pollution as a whole is a major detriment to the U.S. economy, even without taking into account the ravages of climate change. According to the EPA, nutrient pollution costs the tourism industry alone more than $1 billion a year. This is not exactly an issue that has crept up on us. President Kennedy, in a message to Congress in 1963, warned that air pollution was costing the economy $11 billion a year, with agriculture alone losing $50 million. "Crops are stunted or destroyed, livestock become ill, meat and milk production are reduced," he said. "In the light of the known damage caused by polluted air, both to our health and to our economy, it is imperative that great emphasis be given to the control of air pollution by communities, states and the federal government." Of late, more than half of the state governments have been missing from that equation.

* * * *

NO ONE HAS PERSONIFIED the red states' contempt for the environment more than Rick Perry, who was Texas's longest-serving governor and served two years as Trump's energy secretary before resigning amid a scandal related to Ukraine's natural gas industry. He was an abject apologist for Texas's top rankings in most measures of pollution. In 2018, his state's industries released 222 million pounds of toxic chemicals into the air and water, far more than any other state. The amount was nearly six times that of California and ten times that of New York. The state's emissions of carbon dioxide—the most damaging of the greenhouse gases—increased from 606 million metric tons in 1990 to 711 million in 2017, while the second biggest producer, California, increased only slightly, from 357 million to 360 million. Elected officials in Texas protest the loudest about the federal government's "overreach" in regulating polluters or the "junk science" behind climate change studies. In so doing they take their example from Perry, who was once dismissed by his state's Republican establishment as too extreme to be taken seriously as a candidate for statewide office, but who shrewdly anticipated red-state America's lurch to the right and helped usher in a new era of trenchant conservatism in Texas.

Perry was perhaps an unlikely standard-bearer for the far right, given that his career has been more notable for his service to campaign donors, business cronies, and his own ambitions rather than adherence to ideology or a set of policy proposals. He became an anti-government zealot only after gauging that red-state America was headed in that direction, but he took on the role with a panache that captured the imagination of Texas voters. In 2009, as lieutenant governor, his demagoguery was already on full display when he told reporters outside Austin City Hall that Texas might consider seceding from the United States. "We've got a great union," he said. "There's absolutely no reason to dissolve it. But, if Washington continues to thumb their nose at the American people, you know, who knows what might come out of that."

Perry was raised humbly, the child of tenant cotton farmers in Paint Creek, a small town in West Texas, a region whose dominant political ethos was once described by a political consultant and Perry friend as "a sort of Confederate-based, anti-federalism, anti-telling-me-what-the-hell-to-do kind of deal." That was his grounding when he entered politics as a Democrat in the early 1980s. He was conservative by instinct, but uninterested in policy. He admitted as much to an Abilene newspaper shortly after being elected to the Texas House of Representatives in 1984. "I had not one piece of legislation I planned to carry," he said. Even when he became one of the "pit bulls," a group of young legislators on the House appropriations committee pushing for state budget cuts, his worldview was still inchoate. Tom Uher, a conservative Democrat who roomed with Perry in those days, told the journalist Alec MacGillis that the pit bulls were more interested in scoring political points than understanding the agencies whose budgets they sought to cut. "I'm not sure you can ever ascribe a real philosophy to Perry," Uher said. "He can switch colors to whatever he needed to be."

That opportunism explains how he could campaign fervently for Al Gore in the 1988 presidential race and switch parties a year later to run against incumbent Texas Agriculture Commissioner Jim Hightower. He narrowly defeated Hightower by campaigning against the incumbent's stringent regulation of agricultural pesticides. As a state representative, he had sponsored a bill to strip Hightower's department of its pesticide enforcement authority. It was Perry's first full-throated opposition to environmental enforcement, but it would hardly be his last.

In 1989, the Republican Party had not yet fully turned its back on environmentalism, either at the state or federal level. Reagan had been the most anti-environment president in modern history, but his successor, George H.W. Bush, distanced himself from Reagan's positions and proclaimed himself a conservationist in the tradition of Theodore Roosevelt. In his first term, he made good on his promise to protect the environment by signing a set of amendments in 1990 to the Clean Air Act that brought about aggressive action to combat acid rain, ozone depletion, and urban smog.

But Perry, a pathbreaker in the retrograde politics of the red states, was on a different path. While Bush the elder was fortifying the Clean Air Act, Perry reverted to the hostility to environmental regulation that has now become a standard feature of Republican state politics. His campaign against Hightower had closely allied him with agribusiness concerns, including the politically influential Texas Farm Bureau, and as commissioner he watched out for their interests. In 1993, when he was the Texas agriculture commissioner, he appeared before a House committee investigating high rates of chemical-related illness among farmworkers, four times higher than those of the next most hazardous industry. The son of tenant cotton farmers might have been expected to stand up for farmworkers' health, but instead Perry spoke out for agribusiness profits while putting a deceptive populist spin on his position. "American business in general, and American agriculture specifically, have had enough of bureaucracy at both the federal and state levels, but especially bureaucracy out of Washington," he told the committee. "The men and women who feed and clothe this nation are suffocating under the weight of mounting federal regulations."

Perry apparently calculated that he would get further in Texas politics by pleasing the chemical and agriculture firms that poured money into his campaign than sticking up for politically marginal farmworkers. Indeed, in the final days of his campaign for agricultural commissioner, Perry accepted a $25,000 contribution from Voluntary Purchasing Group, a major pesticide manufacturer that was under investigation by Hightower's department for illegally dumping liquid arsenic acid at its plant in Bonham, Texas. Nearby farmers had complained that arsenic-contaminated water was killing their cattle, and Hightower's investigators had amassed voluminous evidence supporting their claim. When Perry became governor, the investigation disappeared, and the department regulator who had headed up the inquiry, Benny Fisher, was eventually fired. "All my life, I always thought that the law was for everyone to follow," Fisher told the *Texas Observer.* "But it don't work that way at the [Texas Department of Agriculture]. If you've got big money, you're cool. If you've got political pull, you're cool." By the end of his term as agriculture commissioner, Perry bragged that he had eliminated 230 regulations and reduced his department's staff by almost 20 percent.

Perry was elected as lieutenant governor in 1998 and quickly elevated to governor after George W. Bush resigned to assume the presidency. And his tutelage of agribusiness continued unabated, as demonstrated by his inaction after one of the worst chemical disasters in the nation's history, the explosion at the West Fertilizer plant on April 17, 2013, that killed fifteen people. The details of the tragedy and the state's lack of response still resonate nearly a decade later.

Volunteer firefighters from the area around West, a small community in Central Texas about eighty miles south of Dallas, had responded to an early evening fire at the plant with little training in hazardous materials and no clue of what they were up against. Their only hint was the surreal wave of heat that confronted them as soon as they stepped out of their vehicles. Having never conducted training drills at the plant, they had no way of knowing that the facility had stockpiled forty to sixty tons of fertilizer-grade ammonium nitrate, a powder so explosive that the federal government has protocols for keeping it out of the hands of terrorists. Within minutes of their arrival, the building exploded, killing twelve firefighters and three others and flattening most of the town. The blast registered 2.1 on the Richter scale and shook the earth forty miles away. Videos of the event show the building there one second and vaporized the next, a crater ninety-three feet wide left in its place, while a black mushroom cloud reminiscent of Hiroshima rose over the town. Two schools, an apartment complex, and a nursing home were so badly damaged they had to be demolished, and 150 other buildings needed repairs.

Residents in the town of less than three thousand people had been complaining for years about ammonia leaks at the plant, including an incident in which a child living nearby was sickened. State and federal agencies visited the plant numerous times but only levied small fines for violations like failing to have a permit or disaster plan and improperly labeling storage containers. The immensity of the tragedy at West Fertilizer and the obvious safety implications for hundreds of similar facilities around the nation prompted immediate action by the federal government. In August 2013, four months after the explosion, President Obama signed an executive order that drew up new guidelines for safe chemical storage and created a working group to assist state and local government in improving their own safeguards.

But the administration got little help from the State of Texas. Perry told a news conference five days after the explosion that he was happy with the state's inspections of West Fertilizer and saw no need for greater regulation of ammonium nitrate, despite large stockpiles of the chemical in 150 Texas facilities, many in close proximity to homes. He said that if the Republican-controlled legislature wanted to take action, it was free to do so. He thus cravenly passed the buck to lawmakers who he knew would never act. Joe C. Pickett, a Democratic state representative from El Paso, proposed a bill to give the state fire marshal authority over storage of ammonium nitrate, but the measure died in committee, with no support from Perry or legislative leaders. They were content with Texas having millions of pounds of highly explosive chemicals haphazardly stored near residential neighborhoods with no state fire code and no ability to compel inspections. In the absence of a new law, all State Fire Marshal Chris Connealy could do was ask fertilizer companies to voluntarily submit to inspections, and he appeared to make excuses for five companies that wouldn't even allow his inspectors on their property. "In their defense," he said in testimony before a legislative committee, "they may have a very good reason."

To this day, Texas has taken no significant measures to protect the public from the enormous hazards of ammonium nitrate, and the Trump administration even reversed the safety controls on chemical facilities that Obama ordered at the federal level. As the *Dallas Morning News* said in a big headline eight months after the West Fertilizer disaster: "It could happen again."

* * * *

EVER SINCE ITS FIRST MAJOR oil well gushed from Beaumont's Spindletop Hill in 1901, Texas has been degrading the planet more prodigiously than most other states. Oil is the gift that transformed Texas from what journalist Richard Parker described as "a broken-down Southern state of impoverished dirt farmers" into an industrial colossus with the tenth largest economy in the world. It lay behind the spectacular growth of Houston, Dallas–Fort Worth, Austin, and San Antonio and the vast fortunes that made the Texas oil man a cultural icon. Texas has paid for that affluence with punishing boom-and-bust cycles, polluted air and water, and huge scars on its landscape that are only grow-ing larger. The six-hundred-mile Gulf Coast in Texas is one of the nation's great natural wonders, but it is studded with oil refineries and chemical plants from the Louisiana border to Corpus Christi. It is jarring for someone used to Cape Cod or the northern Pacific coast to see booming resort towns like Galveston or Port Aransas with chemical smokestacks looming in the background and brown water lapping onto their beaches.

In a nation dependent on oil for its economy and national secu-rity, it once would have been utopian to imagine any other reality for the Gulf Coast and the rest of Texas's petroleum-stained landscape. But therein lies a sad irony. At the very time technology has begun to provide realistic alternatives to oil, a stupendous achievement in engineering has unleashed the biggest Texas oil boom ever.

The "miracle" began in a vast geological formation near Fort Worth known as the Barnett Shale. A wealthy Texas oil man named George Mitchell had been experimenting since the early 1980s with an unproven drilling technique known as hydraulic fracturing. Fracking, as the technique became known, uses highly pressurized water and chemicals to break up dense shale formations and unlock their deposits of oil and natural gas. Mitchell's company, Mitchell Energy, was struggling to meet its obligation to supply 10 percent of Chicago's natural gas and was desperate for a way to access deposits that were known to be pre-sent in shale but had never been extracted in any kind of abun-dance. The conventional wisdom was that it couldn't be done. But Mitchell pressed on through nearly two decades of setbacks and finally perfected the technology in 1998. Mitchell Energy had achieved one of history's biggest breakthroughs in energy extrac-tion, and the company's gas production over the next two years increased sharply. Unfortunately for Mitchell, he did not have the capital to realize the enormous potential of his technique. That was left to Devon Energy, an Oklahoma City company that paid

$3.5 billion for Mitchell Energy in 2002 and combined fracking with horizontal drilling, which utilized drill bits that could pivot underground and fracture chains of oil pockets over a range of miles. Devon's innovation yielded far more gas than Mitchell was able to with fracking alone.

It wasn't long before fracking was adapted to oil drilling, with the same spectacular results, first in the Eagle Ford Shale in East Texas and the Bakken formation in North Dakota and ultimately in the Permian Basin, the nation's true mother lode of oil. The Permian Basin, which sprawls across 86,000 square miles in western Texas and southeastern New Mexico, had been a source of oil since the 1920s, and was particularly productive when the federal government began paying for deep drilling to meet oil needs during the Second World War. But the oil field was considered largely spent by the turn of the twenty-first century, and major oil companies had sold off much of the holdings to small independent speculators and moved on.

Fracking changed everything. It unleashed a new Texas oil boom, fully underway in 2008, and its epicenter was the Permian Basin, where the shale formations were up to a thousand feet thick, relatively close to the surface, within easy pipeline range of the Gulf, and known for decades to contain vast deposits of oil. By early 2019, the dozens of companies tripping over one another for leases in the basin—including ExxonMobil, BP, Shell, and Chevron—were producing four million barrels of oil a day, more than was coming from any of the fourteen OPEC nations except for Saudi Arabia and Iraq. President Obama in 2015 repealed a forty-year-old law barring most U.S. oil exports, and by the end of 2018 the nation had become a net exporter of petroleum for the first time in decades and the world's leading producer of oil and natural gas.

The historic importance of this turn of events is hard to overestimate. American dependence on foreign oil had cost the country enormously in the postwar era. The energy crisis of the 1970s, caused by interruptions in Middle East oil supplies, was one of the major causes of the Great Inflation that shook the nation's economy, undermined the Carter presidency, ended the Keynesian consensus among leading Western economists, and helped pave the way for the Reagan Revolution. Each of the Middle East wars that cost America so much in lives and treasure was somehow related to oil. Energy independence gives the U.S. more leverage on the world stage, not just with other oil-producing nations like Saudi Arabia and Russia, but also with China, whose energy needs are growing as quickly as its economy.

And fracking's economic impact on the country has been huge. According to the author Daniel Yergin, the oil and gas sectors accounted for two-thirds of U.S. net industrial development, and 40 percent of the cumulative growth in industrial output, between 2009 and 2019. The explosion in energy production yielded jobs across the country. "There were jobs in and around oil and gas fields, manufacturing jobs in the Midwest making equipment and trucks and pipes, jobs in California writing software in managing data, and jobs generated by increased income and spending, like real estate agents and cars," Yergin wrote, adding that the "impact has been felt across virtually all states."

But when one takes into account the environmental damage wrought by the nation's rapidly expanding oil and gas infrastructure, the net benefits vanish. The world's economies lose far more dealing with hurricanes, floods, forest fires, algae blooms, water shortages, and other results of climate change than is generated as economic spin-off from oil and gas industries. And hopes that natural gas would be a cleaner fossil fuel than oil or coal have been dispelled by new data showing how much gas companies like Exxon and BP allow to escape into the atmosphere to keep their oil drilling profitable. When companies drill into shale formations, gas and oil come up together. At times when gas prices are depressed or pipelines are not available nearby, companies flare off the gas or let it escape directly into the air, which gives off huge amounts of carbon dioxide, one of the major greenhouse gases. That practice has emerged as a bigger detriment to the environment than the threat to groundwater posed by fracking chemicals. In 2018, the Permian Basin oil fields flared off or vented more natural gas than states like Arizona and South Carolina used in the entire year. And the pipelines used to transport natural gas pose their own environmental hazards and are a blight on America's rural landscapes. Scenic hillsides in Texas's fabled Hill Country have been excavated in recent years to make way for the Permian Highway, a 429-mile pipeline that is to carry natural gas from the Permian Basin to the Gulf Coast. When U.S. District Judge Robert Pitman rejected the Sierra Club's effort to stop the project in August 2020, he said too much had already been constructed to turn back. "Unfortunately," he said, "granting an injunction at this stage of the pipeline's completion would not unring the bell."

* * * *

TEXAS POLITICIANS HAVE ACCEPTED enormous amounts of money from the oil and gas industries in recent years, none more so than Rick Perry and Greg Abbott. In 2017, the National Institute on Money in State Politics published a report showing that Perry, then Trump's nominee for energy secretary, had been given $10.5 million by oil and gas interests since 2000, more than any other state candidate in the nation. He netted more than half of that money, $6 million, in his last run for governor in 2010. Abbott was a close second, with $9.8 million in oil and gas donations. Since then, Abbott has pulled away from Perry, his oil and gas money by 2020 totaling $21.8 million. To put that in perspective, George W. Bush received less than $1.5 million from oil and gas companies in his two presidential campaigns. Other Texas elected officials have also nailed down big bucks from the industry, including Lieutenant Governor Dan Patrick, $5.7 million; Attorney General Ken Paxton, $3.1 million; and former house speaker Dennis Bonnen, $667,000.

And the companies have gotten plenty for their money. Perry made EPA-bashing a staple of his governorship, suing the agency repeatedly during his fourteen years in office. He also larded the Texas Commission on Environmental Quality (TCEQ) and other state agencies with appointees hostile to climate science. He called the 2010 BP oil spill, which the federal government found to be largely the fault of the company's cost cutting, an "act of God" and opposed new federal regulation of offshore drilling. His tactics were aimed largely at keeping federal and state regulators off the back of energy companies, and they worked. For years Perry defied warnings from Obama's EPA that Texas's "flexible permitting" of industrial facilities was too lax in its pollution controls and violated the Clean Air Act, a position the agency had also taken in the previous administration. In issuing permits, the state sometimes even overruled decisions by smog-choked cities like Houston and Dallas. When the EPA lost patience and took over Texas's permitting authority in 2010, Perry lashed out, calling on Obama to "rein in this rogue agency, and stop the EPA from continuing to threaten Texas families, their jobs and cost of living."

But what was actually happening to families, workers, and communities around refineries and petrochemical plants while Perry was carping about federal overreach? Part of the reason we have the answer is that a number of environmental groups, tired of waiting for state regulators to take action against major polluters, filed citizens' lawsuits that have unearthed enormous amounts of evidence about the neglect of environmental enforcement in Texas.

One particularly revealing suit began with a shrimper named Diane Wilson, who had been battling since the early 1990s to prevent the Taiwanese-owned chemical giant Formosa Plastics Corporation from wiping out the legendary shell-fishing industry in Lavaca Bay. The bays and estuaries of the Gulf Coast have long been one of the nation's most fertile shrimping areas, among the only places in the country competing with the flood of cheap farm-raised shrimp from Latin America and Southeast Asia. Shrimping undergirded the local economy in the communities surrounding Lavaca Bay—about eighty miles northeast of Corpus Christi—until the petrochemical industry laid claim to the region.

Wilson, a boat captain whose family had been fishing the bay commercially for four generations, went to war with Formosa in 1993 after the Texas Water Commission issued the company a permit for the daily discharge of fifteen million gallons of toxin-laced wastewater as part of its $1.3 billion expansion of a plant in Point Comfort. The company had already had numerous environmental violations at its existing facility—including a record $3.4 million penalty the EPA issued in 1991—and Wilson heralded the expansion as the death of the local shrimping industry. In case anyone missed the point, she and about twenty other protesters placed a black coffin draped with a fish net outside the office of Governor Ann Richards in the late summer of 1993. Calling her campaign "Diane vs. Goliath," Wilson also waged three hunger strikes and was once on her way to scuttle her fishing boat on top of the company's discharge pipe before the Coast Guard stopped her. Her campaign didn't make her any friends in Calhoun County, many of whose residents were happy that Formosa was going to create jobs to replace what was being lost in the shrimping industry. The political theater worked, at least for a while. Under pressure from Richards's newly minted Texas Natural Resource Conservation Commission and the EPA, which granted Wilson an audience in Washington, Formosa in 1994 announced a goal of "zero discharge" of polluted wastewater and said it would reduce its water pollutants by 32 percent. Wilson became something of a celebrity. She published a book, appeared on TV shows and the lecture circuit, and in 2001 was the subject of a documentary short, *Diane Wilson: A Warrior's Tale.* But all that attention overlooked a sad reality. The pollution quickly resumed, in no small measure because of the fracking boom and the conservative takeover of Texas politics by the likes of Rick Perry.

In 2009, a former wastewater operator at the plant, Dale Jurasek, called Wilson and asked her to meet him at the Hideout, a
little bar on the outskirts of Rockport, Texas. At the meeting, he
told her that the discharge of chemicals was no longer the only
problem. He said the plant had begun polluting the entire bay
with little plastic pellets, known as "nurdles," that are the base in-
gredients of most plastic products. It later became known that fish-
ermen had been commonly finding pellets in the stomach of fish.
That encounter in the Hideout essentially led to Wilson, Jurasek,
and other volunteers scouring Lavaca Bay in kayaks for three years,
filling ziplock bags with nurdles and hazardous PVC powder and
carefully noting the date and time of each collection. The nurdles
would issue from Formosa discharge pipes in Cox Creek, flow into
the bay, and eventually disperse in the Gulf as far south as Corpus
Christi. Those ziplock bags became the core of a federal lawsuit
filed against Formosa by the San Antonio Bay Estuarine, part of
the Waterkeeper Alliance, a national group based in New York.
U.S. District Judge Kenneth Hoyt found the evidence overwhelming, calling Formosa a "serial offender" for the millions of pellets it
dumped into the bay. In October 2019, Formosa agreed to contribute $50 million to a trust fund for environmental restoration proj-
ects in the bay.

But it was something of a hollow victory, because Formosa's serial offending has continued, with little interference from the
State of Texas. Formosa's chairman, Jason Lin, told *Bloomberg
Businessweek* in December 2019 that the company was investing
$14 billion in Texas and Louisiana in part because environmental
regulations in Taiwan had become too stringent. "In Taiwan," he
said, "the government treats petrochemical investment as a polluting industry and stigmatizes us."

The stunning implications of Lin's statement were not lost on the
article's authors, Bruce Einhorn and Joe Carroll. "Formosa's strategy to invest in the U.S. rather than at home represents a reversal of

some long-established roles in the global economy," they wrote. "Petrochemical companies that once focused on Asian nations where governments tolerated pollution in exchange for economic growth are increasingly turning to the U.S., with many pro-industry politicians and cheaper raw materials."

Anne Rolfes, director of the nonprofit Louisiana Bucket Brigade, put it a tad more bluntly: "They are not building this in Taiwan. They are looking at us as a colony."

The Perry and Abbott administrations truly exhibited the kind of subservience that tin-pot dictators once accorded to U.S. corporations, as long as the firms spread around a lot of money. The TCEQ fined Formosa a meager $121,000 in 2019, and only after the citizens' lawsuit was in its final stages. It has since only fined the company $42,000 even though EPA records, as of September 2020, have listed the Point Comfort facility as a "high priority" violator of the Clean Air Act and in "significant non-compliance" with laws governing the disposal of hazardous waste for at least twelve consecutive quarters. The records show that the facility released 13.6 million pounds of toxic chemicals into the air and water in 2018, up from just over a million pounds a year earlier. That $50 million that Formosa turned over to the people of the Lavaca Bay region was not even a blip on the radar for a company with sales of $207 billion in 2019.

Other private suits have yielded evidence just as damning. At the very time Perry was flouting the EPA's permit requirements in 2010, two nonprofit environmental groups, Environment Texas and the Sierra Club, filed suit against ExxonMobil for emissions at a complex in Baytown, Texas, that includes an oil refinery and two chemical plants. It is the largest such facility in the United States, with five thousand employees and enough metal piping to stretch ten thousand miles. It is an enormously complex operation, with the capability of refining 550,000 barrels of crude per day and producing 13 billion pounds of petrochemicals annually. There are 120,000 items in its permit that the company must monitor for compliance with state and federal regulations, and for good reason. In 2018 alone, the three plants together released more than 37 million pounds of toxic chemicals into the air and water.

At trial in 2014, Baytown residents gave testimony about their life with ExxonMobil as a neighbor. They described seeing a toxic haze over their neighborhood and breathing foul odors that caused watery eyes, running noses, and chest constriction. Evidence at the trial showed that the company had illegally released more than ten million pounds of pollutants over sixteen hundred days. In a single event that lasted eighteen hours, one of the facilities released fifty-seven tons of sulfur dioxide, which can cause breathing difficulties and burning of the nose and throat. But U.S. District Judge David Hittner, who was appointed by Ronald Reagan, bent over backward to commend the company's effort to control pollution and found that ExxonMobil should pay no penalty beyond the fines of $1.4 million already assessed by the TCEQ and Harris County, hardly a deterrent for a company that in the first full year after the suit was filed had a net income of $41 billion.

But Hittner's decision was overturned on appeal, and he ended up fining the company nearly $20 million, believed to be the largest verdict ever against a polluter in a citizen lawsuit. The State of Texas wouldn't hold ExxonMobil accountable. It took two scrappy environmental groups and an appellate court. But without the state or the EPA continuing the pressure, it is questionable how much is likely to change. EPA records from 2020 show that all three of the Baytown facilities had twelve consecutive quarters with "high-priority violations" of the Clean Air Act. In the facility known as the Olefins plant, the previous five quarters of violations had gone unaddressed. During those five quarters, the TCEQ fined the company less than $140,000.

* * * *

WAYS OF LIFE that have persevered for decades along the Gulf Coast of Texas and Louisiana are being wiped out. Port Lavaca was once an idyllic fishing village with seafood shacks lining its shorelines and hundreds of flat-bottomed trawlers plying the bays and estuaries for pink and white shrimp. Tourists came for the sand dunes and the salt marshes and the sea turtles. They came because there was something indigenous and authentic about the place. But shrimping was more than just a cultural artifact. It was the engine of the local economy. A quarter of a century ago, the Gulf of Mexico was the predominant source of domestic shrimp in America and a $55 million industry in the region surrounding Lavaca Bay.

The first blow to this way of life was Alcoa. Between 1966 and 1979, the aluminum company dumped an estimated 1.2 million pounds of mercury into Lavaca Bay and other nearby waterways. That part of Lavaca Bay, near Point Comfort, is now one of the nation's largest Superfund sites, a 3,500-acre dead zone with signs warning against fishing and a huge mound of stored toxic waste called Dredge Island.

About an hour and a half drive up the coast from Lavaca Bay is the little island of Quintana, a beach town that was another favorite of tourists. Quintana Beach was beloved for its fishing, sand dunes, bird watching, and the nesting every year of the endangered Kemp's ridley sea turtles, one of the only places in the world where that species can be seen. Generations of families had memories of renting bungalows on the island, and for some those experiences led them to retire there over the decades. But sometime around 2015, the town of their memories virtually ceased to exist. A company called Freeport LNG announced plans for a massive natural gas export facility, purchased most of the seventy homes on the island, demolished more than two dozen, and set aside others for company employees. Over the next several years, a two-mile stretch on the western half of the island was leveled to make way for the new plant. Face west on the beach now, look past the low dunes that still have signage warning that "Dunes and Christmas Trees Are Protected," and the landscape is an industrial colossus—thousands of miles of steel piping for gas liquefaction and storage tanks as tall as fifteen-story buildings.

For years, Freeport LNG had a small natural gas import facility that was a mile away from homes and did little to disturb the serene lifestyle of the island. But after the shale revolution, the country was awash in cheap natural gas, so the company did an about-face and regeared for a $14 billion export plant that would make their previous facility look quaint. The company signed contracts with Dow Chemical, Conoco, and others to have their gas piped to the facility from the fracking fields in the western part of the state. The people of Quintana tried to fight. Harold Doty, then on the town council, knocked on the doors of all sixty-six permanent residents in the summer of 2013 and got most of them to sign a petition opposing the project, according to the *Texas Observer*, the only major news organization that covered the issue. But they were quickly overwhelmed by Freeport LNG's industrial might. The company not only bought up the homes, but also offered remaining residents $25,000 apiece to keep quiet. Eventually, Doty and other members of the council gave up, selling their homes like the rest and moving on. Now the council is made up of company employees. Freeport LNG runs the town. Hardly anybody remembers the sign that hung on one resident's house: "SOLD Quintana for LNG Chump Change."

Champions of Texas's indigenous culture are fighting a losing battle against the power of the oil, gas, and chemical industries and their patrons in the Texas statehouse, even as society begins to move away from fossil fuels and the new wariness of investors exposes a chink in the industry's armor. The Port of Corpus Christi, a state-chartered entity with an unelected board, was moving ahead with plans at the end of 2021 to spend more than $500 million dredging its ship channel to make way for LNG tankers docking at a planned export facility on Harbor Island.

The port doesn't care that the biggest investor, the Carlyle Group, bowed out of the project. It was pressing on, even though the complex sits just across a small channel from Port Aransas, the world's longest barrier island and one of the most cherished beach towns on the Gulf Coast. To accommodate natural gas, it was willing to lay waste to the region's tourism. Richard Parker said it best: "The coastline of the Gulf of Mexico is a working person's waterway. It's not fancy. It's a simple place of crab boils, bars and bays. ... The decision hanging over Harbor Island and Port Aransas is a test of our values as modern Texans. Will we sink good money after bad for a dying fossil fuel business, enriching a few, as we have for a century? Or, in hard economic times will we flash a new set of values to preserve the natural and cultural heritage of Texas?"

5

Code Red: The Shame of Health Care in the Red States

ON THE DAY SHYTERIA SHOEMAKER DIED, SHE was trying to overcome the limits of her life. She was twenty-three years old, unmarried, and pregnant with her second child, and she was getting off the night shift at a McDonald's in Houston, Mississippi, with the dew freezing into ice crystals in the parking lot and the little town as cold and fallow as the dormant cotton fields that lay around it. She wanted to make something of her Saturday night, to break the ties that bound her to frustration, but the prospects were not good.

Then again, they never were. Shoemaker's life had been a constant struggle with poverty and ill health. She lived with her mother and three-year-old daughter, A'Dore, in an apartment complex in nearby Aberdeen that was little more than a cluster of drab brick buildings with yards made of dirt and gravel. Born with severe asthma, she had spent much of her life sleeping with an oxygen mask, and never knew in the course of a day when she'd suddenly be gasping for breath. Her daughter inherited the same ailment and had an oxygen mask of her own.

But Shoemaker didn't let her life's challenges overwhelm her. It was as if the petite young mother knew her days were short, had been short from the day she was born, and that every one of them had to count. She loved to laugh and dance and poke fun at her friends, and made everyone want to do those things with her. "She loved to party," said her mother, Makeska Shoemaker. "My baby loved to have fun." On the night of January 26, 2019, the party was the same place it always was, at a house her brother and two male cousins were renting just south of Houston. That was where she could relax, if only for a little while. She had no way of knowing that a political vendetta being waged in Republican-controlled statehouses across the country was about to make her its victim.

Just after one o'clock in the morning, as she sat by herself on a bed inside one of the rooms, she was seized by an asthma attack so severe she could barely manage to open the door and stagger into the hallway, where she collapsed. Her brother and cousins wasted no time in bundling the gasping Shoemaker into a car for the ride to the Trace Regional Hospital emergency room eight minutes way. But when her cousin, LeKearis Shoemaker, called 911 to report that they were on their way, the group got a surprise that none of them will forget. The building was closed. The facility's owner, Southern Hospital Corporation of Houston, a subsidiary of the publicly traded SunLink Health Systems, had grown tired of the millions of dollars it was losing in the treatment of uninsured patients. It shuttered the emergency room in 2014 and turned the hospital into a family health clinic, leaving Chickasaw County— an area the size of Los Angeles—without a facility for medical emergencies.

Rural hospitals have been closing across the country, but the crisis is particularly acute in states, like Mississippi, where Republican governors have refused federal funding under the Affordable Care Act for the expansion of their Medicaid systems. Chickasaw County is the kind of place where that political grandstanding hurts the most. Black people make up nearly 50 percent of the population, and their median household income in 2018 was $23,000, half that of the county's white households and below the federal poverty level for a family of four. Of the county residents in that income range, Blacks and whites combined, 15 percent had no medical coverage; most of them were adults who ended up in the emergency room sooner or later. The *Chickasaw Journal* reported that Trace Regional absorbed $3 million in unpaid medical bills in the year before it closed the emergency room. "They could not keep that emergency room open because they couldn't get paid," said Russell Jolly, the Democrat who represented Houston in the state senate. Had Mississippi expanded Medicaid coverage, the poor of Chickasaw County would have had universal coverage, and the emergency facility would have had a new stream of revenue.

But Shy Shoemaker's brother and cousins knew none of this. All they knew was that she was dying. As she faded out of consciousness, the 911 dispatcher directed LeKearis to the Houston Fire Department, where he was told an ambulance would meet them. In the meantime, they flagged down a police officer in the town square. As he and Shy's other cousin, LeParishe Shoemaker, got out of the car, the officer mistook the agitation of the two African American men as a threat and, placing his hand on his Taser, ordered them to lie down on the roadway. "He looked like he was shocked . . . like he was scared, like we were going to rob him," LeParishe told a Mississippi newspaper.

Ambulance service in Chickasaw County has long been provided by private medical companies who get most of their revenue from the people they transport. They are hampered by the same issue of unpaid bills as the hospital. MedStat, the company that held the contract until 2017, dropped out after reporting it had lost $182,000 in a year. Its successor, CareMed, has attempted to keep two ambulances at the ready at all times, one in Houston and the other in Okolona, twenty-one miles away. But the driver in Houston had a family emergency that night and clocked out at midnight, according to the company's owner. The ambulance dispatched from Okolona arrived to pick up Shy Shoemaker twenty-four minutes after getting the call. It still had to drive twenty miles to Baptist Memorial Hospital in neighboring Calhoun County.

Along the way, Shy was no longer gasping for breath. She no longer had the joys and burdens of being a mother while little more than a child herself. She and her unborn child were dead. The pronouncement was made more than an hour after the first 911 call.

It doesn't take an expert to know that something has gone wrong with health care in the red states. It just takes sitting with Makeska Shoemaker on her threadbare sofa as the three-year-old she has to raise alone bounces on her knee. In the fading afternoon light of her apartment, the giggling and playfulness of the child were not enough to dispel the sadness of her grandmother, which more than a year after her daughter's death was still as fresh as flowers on a grave. "They could have saved my baby," she said quietly, "and they could have saved my granddaughter. Nobody can tell me that they had to die."

* * * *

SINCE THE JIM CROW ERA, there have been few acts of political spite more damaging to the lives of ordinary citizens than the red states' sabotage of the Affordable Care Act. As of this writing, Mississippi is one of twelve states still rejecting the federal government's offer under the ACA to fund the expansion of their Medicaid programs. By boycotting expansion, these states have turned away billions of dollars of investment in their health care systems, while giving up the enormous economic spin-off that would have come with it. It is governmental malfeasance of the highest order, and it arises quite simply from a brute desire to undermine President Barack Obama's legacy. As one of Mississippi's newspapers editorialized, "Had the Affordable Care Act . . . been pushed by a Republican president instead of Barack Obama, Mississippi would have been first in line to sign up." For years, most Republican-dominated states have been inflicting deep budget cuts on their health care systems, and the loss of rural hospitals heavily dependent on Medicaid and Medicare funds is the most glaring result of that austerity. Mississippi has seen five rural hospitals close since 2010 and is at risk of losing thirty-one of the sixty-four it has left. And that doesn't include partial closings, such as the disappearing emergency room at Trace Regional that cost Shy Shoemaker her life. Medicaid expansion opens up a new revenue stream for struggling hospitals, whose patients are often poor and otherwise uninsured. It also benefits smaller medical clinics and individual physicians. But leaders of the boycotting states refuse to throw their medical communities a lifeline, and their intransigence has cost thousands of lives. To score political points with their donors and indulge a visceral hatred of Obamacare, Republican elected officials have chosen to let people die.

The true death toll accruing from the expansion boycott may never be known, especially after the onset of the COVID-19 pandemic. But there has been enough research to suggest the impact is huge. A major study for the National Bureau of Economic Research, which looked at a four-year period between 2014 and 2017, found that the deaths of more than nineteen thousand people ages fifty-five to sixty-four were prevented in the states that adopted Medicaid expansion. In those states that blocked expansion, nearly sixteen thousand low-income people died because they lacked medical coverage. Imagine that number after four more years, 2018 to 2021, and factor in the deaths of younger people, and you get some idea of the magnitude of lives lost. What is impossible to quantify is how many others will die prematurely in the years ahead because of care and medication that is denied them now, as the states rebuff a historic infusion of health dollars into their economies. There is almost no element of public health—prenatal care, mental health services, cancer screening, the availability of medication for diabetics and HIV patients—that is not stunted by the states' failure to expand Medicaid.

Before the creation of Medicaid in 1965, one of Lyndon Johnson's Great Society programs, the United States had been an outlier among developed nations in its failure to guarantee health care as a basic human right. This was not just a moral failing on the part of a supposedly enlightened nation, but also a detriment to its economic future. Voluminous research has linked a healthier workforce to economic gains, including a 2018 report by the non-profit Milken Institute, which found that preventable chronic diseases cost the U.S. economy $1.1 trillion in 2016, or 5.8 percent of that year's gross domestic product. Medicaid was only a partial fix. It provided matching funds for state-run health insurance for the poor, but eligibility requirements and benefits varied from state to state, and the programs generally covered only low-income pregnant woman, children, and the disabled, not childless adults. The Affordable Care Act sought to bring the United States a step closer to the models of other developed nations by agreeing to fund states' expansion of Medicaid to cover anyone whose income was less than 138 percent of the federal poverty line. A state's contribution to the expansion would be zero for the first three years before increasing to only 10 percent in subsequent years.

It might be expected that states with chronically underfunded health budgets and, in the case of the Deep South, embarrassingly high rates of death and morbidity, would jump at the chance to erase a moral stain on their reputations. But the Affordable Care Act has been a political lightning rod since its passage in 2010, seized upon by the Tea Party and other elements of the far right as a potentially divisive issue with which to undermine a Black president whose 2008 landslide frightened Republicans. Early backers of the Tea Party such as the Koch brothers' Americans for Prosperity and FreedomWorks, a right-wing group founded by former Republican House majority leader Dick Armey of Texas, threw millions of dollars into an effort to block passage of the law. As Jane Mayer noted in her book *Dark Money*, the citizens who heckled Democratic lawmakers holding town halls in their districts in the summer of 2009 were not the spontaneous grassroots opposition to Obamacare that they appeared to be. A volunteer for FreedomWorks circulated a memo giving instructions on how to disrupt the town halls, and Americans for Prosperity hired professional agitators to fill the meetings with opponents. "We packed these town halls with people who were just screaming about this thing," Sean Noble, a former Koch brothers' adviser, told *National Review*. Americans for Prosperity also blanketed the airwaves of targeted media markets with anti-Obamacare ads that created a false narrative in much of red America that the law would cause hardworking people to lose their medical insurance or pay higher premiums while the benefits would go primarily to the inner-city poor. Unable to block the ACA in Congress, Americans for Prosperity has pressured elected officials in Republican states to hamstring the law by boycotting Medicaid expansion. It is not a hard sell. Obamacare is politically toxic in the red states, which helps explain why officials in nineteen of them joined a federal lawsuit in 2018 that sought to have the law declared unconstitutional. Ironically, nine of the states that took part in the lawsuit accepted Medicaid expansion at the same time and saw demonstrable improvement in their health care systems. That they would seek to throw out a law that has eased the suffering of the poor and boosted their economies has had health care experts scratching their heads in every one of those states.

Arkansas is a case in point. During the time it still had a Democratic governor, Mike Beebe, the state used expansion funds in 2014 to set up Arkansas Works, a program that buys private health plans for people who make less than 138 percent of the poverty line. The success of the program has been grudgingly acknowledged even by many Republicans, including Governor Asa Hutchinson. Between 2013 and 2015, the percentage of uninsured in Arkansas dropped from 22.5 to 9.6, making it tied with Kentucky for the largest reduction in the country. The program has ensured the flow of billions into the state's economy and helped shore up struggling rural hospitals. In a single fiscal year, 2018–19, the federal contribution to Arkansas Works was $1.95 billion. Moreover, the National Bureau of Economic Research's study found that the lives of 440 people between ages fifty-five and sixty-four were saved as a result of expansion over a four-year period. Dr. Joe Thompson, who was Arkansas's surgeon general when the program was enacted, called it "a triple win: a benefit to the working poor, hospitals, and state economies."

And yet, Leslie Rutledge, the first woman and first Republican to serve as the state's attorney general, was a key player in the federal lawsuit against Obamacare, which, if successful, would have meant the end of Arkansas Works. *Arkansas Times* editor Max Brantley spared no irony in a column he wrote about her role in the lawsuit. "What does Rutledge want? Medicaid expansion that has provided health security for 300,000? Dead. Coverage for pre-existing conditions? Dead. Extended coverage for older children? Dead. All the pro-health provisions such as coverage for birth control and preventive health care, limits on insurance company profiteering? Dead."

Then there are zealots like Mississippi Governor Tate Reeves, who will oppose expansion until his last breath. Reeves, a stout, ruddy-faced former banker with a Trump-like combativeness, is an arch conservative even by Mississippi's standards. He rails at GOP members of the legislature as "liberal Republicans" and has wielded his veto power like a bludgeon. He used the pandemic as an excuse to halt abortions at the state's last remaining clinic, saying they were elective surgeries. He blasted a federal judge for ruling that county clerks cannot refuse marriage licenses to gay couples. He has sought to defund public education in favor of "school choice." He leads his state in public prayer, supports concealed carry of handguns, and wants local police to investigate Mississippians' immigration status. In short, Tate Reeves is about as far to the right as you can get as an officeholder in the United States.

And on the issue of Medicaid expansion, he has been no less extreme. His predecessor, Republican Phil Bryant, a Tea Party adherent who was one of the plaintiffs in the federal suit against the

ACA, had quietly been in talks with health care executives about backing some form of expansion. His evolution on the subject reflected the mood of his state. There was growing support for expansion even among Republicans in the legislature, and the three people who ran against Reeves in the 2019 primary and general elections— as well as the Mississippi Hospital Association—were all in favor. But Reeves's imposing mass stands squarely in the doorway to progress. He ran ads during his campaign deriding "Obamacare expansion" and warning against "a slide toward socialism."

He has never really presented a full exegesis of his reasoning for opposing expansion beyond vague and inaccurate claims about its impact on the state budget. This argument doesn't hold water because Mississippi hospitals volunteered to pony up the money themselves for the state's 10 percent share of expansion costs. Expansion opponents elsewhere say the federal government cannot be trusted to come up with its 90 percent share and that the care provided through Medicaid is substandard. But these claims are belied by the experiences of small conservative states that have approved expansion and, like Arkansas and Kentucky, have seen marked benefits. Asked about his opposition at one news conference, Reeves had no facts at his disposal to back up his position. He just robotically repeated the same phrase three times: "I am opposed to Obamacare expansion in Mississippi." His obstinacy might have something to do with the campaign contributions and other support he has received from Americans for Prosperity and closely allied groups like Empower Mississippi. But whether it was this or just his blind enmity toward Obamacare, Reeves made opposition to the plan central to his campaign and, in the first part of his governorship, made sure that expansion never saw the light of day. The question is whether citizens will eventually force his hand. Proponents of Medicaid expansion, inspired in part by the success of a ballot initiative that had legalized medical marijuana in 2020, had hoped to put the Obamacare issue before the voters in November 2022. But the Mississippi Supreme Court ruled in

May 2021 that the state's ballot initiative process was constitutionally flawed and overturned the legalization of medical marijuana. The same ruling stopped the campaign for Medicaid expansion in its tracks. The "Yes on 76" campaign, named after the Medicaid initiative the group was seeking to place on the ballot, stopped gathering signatures after the ruling and turned its attention to lobbying the state government for a fix to the ballot initiative process. "Our broad coalition of doctors, nurses, businesses, faith leaders, and voters from across the political spectrum is not going away," the group said after suspending its campaign. "We will keep up the fight until Mississippians receive the health care they need."

* * * *

WHAT MAKES THIS SABOTAGE of Obamacare especially tragic is that most of the states participating in the expansion boycott or the legal effort to overturn the ACA are political backwaters whose health care systems need the most help. Every year the Commonwealth Fund, a New York nonprofit whose board is made up of internationally recognized experts, releases a report that ranks the quality of state health care systems. Of the twenty states the group rated in 2020 as having the worst health care, fourteen were fully under Republican control, and seventeen had GOP-controlled legislatures holding the purse strings. Ten of the states had not expanded their Medicaid systems, and twelve were part of the lawsuit to overturn Obamacare.

Making comparisons of public health spending across states is notoriously difficult. Each state's health apparatus is set up differently, and the services included under the rubric of "health" often vary. Most state health systems get a large share of their funding from the federal government, and that allotment varies both by need and how competently the state manages the competition for grants. Tracing where those grants end up, at the state, county, or local level, muddies attempts at tallying any state's public health expenditures. One team of researchers that set itself to the task of quantifying federal, state, and local health outlays for the period of 2000 to 2018 had to code some 2.7 million administrative spending records.

But rigorous studies of how much states spend of *their own* funds for health care invariably show red states ranking at the bottom. One study of 2019 state spending by the nonprofit Trust for America's Health listed nine Republican-controlled states among the ten with the lowest per capita expenditures for public health. Missouri ranked the lowest with outlays of $7 per citizen. Texas, Florida, Arizona, and other large states spent less than $20. Six of the ten highest-spending states were blue states, including two often cited as the healthiest, Massachusetts and Hawaii, which spent $83 and $128 per person, respectively.

Another way of assessing states' commitments to public health is to look at how much they dedicate to their poorest citizens. A study of 2017 spending by the Kaiser Family Foundation compared the percentage of low-income people in each state—those making less than 200 percent of the federal poverty level—with the percentage of their citizens covered by Medicaid or the Children's Health Insurance Program (CHIP), also administered by the states. That study was even more damning for the red states. The twenty-two states with the biggest gaps between need and funding were all Republican-controlled, with Oklahoma having the largest gap at seventeen points and Alabama, Georgia, Mississippi, and Texas tied for second with gaps of fifteen points. The sixteen states with the smallest gaps were all blue states except for Alaska. California, Hawaii, Maryland, New York, Rhode Island, Washington, and Connecticut all had gaps of one or zero points, and Vermont and Massachusetts actually covered a higher percentage of people than were listed as low-income.

Red-state leaders like to argue that big government, throwing money at social maladies, is less effective than letting the problems solve themselves through the magic of the free market. But the fact is that most of the states that rank toward the bottom in health spending also fare the worst in health outcomes such as infant mortality, life expectancy, cancer rates, obesity rates, mental illness, and suicide. People who are used to thinking of the United States as the world's most successful nation might be surprised to learn that many red states have public health profiles more in common with nations in Eastern Europe and parts of Latin America and the Middle East than with developed countries in Western Europe and Asia. After four rural hospitals shut down between 2012 and 2014 in Georgia, another state that has not expanded Medicaid, Jimmy Lewis of HomeTown Health, an organization of rural hospitals, told a state committee exploring the issue: "We're approaching Third World care in the state of Georgia."

Mississippi is the poorest and sickest state in the country, consistently rated at the bottom in the quality of its health care by the Commonwealth Fund and other organizations. In some key health measures, Mississippi truly does not resemble a developed nation. Its infant mortality rate in 2018, the highest in the nation at 8 deaths per 1,000 live births, exceeded that of Bahrain (6), Kuwait (7), Chile (6), Bulgaria (6), and other developing nations, and was well above the European Union (3). Its life expectancy in 2018 was the second lowest in the United States at 74.9 years (the fifteen worst were all red states), and was inferior to that of Cuba, Albania, Chile, and many other developing nations. Mississippi also ranked miserably in its rates of cancer, diabetes, obesity, and mental illness, with some of the measures skewed heavily against African Americans. As *The Atlantic* magazine put it a few years ago: "A black man in Mississippi has a shorter life expectancy than the average American in 1960." Studies have also shown that states in the Deep South have significantly worse mortality rates for people of color. "Racial and ethnic minorities in Arkansas, Georgia, Indiana, Mississippi, and North Carolina faced some of the widest disparities relative to the national average across all of the indicators assessed in our Equity dimension," said a Commonwealth Fund report in 2014.

Mississippi's persistent poverty bears much of the blame for its ill health, but the state's Republican leaders have been studied in their refusal to deal with the problem, even beyond boycotting Medicaid expansion. Their response to epidemic levels of obesity and diabetes and rising death rates has been to spend years cutting funds for health care. They have slashed budgets for the state university medical center, the state trauma system, hospitals for indigent care, and the state's tobacco-free program.

It is almost as if the state's dedicated response to health crises is to make them worse. Recent research has placed Mississippi among the states with the highest rate of mental health disorders in children and the lowest percentage of such children who receive treatment. What was the state's response? In 2017, it announced plans to lay off 650 employees in its Department of Mental Health, which included closing the adolescent psychiatric program at East Mississippi State Hospital in Meridian and combining its services with a psychiatric unit at the Mississippi State Hospital in Whitfield, more than an hour's drive from the Meridian facility.

What does a state do when 40 percent of its population is obese and it has the second highest diabetes mortality rate and second highest cancer mortality rate? Governor Phil Bryant knew just what to do. In 2016, he cut the state health department budget from $40 million to $31 million, which included an $8.2 million reduction for the University of Mississippi Medical Center and the loss of 280 of its jobs. On top of this, UMMC, the state's largest employer, lost $35 million more of its budget after the state reduced Medicaid reimbursements for the treatment of uninsured patients. There would be far fewer uninsured patients, of course, if the state had accepted Medicaid expansion.

Bryant and the two most powerful legislative leaders—House Speaker Philip Gunn and Tate Reeves, who was then lieutenant governor and the senate president—blamed the cuts on budget shortfalls that forced them to squeeze savings from state agencies across the board. The state's shortfall in 2017 was $169 million. "Like hardworking Mississippi families and businesses, government must live within its means," Bryant said in March 2017 after making emergency cuts to the budget for the sixth time in two years. Reeves was even less empathetic about the hardship the reductions were inflicting on ordinary Mississippians. "If you define the success of our state by how much money our government spends," he said, "then you ain't gonna be happy with this budget recommendation."

But there was something they weren't telling their constituents, even if it was obvious to anyone who closely followed the state's politics. The budget shortfall was entirely due to a binge of corporate tax cutting they had engaged in for years. Mississippi Today, an online news organization, reported that between 2012 and 2017, Republican leaders had pushed through fifty-one tax cuts or tax breaks that had cost the state $577 million in revenue. In fiscal year 2017 alone, the cuts had cost $324 million, nearly twice the budget shortfall that was the cause of so much pain in Mississippi. Most of the tax reductions were geared toward corporations rather than individual taxpayers. And it was Lieutenant Governor Reeves leading the charge all the way. "I would reject the notion that we are giving anything to corporations," Reeves told the news site. "We are simply choosing to take less than what the Democrats, who were in control for 100-plus years, chose to take from them."

Reeves said the tax cuts were necessary for Mississippi to be competitive with other southern states in attracting businesses and jobs. This, of course, flies in the face of academic research showing that corporations base their decisions on where to locate on a number of factors, and tax policy is less important to them than the quality of a region's workforce. "Corporate site selection professionals rank the availability of skilled labor and adequate land and infrastructure higher than they rank tax policy," the Tax

Policy Center, a nonpartisan think tank, said in a review of the research. In any case, it didn't work for Mississippi, whose job growth of 0.4 percent between 2018 and 2019 ranked fortieth in the country. Job growth in the state had actually declined from an annual average of 0.75 percent for the previous five years, despite the booming economy. Apparently, it did not occur to Reeves that failing to invest in the health and education of your citizens is not a way to attract good-paying jobs.

* * * *

IT SHOULD HARDLY come as a surprise that most of the states boycotting Medicaid expansion, and devoting the lowest amount of state tax dollars to public health overall, were among those least prepared for the coronavirus pandemic. Worse still, their governors tended to be the most arrogant in resisting mask mandates and stay-at-home orders. That they would flaunt their incompetence and recklessness as their citizens died unnecessarily is one of those outrages of the Trump era that will occupy future historians. "The reality, unfortunately, is people are going to die because of the irresponsibility of the decisions being made by the people crafting the budgets," Ron Bialek, president of the nonprofit Public Health Foundation, said in the summer of 2020. His prophecy proved to be correct when the Centers for Disease Control reported in March 2022 that the fourteen states with the highest Covid death rates in the previous eight months had Republican governors.

Florida, the second most populous of the states rejecting Medicaid expansion, had been cutting public health since the 1990s, under a succession of Republican governors dedicated to shrinking the size of government. As its population grew by some 2.4 million between 2010 and 2019, Florida's budget cuts reduced staff at state-run local health departments from 12,422 to 9,125, with the amount the agencies spent per resident dropping 41 percent. Duval County's former health director, Dr. Jeff Goldhagen, told

Kaiser Health News that the department he once headed had been "dismantled to the extent that it could not really manage an outbreak." Former governor Rick Scott, now a U.S. senator, made no apologies, saying he was happy with the cuts he made in his state's public health apparatus, which he said were about "making government more efficient."

It is hardly surprising, then, that Florida, at least in its top leadership, took the pandemic less seriously than most other highly populated states. As late as August 2020, when the state had over a half-million coronavirus cases, including highly publicized infections within the Miami Marlins baseball franchise, Governor Ron DeSantis still had not issued a mask mandate and mocked other state's officials, like New York Governor Andrew Cuomo, who had enacted more stringent protective measures. By the end of November 2020, Florida ranked twenty-sixth among the fifty states in the rate it tested its population for coronavirus. Testing and contract tracing are two of the key strategies in combating the spread of COVID-19, and this really "efficient" state, with the fourth highest gross domestic product in the country, was doing a worse job of it than poorer states like West Virginia, Tennessee, and Louisiana. Even with that low rate of testing, it still reported the third highest number of coronavirus cases, 962,000, while New York's was about two-thirds of that number.

Florida ended up in the middle of the pack in its rate of Covid vaccination and per capita number of deaths, but DeSantis appalled health experts throughout the pandemic with his public stances on vaccination, social distancing, and mask wearing, positions that were blatantly more geared toward firing up his base and laying the groundwork for a presidential run than safeguarding Floridians. His negligence took its toll. The CDC found in March 2022 that Florida was one of three states with the highest Covid death rates in the previous eight months, 153 deaths per 100,000 residents, compared to California's 58 per 100,000. While DeSantis began as an advocate for vaccination, he later questioned its efficacy, putting himself more in line with the disinformation that animates Republican primary voters. In November 2021, he signed legislation that restricted businesses from requiring vaccination and ordered schools not to implement mask mandates, saying that getting vaccinated was a personal choice. "It's about *your* health," he said, "and whether you want that protection or not. It really doesn't impact me or anyone else." His statement drew a blistering rebuke from the *Miami Herald* editorial board: "Doesn't impact anyone else? Talk about a profile in selfishness. Almost 46,000 have died of Covid in his state since the pandemic began. Too bad we can't ask the thousands who have died since vaccines became available if they wished everyone around them had gotten vaccinated."

Texas, with the world's tenth largest economy and a booming energy sector, is another wealthy state that has starved its public health agencies, leaving it unprepared for a pandemic. The state's bravado in attacking Obamacare has been unsurpassed. Texas spearheaded the lawsuit seeking to overturn the law and crowed the loudest about its rejection of Medicaid expansion. "If anyone was in doubt, we in Texas have no intention to implement so-called state exchanges or to expand Medicaid under Obamacare," then governor Rick Perry said in a statement in 2012. "I will not be party to socializing healthcare and bankrupting my state in direct contradiction to our Constitution and our founding principles of limited government." The irony was that Texas needed federal help more than most states, given how miserly it was in doling its own funds for health care. Despite its vast resources, Texas ranked fortieth out of the fifty states in 2019 in the amount per capita it spent from its own budget on health care—$17 per person, compared with $84 in New York and $72 in California. Nearly a third of its population is low-income, and in the summer of 2020 its rate of uninsured adults was 29 percent, the highest in the nation.

Federal funding has been a bulwark of the Texas public health system, accounting for about a third of its spending. Because it is a huge state with major university medical systems that secure their own federal funding, outlays from Washington allowed it to maintain a modern public health system, with better health outcomes than most red states. But its outsized reliance on federal funding means that the closing of the spigot in Washington over the last decade has hit Texas particularly hard, especially since it is among the states that have rejected Medicaid expansion under Obamacare. Staffing for local health departments in Texas dropped by 16 percent between 2008 and 2020, at a time when its population grew by more than two million people.

The effect on the state's preparation for a pandemic like COVID-19 has been especially dire. Federal funding for Texas under the Hospital Preparedness Program dropped 40 percent between 2013 to 2019, going from $26 million to $15 million, and those funds have traditionally made up nearly a quarter of the state's budget for hospital disaster preparedness. Federal funding under the Public Health Emergency Preparedness program saw similar reductions. State employees were forced to rely on outdated technology to understand where the outbreaks were occurring in Texas and make decisions on shutdowns and allocation of resources. The state's stockpile of personal protective equipment (PPE) was so denuded at the outset of the pandemic that doctors and hospitals were on their own in trying to purchase masks, gowns, sanitizer, and other protective equipment. Tom Banning, chief executive of the Texas Academy of Family Physicians, told the *Texas Tribune* that a golfing buddy made him aware of a half-million surgical masks available in Mexico. His organization and the Texas Association of Rural and Community Hospitals arranged for a rented truck to bring them to Texas, and Banning personally put boxes in his car and drove around to doctor's offices and medical clinics in Austin and Houston. Banning said that "it shows how broken our acquisition and distribution model was for PPE if you were having to rely on two professional associations to handle that." When the virus rolled into Texas like a tsunami in July, the lack of preparedness was on full display as hospitals reached 100 percent capacity and had to turn people away from their emergency rooms and evaluate patients for "survival potential" before admitting them. On July 4, 2020, after the number of cases in the Rio Grande Valley tripled over two weeks, ten out of twelve hospitals in Hidalgo, Cameron, and Starr Counties were out of beds and turning people away. After months in the grip of the coronavirus, Texas had tested fewer people per capita than all but seven states, and its numbers of cases and deaths were considered suspect.

A special place in the history books will go to South Dakota Governor Kristi Noem, the biggest Trump enabler on the Great Plains, the quickest to defend his outrages and parrot his talking points, and one of the last governors to continue repeating the Big Lie—that massive electoral fraud cost him the presidency. She has also been the most shameless in her neglect of a science-based response to the pandemic. South Dakota is one of seven states that never issued stay-at-home orders, and Noem exhibited more defiance than any of the other governors, telling her citizens during the deadliest outbreak of disease in a century to do as they saw fit and expect no guidance from their state government. "The people themselves are primarily responsible for their safety," she told a news conference in April 2020. "They are the ones that are entrusted with expansive freedoms. They're free to exercise their rights to work, to worship, and to play. Or to even stay at home, or to conduct social distancing." She said that South Dakota, with its low population density, would never end up like New York City. "It's so important not to turn on the news and look at NYC and think that that's what Lemmon, South Dakota, is going to face in a month. It's absolutely not true."

In August, Noem overruled the recommendations of infectious-disease experts and allowed the eightieth annual motorcycle rally in Sturgis, South Dakota, to go ahead as planned, and 460,000 people showed up. It is not known how many people contracted the virus because attendees were from all over the country, and South

Dakota did no study of any possible outbreak. But neighboring Minnesota did. It found "51 confirmed primary event-associated cases, 21 secondary cases, and five tertiary cases" stemming from the rally. The toll nationwide can only be imagined.

Noem expressed no contrition after her prediction that South Dakota would not end up like New York City proved to be disastrously wrong. Her state ended November 2020 as the epicenter of coronavirus in the United States, second only to North Dakota in the highest number of cases per capita. But those numbers should be treated with extreme caution since only eight states tested fewer citizens per capita than South Dakota, and North Dakota's testing rate was second only to Rhode Island.

It is a reflection of how untethered from reality the Republican Party has become that Noem has been treated as a hero in the party and is mentioned as possible candidate for president in 2024.

* * * *

EVEN WHEN COVID-19 is finally behind us, the crisis in rural health care will remain. It is a gaping hole in the country's health care system that we ignore at our peril. What is most disheartening is this: it's a problem that previous generations of national leaders had largely overcome. The modern infrastructure of rural medicine grew out of the Hill-Burton Act of 1946, which rested on the belief that every community in the country deserved a hospital. Harry Truman was the first U.S. president to throw his full support behind establishing universal health care, modeled on national insurance programs being assembled piece by piece in Western Europe. After the GOP captured the House and Senate in 1946, his broader proposal ended up on the legislative scrap heap. But Truman won bipartisan support for Hill-Burton, known formally as the Hospital Survey and Construction Act, which provided grants and loans for hospital construction in communities that had enough wealth and population to sustain such a facility. At the time of the bill's passage, 40 percent of the nation's counties had no hospital. By the turn of the twenty-first century, the construction of about 6,800 medical facilities in 4,000 communities had been funded in whole or part from funds originating with the act, the nation's biggest achievement in public health prior to the establishment of Medicaid and Medicare.

Unfortunately, many of the hospitals were in trouble by the late 1980s. Rural areas have been in gradual decline for decades, afflicted by losses in manufacturing and agricultural jobs and an exodus of young people. Those left behind in rural America tend to be older, poorer, and often without insurance to pay their medical bills. As a result, their community hospitals have become burdened with rising caseloads of indigent care. At the same time, the advanced medical technology that hospitals need to compete has become out of reach, forcing many patients to seek care in metropolitan areas. "Most of what we knew how to do in the 1970s and 1980s could be done reasonably well in small towns," said Dr. Nancy Dickey, president of the Rural and Community Health Institute at Texas A&M University. "But scientific developments and advances in neurosurgery, microscopic surgery and the like required a great deal more technology and a bigger population to support the array of technology specialists."

But pinning too much of the blame on shifts in population and technology lets right-wing politicians off the hook. In 1946, we were paying our war debt, funding the Marshall Plan, and maintaining our commitment to New Deal programs, and yet we still found the resources to build thousands of community hospitals. In the post-Reagan era, the United States is still the world's wealthiest nation, but the Republicans who have dominated public policy for decades have shown far less concern than Harry Truman for the plight of ordinary citizens, choosing tax relief for the wealthy over adequate health care for the poor and working class. Health care funding has been taking a hit for decades. From 2010 to 2019, funding for the Centers for Disease Control and Prevention, which oversees the nation's public health programs, was reduced by

10 percent when adjusted for inflation—at a time when the nation was newly saddled with the opioid crisis and the epidemics of obesity and diabetes.

Many rural hospitals received a jolt to their finances with the passage of the Affordable Care Act, which freed up money for Medicaid expansion by cutting funds hospitals receive in Medicare reimbursements—a reduction the Congressional Budget Office estimated in 2012 would exceed $500 billion over a decade. The American Hospital Association supported the ACA because the Medicare cuts would be more than offset by the steep decline in uninsured patients that would come with Medicaid expansion. This was especially true because the bill signed by President Obama *required* states to expand their Medicaid systems. But things didn't go as planned for hospitals in some red states, after the U.S. Supreme Court ruled in June 2012 that the mandate was unconstitutional and that state Medicaid expansion would be optional. In states that rejected expansion, hospitals were put in a bind. They lost part of their Medicare reimbursements without benefiting from the new flow of insured patients. The blow was particularly painful for rural hospitals, which in many cases were already struggling.

This helps explain why 89 of the 134 rural hospitals that closed between October 2010 and October 2020 were in states that either had not expanded Medicaid or did not do so until 2020. A study by the Chartis Center for Rural Health found that 162 of the 216 rural facilities most vulnerable to closing before the pandemic were in non-expansion states. Some hospitals have closed in regions so denuded of population that their loss was inevitable, and in other cases the closings had a negligible impact on health care because alternatives were available. But more is at stake than just health care. Hospitals are often the linchpin of rural economies, offering the highest paying jobs and propping up other businesses such as pharmacies and nursing homes. One study of fifty-five rural hospital closings estimated an average loss of

$5.3 million in salaries and benefits for each closing. The lack of a nearby hospital can also be a disincentive for business investment and a deterrent for retirees thinking of settling in an area, and can make it difficult for a school system to recruit teachers. "A hospital closure is a frightening thing for a small town," Patti Davis, president of the Oklahoma Hospital Association, told a GateHouse Media reporter in 2019. "It places lives in jeopardy and has a domino effect on the community. Health care professionals leave, pharmacies can't stay open, nursing homes have to close and residents are forced to rely on ambulances to take them to the next closest facility in their most vulnerable hours."

Just how frightening was demonstrated when Mercy Hospital Fort Scott closed in February 2019 after 132 years of serving its rural community in southeast Kansas. Sarah Jane Tribble, a reporter with *Kaiser Health News*, embedded in the town for weeks to see how residents were coping with the loss of the cancer care center, dialysis center, and emergency room. She met some of the two hundred people who had been cancer patients, joining a sixty-five-year-old woman with a rare form of multiple myeloma—cancer of the plasma cells—as she drove nearly an hour to Chanute for her weekly chemotherapy. There were others:

> Barbara Woodward, 70, slipped on ice outside a downtown Fort Scott business during the early February storm. The former X-ray technician said she knew something was broken. That meant a bumpy and painful 30-mile drive to a nearby town, where she had emergency surgery for a shattered femur, a bone in her thigh. About 60 percent of calls to the Fort Scott's ambulances in early February were transported out of town.... The calls included a 41-year-old with chest pain who was taken more than 30 miles to Pittsburg, an unconscious 11-year-old driven 20 miles to Nevada, Missouri, and a 19-year-old with a seizure and bleeding eyes escorted nearly 30 miles to Girard, Kansas.

None was more tragic than Robert Findley, the seventy-year-old owner of a popular auto body shop who slipped on the ice and banged his head as he was checking his mailbox. He thought he was fine and went to bed as if nothing had happened. But in the morning, his wife, Linda, couldn't wake him. The EMS crew that responded took one look at his eyes and suspected a brain hemorrhage. He was taken to the helipad of Mercy Hospital, where they planned to summon a helicopter to fly him to Kansas City. But the crew had trouble getting a unit to respond. "My Nevada (Kansas) crew is not available and my Parsons crew has declined," the helicopter dispatcher told them. By the time a helicopter landed, Findley had been lying in the ambulance for thirty minutes. He never made it to Kansas City. When his wife listened to the dispatcher's comments on a recording, she was puzzled: "I didn't know that they could just refuse."

Not only is it disturbing that this is happening in the world's richest nation. It is also important to remember that Kansas, which has not accepted Medicaid expansion, is the state whose former Republican governor, Sam Brownback, gutted the public sector in 2012 to pay for a reckless tax cut slated to cost a billion dollars over six years, a move even his own party came to recognize as a disaster. How many of the five rural hospitals that have closed recently in Kansas could have been saved with a billion dollars? It's not like the state's strategy of low taxes and low spending was paying dividends. Innumerable studies have shown that the state's GDP and job growth lagged behind neighboring states in the years following the tax cuts. The state's pain was for nothing.

Mississippi and Kansas are rural states struggling with aging populations and limited business growth. But the same problems are also afflicting rural health care facilities in wealthy, high-growth states that have not expanded Medicaid, like North Carolina, Florida, and Texas. With all of its resources, Texas has no excuse for neglecting health care in its vast rural areas. The state lost twenty rural hospitals over the decade and, as of January 2020, had seventy-seven more on the brink—the most closures and threatened closures of any state. The deficiency of rural health care in Texas is staggering. Of the 254 counties in the state, 170 are rural, and those comprise 20 percent of the state's population, about three million people. A recent report by the Texas A&M Rural and Community Health Institute portrayed many of them as medical deserts: thirty-five counties had no physician and 80 had fewer than six; 58 counties had no general surgeon, 185 were without a psychiatrist, and 147 had no obstetrician/gynecologist.

One hundred forty-seven counties without a doctor specializing in childbirth. That doesn't sound like America, at least not the America most of us picture in our minds. The problem of inadequate health care has a solution as readily as it did in Harry Truman's day. We just have to find it. As a country, we are not smaller or less resourceful or less compassionate than we were in 1946. It is just our leaders who are smaller, and those we can do something about.

6

Defund the Children:
The Attack on Public Schools

In 2018, when *U.S. News and World Report* pub-
lished its annual ranking of the nation's best high schools, a list
that can catapult schools to national stardom, the results amounted
to a stunning rebuke for advocates of public education. The top five
were all Arizona schools operated by BASIS Educational Group, a
for-profit company in Scottsdale that manages a chain of taxpayer-
funded charter schools. The results not only gladdened the hearts of
state officials in Arizona, which perennially lands at the top of anyone's list of states with the lowest-quality and worst-funded public
schools. It was also a major victory for wealthy conservatives who
lead the national school choice movement and make no secret of
their plans to disrupt or even destroy American public education.
If the top high schools in the country were run by a for-profit corporation, what did that say about the potential for privatization to
transform schooling nationwide? Two days after the rankings were
published, the American Federation for Children, an advocacy
group founded by Betsy DeVos, Donald Trump's secretary of education, posted what seemed to be a heartfelt essay by a "charter school
mom," Sarah Raybon, who wrote of her daughter's "amazing education" at the BASIS school in Peoria, Arizona. She declared the case
closed on charter schools: "School choice—just one more reason Arizona is a great place to raise children."

The website failed to mention that the "charter school mom" was a former lobbyist for the federation and, at the time, one of the directors in its Arizona office. But that didn't detract from the essential truth of Raybon's essay. BASIS charter schools *do* offer an extremely rigorous curriculum, which puts students on a track toward high academic achievement before they even reach puberty. Students are assigned four hours of homework daily and exposed to challenging concepts in math, science, and other subjects beginning in middle school. By high school, they are steeped in Advanced Placement courses. When *U.S. News* rated BASIS Scottsdale the second-best high school in the nation in 2016, it noted that the school had a 92 percent participation rate in Advanced Placement courses, with an average of ten AP exams per student. The students passed those exams at a rate of *100 percent.* In a ranking of Arizona's best high schools based on SAT scores in 2017, BASIS schools nailed down eight of the top ten spots. BASIS classrooms are housed in architecturally stylish buildings—more like office campuses than schools—with state-of-the-art science labs, cavernous gymnasiums, and the latest in computer technology. It's almost a letdown when the students leave for college—except they go off with an average of $100,000 in scholarships, according to a company website.

That kind of academic rigor was what BASIS founders Michael and Olga Block envisioned in 1998 when they launched their first school, BASIS Tucson. Olga is a native of the Czech Republic and a former dean of students at the University of Prague, and her husband is a retired professor of economics at Arizona State University. According to the website for BASIS Educational Group, which also calls itself BASIS.ed, Olga was looking for a school for her daughter Petra and was frustrated that Arizona schools fell short of the academic standards commonly found in Europe. The couple's answer was BASIS Tucson, which opened with fifty-eight middle school students in a modernistic blue-and-terracotta complex amid the banal subdivisions of East

Tucson. The Blocks were getting in on the ground floor of what would become a growth industry in their state. Arizona's former Republican governor, Fife Symington, scion of a wealthy Maryland family and a free-market purist since he was introduced to the writings of F.A. Hayek in college, signed legislation in 1994 that set up the loosest regulations for charter schools in the nation, putting the state at the forefront of the school choice movement. Unlike many other states, there is no cap in Arizona on the number of charter schools and no limit on how many can be managed by the same entity. Arizona now has the greatest penetration of charter schools in the fifty states. As of 2020, the state's 556 charters accounted for 28 percent of its public schools and 19 percent of the students, according to the Arizona Charter Schools Association.

Arizona law frees charter schools from many of the regulations that constrain traditional public schools. Their teachers are non-union and may be hired without education certificates. The schools are free to develop their own curricula as long as they meet the state's educational standards and the students participate in standardized tests. Because they get no money from local tax levies or bond issues, and are forbidden to charge tuition, they are completely funded by the state, including for the construction of their buildings. Although the charter schools are nonprofit, they are often managed by for-profit companies whose finances are shielded from public view. The state pays for their facilities, including the lavish BASIS campuses, but once they are built, they are the property of the management firms, on their books as assets. What the owners of the for-profit companies do with their management fees and how they are able to monetize the school buildings the state bought for them is not considered the public's business.

Thus an advocacy group, Arizonans for Charter School Accountability, and the *Arizona Daily Star* were able to get state audit documents in March 2019 showing that the BASIS charter schools had a deficit of $44 million, which forced them to obtain loans to cover their expenses. But there are no public documents showing where

Michael and Olga Block got the money at the end of 2017 to make a $1.68 million down payment on an $8.4 million condominium in Manhattan. The apartment is in a sixty-floor building with "breathtaking panoramas" of the city, an infinity pool, and an indoor/outdoor theater, according to the *Arizona Republic*. The Blocks plunked down the money at about the same time parents of BASIS Scottsdale were receiving letters asking them to donate $1,500 per child to help boost teacher pay, despite BASIS.ed having earned its usual $10 million in management fees from the state that year. Perhaps realizing the poor optics arising from the Blocks' condo purchase, Peter Bezanson, BASIS.ed's chief executive, and the company's chairman, former Intel CEO Craig Barrett, fired off a letter to parents in March 2018 that sought to paper over the couple's lavish lifestyle. "The Blocks have put their heart and soul—and personal money—into growing BASIS Curriculum Schools for more than twenty years," they wrote. "To claim that they should not profit from their life's work is unkind and, frankly, un-American."

They would get no argument from the state's Republican leadership, which has been steadfast in its commitment to expand the number of charter schools. Governor Doug Ducey is a ferocious advocate not only of charter schools but also private school vouchers, convinced that traditional public schools are an impediment to the state's economic future. After the *U.S. News* rankings for 2017 put the five BASIS schools at the top of the list, he viewed it like the former corporate chieftain he is rather than through the eyes of the low-income Arizonans who will never attend those schools. "National recognition like this," he said, "is what attracts new, exciting companies to our state."

* * * *

THIS WOULD ALL be very good for the people of Arizona if the success of the BASIS schools were not a grand deception, if the charter school movement in the state were not rife with corruption and profiteering, and if the state's traditional public schools—the ones that teach the majority of its children—did not end up as the losers.

Start with the *U.S. News* rankings. The notion that the top five schools in the country would end up being in the same state and run by a single company should, in the apt words of *Tucson Weekly* writer David Safier, set off a citizen's "bullshit detector." "Does that statement trigger your detector's smell alert?" he wrote. "Are red lights flashing? I hope so. Such ridiculously lopsided results should raise suspicions that someone is gaming the system."

Safier, like others who have studied the BASIS curriculum, like Carol Burris, an acclaimed high school principal in New York who became executive director of the nonprofit Network for Public Education, has figured out exactly how the company games the system. Before 2019, the method *U.S. News* used to choose the best high schools amounted to measuring what percentage of students took Advanced Placement and International Baccalaureate courses and what percentage passed them. BASIS figured out early that AP and IB courses were the ticket to the "best high school" list and the prestige that served as currency for BASIS.ed. So the company pushed hard to prepare students for a barrage of those tests from the time they were in middle school.

But just as importantly, it made sure that only the right students were left in the senior class to take those tests. BASIS officials are quick to point out that they accept anyone who applies and do not "cherry pick" the best students. The fact is that any students perceived to be unfit for the rigorous curriculum are discouraged from coming to the school, and each year those not making the grade are encouraged to leave. Gradually the classes are winnowed down until only the highest-achieving students are left in the graduating class. "BASIS schools operate on a tournament model, where only the strongest survive," Burris wrote in an essay for the *Washington Post*. "Ironically, however, the prize at the end goes to the BASIS chain. The 'best high school' rankings that put BASIS near the top are the catalyst that allowed the Blocks to build an empire." Safier obtained figures from the state showing the decline in enrollment for the 2018 senior class for each school compared with where the class started. The numbers tell the story:

BASIS Scottsdale: 5th grade: 140 students. 12th grade: 63 students

BASIS Chandler: 7th grade: 139 students. 12th grade: 57 students

BASIS Oro Valley: 6th grade: 148 students. 12th grade: 63 students

BASIS Tucson North: 8th grade: 131 students. 12th grade: 51 students

BASIS Flagstaff: 7th grade: 93 students. 12th grade: 31 students

The curating of the students begins by siting the schools for the most part in predominantly white middle-class neighborhoods. Since the schools do not provide transportation, low-income students would have trouble attending the schools for that reason alone, even if they could afford application fees, the cost of books, and the "suggested" donation of $1,500 annually. BASIS Chandler, which *U.S. News* chose in 2021 as the best charter high school in the country, was 77 percent Asian, 14 percent white, 3 percent Black, and 3 percent Hispanic. The school theoretically could draw students from a wide area of Maricopa County, which is roughly a third Hispanic. BASIS Phoenix was 44 percent Asian, 44 percent white, and only 7 percent Hispanic, even though Phoenix was 43 percent Hispanic in 2019.

BASIS charter schools take public money but by no traditional definition are public. They may do a brilliant job of training affluent students to ace AP exams, but there is more to education than AP exams, more than simply preparing students for college and careers in the corporate sector. It is about shaping human beings, training them to understand and contribute to society, within the confines of their abilities. The Blocks have earned their riches to the degree that they succeeded in the mission they set out for themselves, creating a regime of social Darwinism in the classroom for the benefit of the economic and intellectual elite, but theirs is not a model for educating the masses.

* * * *

BUT EDUCATING THE MASSES is not the point. The point is destruction. Eviscerating public education is a prime objective of the Koch network, Betsy DeVos, the Scaife Foundation, and other wealthy advocates for school choice. The system of public education is a big, fat line item in the government budgets that corporate libertarians want to squeeze down to size so that taxes on the wealthy can be all but eliminated and the privileged class can hold full sway in society. The right's hatred of public education is visceral, if for no other reason than that public schools are the province of teachers' unions that conservatives believe indoctrinate students toward progressivism, toward suspicion of big business and its vision of a society organized around corporate profits. That's one reason Republicans have such fear of critical race theory being taught in the public schools. They see it as the vilest form of indoctrination yet, rather than what it really is: a light shining on an uncomfortable truth about our nation's history.

"School choice" is a benign-sounding term that seems to offer more for everyone. And there are charter schools that even progressives describe as success stories, in states red and blue, particularly those that have been shown to boost education outcomes among low-income students in the inner-city. But those schools tend to be highly regulated and run by nonprofit companies. That is not the model that attracts Republican politicians and their corporate donors. What the far right is contemplating, and spending huge amounts of money to achieve, is the elimination of public education. Bryan Caplan, an economist at George Mason University's Mercatus Center—which has been heavily funded by the

Koch brothers—published a book in 2018 whose title stated it plainly: *The Case Against Education: Why the Education System Is a Waste of Time and Money*. The book, with its nihilistic thesis that "government should stop using tax dollars to fund education of any kind," is a thrust into a new Dark Ages. And yet, as Jennifer Berkshire and Jack Schneider point out in their own book, *A Wolf at the Schoolhouse Door: The Dismantling of Public Education and the Future of School*, Caplan's book strode into the mainstream, "published by Princeton University Press, excerpted in *The Atlantic*, and declared 'bold' and 'provocative' in book reviews." As they also note, the crusade against public schools doesn't end with a push for private schools. There is a nascent movement for getting rid of schools altogether and replacing it with homeschooling. Paul Mosley, a Republican congressman from Arizona who was turned out of office in 2018, advocated for the repeal of his state's compulsory education law, a sentiment that has been echoed by other libertarians. "What is gaining traction," Berkshire and Schneider write, "is the even more radical notion that parents, not the state, should control their children's education. The insistence that the history of public education in the United States is one of government overreach is no longer relegated to the libertarian fringe; it is now shaping government policy in a growing number of states."

The arena for the battle over school choice is very much at the state level, which is why Arizona's unprecedented expansion of charter schools is of such import to conservatives. As the governor most prominently identified with school privatization, Ducey is a darling of the Koch network and a major recipient of its support. He was an enthusiastic attendee of Americans for Prosperity seminars even before becoming governor, and has forged a tight bond with the organization. "He is one of the best governors in the country," Tim Phillips, AFP's president, told the *Phoenix Business Journal* as Ducey campaigned for reelection in 2018. The Ohio native was elected in 2014 after a long sojourn in corporate America, including more than a decade as CEO of Cold Stone

Creamery, a national chain of ice cream stores. His support for deregulation and successive tax cuts made him the perfect governor for Arizona as it reached the apex of its capture by the far right. The Grand Canyon State was always marked by its own brand of southwestern conservatism, but it never hewed completely to the Republican party line. The state that gave the world Goldwater conservatism also elected Democratic governors Bruce Babbitt and Janet Napolitano, who later served in the Clinton and Obama administrations. But Arizona took a sharp right turn in 2009, when Obama appointed Napolitano as his secretary of homeland security and Arizona's secretary of state, Republican Jan Brewer, filled the governor's seat.

Brewer was an unelected governor, assuming the position as the person next in the line of succession, but her rabid conservatism quickly gained national attention. She is best remembered for signing a law in 2010 that made it a misdemeanor to be an undocumented immigrant in Arizona and essentially turned state and local police into immigration agents. The law prompted a spate of civil rights lawsuits alleging that it unleashed racial profiling, and most of its provisions were tossed out by the U.S. Supreme Court. The Justice Department filed a lawsuit against Maricopa County Sheriff Joe Arpaio that cited widespread abuse of Hispanic detainees that "starts at the top and pervades the organization." A federal judge charged Arpaio with criminal contempt after he refused to desist in his department's immigration roundups. But Trump pardoned Arpaio in 2017 and he remains a heroic figure for many Arizona Republicans. Ducey calls Arpaio a friend and received a key endorsement from him in his first campaign for governor.

Conservatism may have reached its peak in Arizona. The growing Hispanic population and an influx of tech and financial professionals into the Phoenix area from other states, particularly California, is changing the political complexion of the state. The elected positions of secretary of state and superintendent of public instruction have recently been captured by Democrats, as have the state's two U.S. Senate seats. And in 2020, Joe Biden narrowly defeated Donald Trump, who was apoplectic when Fox News called the state for Biden. But for the moment, the state's progressive impulses are stymied by its far-right leadership, as exemplified by the bizarre Cyber Ninjas audit of the 2020 election.

It was under Brewer that Arizona began a headlong push into school privatization. She signed a bill in 2011 that made the state the first in the country to establish education savings accounts, or ESAs, which allow parents sending their children to private schools to receive state funds that would have gone to public school districts. The original law limited the program to disabled children, but it was gradually expanded to include many others, including children who are in failing schools, living on tribal lands, or had siblings in the program. By early 2017, there were about 3,200 children in the program and it was costing the state—and local school districts—an annual $40 million. But that wasn't enough for detractors of public education, especially after Trump's appointment of DeVos as education secretary gave them a key advocate in Washington. In 2017, Ducey, with a strong backing from AFP, signed legislation expanding eligibility for ESAs, now grandly renamed "empowerment scholarship accounts," to all 1.1 million Arizona schoolchildren, though actual participation would be capped at 30,000. Ducey's signature was seen as a national victory for school choice. The bill was sponsored by a state senator, Debbie Lesko, who was the national treasurer and state chair of the American Legislative Exchange Council, and it was based on ALEC's model legislation. DeVos applauded Ducey for what she called "a big win for students and parents in Arizona." But the state teachers' union and other advocates rightly saw the bill as an existential threat to the state's public schools and formed a coalition, Save Our Schools, that collected enough signatures to have the measure placed on the ballot in November 2018.

Americans for Prosperity geared up for battle. While the organization had long poured money into higher education to promote conservative scholarship—amounting to about $100 million for 350 colleges and universities in 2017 alone—K-12 was relatively new territory. In January 2018, Charles Koch told donors at an AFP conference in Indian Wells, California, a desert resort outside Palm Springs, that he planned to double the group's investment in K-12 that year, along with committing $400 million toward the upcoming congressional midterm elections. "We've made more progress in the last five years than I had in the last fifty," Koch said. "The capabilities we have now can take us to a whole new level. . . . We want to increase the effectiveness of the network . . . by an order of magnitude. If we do that, we can change the trajectory of the country." Ducey, at the same conference, told the donors that the voucher referendum, known as Proposition 305, was a pivotal moment for the school choice movement. "This is a real fight in my state," he said. "I didn't run for governor to play small ball."

Supporters of the voucher expansion put forth the argument that it would help low-income students escape failing schools, but an analysis by the *Arizona Republic* put that fiction to rest. The paper found that 75 percent of ESA funds were pulled out of districts with "A" or "B" ratings and only 4 percent from districts with "D" ratings. For opponents of the expansion, the report vindicated claims that it would simply allow affluent families who send their children to private schools anyway to siphon off money from a badly underfunded school system. The last thing the Koch network wanted was to let the public decide the issue. AFP funded a lawsuit seeking to block Proposition 305, but it was thrown out of court and, at the ballot box, two-thirds voted against the expansion.

Having lost the fight over ESAs—which continued to expand nonetheless, covering more than eleven thousand students by 2021, triple the number of students in 2017—Ducey and his allies continued to push for a proliferation of charter schools, at this point their main vehicle for achieving de facto privatization. Ducey has been intertwined with the leadership of the state's largest charter school chains from the start of his administration, particularly BASIS.ed and Great Hearts Academies, a conservative nonprofit with twenty-three charter schools in Arizona.

Michael Block and BASIS board member Don Budinger have contributed heavily to Ducey's campaigns. BASIS.ed itself gave $100,000 over two years to Republican committees, half of it to Arizonans for Strong Leadership, a committee Ducey set up to benefit GOP legislative candidates. In December 2018, the *Arizona Republic* reported on other ties between the governor and the two companies: Ducey appointed a former BASIS board member, Clint Bolick, to the Arizona Supreme Court. BASIS's chairman, Craig Barrett, has been a political supporter of the governor since at least 2012.

Ducey's former campaign manager and policy adviser, J.P. Twist, is the brother of Erik Twist, Great Hearts' president and a former BASIS employee; another key supporter of the governor, Maricopa County Attorney Bill Montgomery, was on the Great Hearts board, as was Arizona Diamondbacks CEO Derrick Hall, who donated more than $10,000 to Ducey's reelection campaign in 2018.

Meanwhile, the state has taken a number of actions to help the two companies remain the dominant players in Arizona's charter school industry. In Ducey's 2016 State of the State address, he unveiled programs through which the state would help the "best public schools" obtain low-cost loans and earmark special funds for schools whose students are most successful in completing AP courses. There is little doubt as to what schools he had in mind. *The Republic* reported that BASIS and Great Hearts gobbled up the majority of the AP performance rewards and two-thirds of school-construction loans, even though there are more than five hundred charter schools in the state. At the same time, the state made it harder for smaller companies to enter the industry by assessing a $6,500 application fee and other costs to make sure only serious entities apply. These and other factors explain why ten companies, including BASIS and Great Hearts, accounted for 73 percent of the growth in the number of students attending Arizona charter schools between 2014 and 2017. The newspaper concluded: "BASIS Charter Schools Inc. and Great Hearts Academies, two booming charter chains, were the clear winners in Ducey's plans."

Arizona's loose regulation of charter schools has bred corruption and profiteering, which is always the danger when a sizable segment of the public sector is placed into the hands of for-profit companies. The efficiencies promised by advocates of privatization often never materialize, decent-paying civil service jobs are lost, and a large portion of taxpayers' money—which once went directly to government services—ends up in the pocket of entrepreneurs, who may or may not be of the most pristine character. It is a reality in states red and blue that well-timed political contributions can put even unsavory vendors in good stead with elected officials. That symbiosis becomes particularly questionable when the government service is not road paving or garbage collection but the education of children.

In 2018, the *Arizona Republic* published a series of articles showing that the founders of BASIS and other charter school operators—including American Leadership Academy, Primavera, and Benjamin Franklin—pocketed millions of dollars in profits from the taxpayers for fees and property deals that took advantage of the state's lax oversight.

One businessman who came under the paper's scrutiny was Glenn Way, a former Utah state legislator and founder of American Leadership Academy, which operates a dozen charter schools in Phoenix's East Valley that serve more than eight thousand students. The schools don't show up at the top of *U.S. News* rankings, but Way told the paper they provide a good education in a "moral and wholesome environment," complete with red-white-and-blue student apparel. The emphasis on patriotism is popular in the conservative East Valley, and the schools have made Way a rich man.

In nine years of expansion, Way made $37 million in profits on land deals associated with taxpayer-funded school buildings, according to state records. On top of that, his company was paid $6 million a year to manage the schools. In one case, Way's development company, Schoolhouse Higley, a subsidiary of Schoolhouse Development, built a K-12 school in Gilbert, Arizona, after buying the property for $11.25 million and obtaining a $36.1 million construction loan. His big payoff came when the state-funded American Leadership Academy bought the school for $62.5 million. He essentially used state funds to pay himself to build the school, which is apparently legal under Arizona law. No public bids for construction are required. Although Way disputed the $37 million figure—saying without offering proof that the actual profit was $18.4 million—he told the paper that the profit motive benefits the state's education system: "The law is silent on the question of profit, and for good reason. Arizona families will only benefit if more operators of quality charter schools are enticed to expand their offerings in our state."

Way made sure some of his bounty made it into the campaign funds of Republican elected officials. Public records show Way personally contributed more than $145,000 to GOP candidates and committees in recent years, including $50,000 to the Arizona House Republican Victory Fund committee and $50,000 to the Republican Legislative Victory Fund. He has also given on the national level, including to Donald Trump.

Another businessman who cashed in on state education funds was Damian Creamer, founder and chief executive of the Primavera online charter school. Online charter schools have been cited by watchdog groups as a detriment to their students and a drain on public school funds. They offer little in the way of quality instruction, but their owners reap huge profits because they have no buildings, no school lunches, and few other expenses. As Craig Harris of the *Arizona Republic* reported, Primavera can't claim to offer a sound education. In 2018, it had the third highest dropout rate in the state, 49 percent, and student-teacher ratios and test scores were well below the state average. But Creamer has made a pile of money. Primavera started out as a public charter school, but around 2012 began transferring big chunks of the annual $30 million it received from the state into private investment accounts. In 2012, 70 percent of its state funding, or $22.4 million, went into such investments. When the investment account reached $36 million in 2015, Creamer took the company private and paid himself an $8.8 million shareholder distribution from the new for-profit company. All this was apparently legal. Creamer was also generous in his donations to elected officials, to the tune of $114,000 he gave over thirteen years, including $8,000 he and his wife contributed to Ducey. When asked about Creamer's profiteering, Ducey deflected the question. "I'm not concerned about the CEO," he said. "That is of very little interest. I'm concerned about the child and the parent and what the child is equipped to do after 12 years of education." In fact, Creamer's profiteering was of such little interest that in December 2018, the state's charter school board approved an application by one of his companies to open another charter school.

But perhaps the most eye-popping case of taxpayer dollars going into the pockets of charter school operators involved a longtime Republican state representative, Eddie Farnsworth. Farnsworth owned Benjamin Franklin Charter School, which has four campuses in the East Valley. In September 2018, the charter school board voted unanimously to approve Farnsworth's application to transfer the campuses to a newly formed nonprofit company. As part of the deal, he would sell the campuses, paid for by the taxpayers, for nearly $14 million.

The state charter school board also does little about complaints that parents and others file against schools. One of the biggest complaints is lack of transparency. The charter schools each have a board, but it is typically made up of the owner's colleagues and sometimes just the owner. The boards routinely violate the state open-meetings law by not allowing parents to speak. The sala-

ries of executives and other finances in the management companies are a secret. The state charter school board does not allow the
public to view the complaints made against the schools. The *Republic*
had to file a request under the state's public records law to find out
that of the eighty-nine complaints the board received over a four-year
period, only 12 percent were investigated. With all the pilfering of
state funds, it is no surprise that Arizona's charter schools often fail,
sometimes shutting their doors in the middle of the school year. In
the 2016–17 school year, 138 of the state's 538 charter schools were
in some kind of financial distress.

There is no shortage of progressives in Arizona appalled by the
stunning ethical breaches in the charter school industry that are
tolerated, if not encouraged, by state officials. But their voices are
not heard by Republican leaders in the statehouse. "Charter
schools were not designed for people to make a profit," said
Chuck Essigs, government relations director of the Arizona
School Association of Business Officials. All of the reporting by
the state's largest newspaper on abuses in the charter school industry was bound to generate a clamor for reform, and that's exactly
what happened. In March 2019, a Republican state senator proposed and won passage of a "reform" bill. It contained nothing
that would stop charter school companies from awarding no-bid
construction or management contracts or from keeping executive
compensation secret. The bill, which passed on a party-line vote,
was applauded by the charter school industry. After all, the industry's lobbyists helped write it.

* * * *

WHAT HAPPENS TO FUNDING for traditional public
schools while Arizona's public officials are diverting more and
more money to charter schools and allowing for-profit companies
to siphon off tens of millions of dollars? The answer to that question goes to the heart of the school choice travesty in Arizona and
requires looking at the bigger fiscal picture in the state.

The last decade in Arizona, the period of far-right ascendancy, has been one of lost opportunity. The state's growth has been enormous, largely owing to the continuing migration of West Coast and Midwestern retirees and the new influx of tech and finance businesses from other states. Between the first quarters of 2010 and 2021, the state's real gross domestic product shot up by 32 percent, far outpacing the country as a whole (23 percent) and nearly equaling Texas and California (37 and 38 percent, respectively). New York's growth was a mere 14 percent.

That growth could yield new resources to invest in the building blocks of a state's prosperity—K-12 education, higher education, health care, infrastructure, job training, and environmental protection. But Arizona's leadership has chosen to invest in little of that. It has continued the historic neglect of its public sector and focused almost entirely on tax relief for corporations and wealthy individuals. Arizona's legislature cut taxes *every year* between 1990 and 2019. Those cuts added up to a $4.4 billion annual loss to the state treasury when accounting for inflation, and it has resulted in a tax system heavily skewed to benefit the wealthy, according to the Arizona Center for Economic Progress, a progressive advocacy group. "While our tax code is filled with loopholes and tax breaks for corporations and the wealthy, a recent study showed that low- and middle-income Arizonans pay a larger portion of their income in state and local taxes than do wealthy families," the center said in April 2019. "Arizona's upside-down tax code is pushing the state's low-income taxpayers deeper into poverty, while corporations and the rich are not paying their fair share for things like education, public safety, and infrastructure which we all benefit from."

A 2017 study by the Center for Budget and Policy Priorities in Washington found that Arizona slashed its K-12 funding by an inflation-adjusted 36.6 percent between 2008 and 2015, by far the deepest cuts of any state. The study said that thirty-one states had reduced school funding in that period, but it singled out seven Republican states—Arizona, Idaho, Kansas, Michigan, Mississippi,

North Carolina, and Oklahoma—for enacting repeated income tax cuts while starving their schools. Ducey promised to increase school funding when he became governor in 2015, even saying Arizona would be "one of the leading states in the nation" for "new dollars" flowing to education. But he also vowed not to raise taxes, which under Arizona law requires a two-thirds supermajority in any case. The governor did in fact secure increases in school funding through 2019, but it was mostly to restore the cuts enacted after the 2008 recession, and much of the new money has gone to charter schools. As of 2018, Arizona was spending $900 less per pupil than it was a decade earlier, when adjusted for inflation.

Depending on the calculation method, Arizona also ranks at the bottom or near the bottom in teacher salaries. Arizona State University's Morrison Institute for Public Policy calculated the state's median pay for elementary school teachers in 2016—when adjusted for regional cost of living—as $42,474, the worst in the nation. Arizona's schools had been rated poorly for years, but the issue emerged as a full-blown political crisis for Ducey as he campaigned for reelection in 2018. A teacher walkout in West Virginia early that year prompted an awakening among other poorly paid teachers around the country, with strikes spreading to Oklahoma and Kentucky. Their walkouts and protests became known as the Red for Ed movement, so named because the teachers wear red at their demonstrations. Arizona soon joined the fray. Weeks of demonstrations in the late winter of 2018 culminated in a major protest on April 11, with tens of thousands of teachers, parents, and students gathering outside schools. A week later, 57,000 teachers voted to strike, even though only 20,000 of the state's 90,000 certified teachers belong to the Arizona Education Association, the teachers' union. The strike lasted for five days, ending after Ducey agreed to a 19 percent pay raise and other concessions.

Frustration had been building for years. The Arizona School Personnel Administrators Association reported that 866 public school teachers had quit in 2017 alone, 156 simply abandoning their classrooms. The schools had nearly 8,600 teacher vacancies that year, 62 percent of which were either unfilled or filled with teachers without certificates. The Morrison Institute reported that 42 percent of teachers hired at traditional public schools were gone within three years, and 52 percent of charter school teachers quit after the same number of years. Teachers at traditional schools had taken to posting photographs on the internet showing broken desks, worn-out textbooks, and duct tape holding together carpets. One photo showed a tile wall with a sign reading, "Please leave lights on at all times due to roaches." A June 2019 audit of the state's School Facilities Board, which oversees grants for school-building renovations, found poor monitoring, chronic project delays, and "monies sitting idle for years." The audit said that 628 projects had been open for more than a year and $1.6 million was sitting unspent. All this came as the state continued to spend more per pupil at charter schools whose websites included virtual tours showing gleaming new facilities.

All the bad publicity arising from the strike threatened to make a mockery of Ducey's claim to be the "education governor" as the 2018 election drew closer. Arizona business groups raised more than $1 million for an advertising blitz that claimed he had made significant progress in improving the state's public schools. But the pay raises and modest increases of funding under Ducey were not enough to overcome years of neglect. In 2021, Arizona still had the third-lowest per-pupil spending of the fifty states— $8,044—just behind Florida and ahead of only Utah and Idaho. By comparison, New York spends $23,321 per pupil. Even poor states like West Virginia and Mississippi had higher per-pupil spending.

Ducey was reelected handily. But the Republican leadership had been so profligate in its giveaways to the rich that public opinion began to run against them, especially as Hispanic immigration and the influx of younger professionals from other states continued pushing the state from red to purple. The fervor of the Red for Ed movement had not gone away. In 2020, the progressive group Stand for Children won approval for a ballot measure, Proposition 208, that called for a major income tax hike on the wealthy to be used exclusively for school funding. Individuals making more than $250,000 and couples more than $500,000 would pay a 3.5 percent surcharge on top of the state's existing 4.5 percent income tax on the highest earners. It was estimated that the resulting 8 percent income tax at the top margin would generate $827 million annually for the schools. But it would also give Arizona the ninth highest marginal income tax rate in the country, which prompted business groups to protest that it would drive away investment. None of the business groups explained why one of the fastest-growing economies in the country could not absorb the ninth highest income tax rate, especially since it would only kick in at high margins. Robert Robb, a columnist at the *Arizona Republic*, called it a "gigantic gamble with Arizona's economy." But the voters didn't agree. Proposition 208 was approved by just under 52 percent of the voters, the second time in two years they had registered discontent with the Republican leadership's plans for neutering public education.

Their timing should have been perfect. Federal assistance had helped Arizona emerge from the pandemic with a surplus of more than $1 billion, the best fiscal shape the state had been in for many years. No longer would tight budgets be an excuse for neglecting crucial public services. Proposition 208 would generate new money for schools. There would be money for health care and infrastructure and public-employee pay raises, if the legislature so chose. But that's not what the Republican leadership had in mind. In the judgment of Ducey and his allies, the best use of the surplus was yet another tax cut for the wealthy. And the way they went about getting it, through a maneuver that also undercut the intent of Proposition 208, was as much an affront to democracy as the audit of the presidential election results.

In July 2021, Republicans didn't just enact a new tax cut. They approved a package that Ducey's office bragged was "the largest tax cut in state history." The main tax cut bill was crafted with no participation by Democrats and almost no public debate of any kind. It was passed on a party-line vote, buried in a budget reconciliation bill. But its impact on Arizona's revenues could echo for years to come. The bill replaced the state's graduated income tax with a "flat tax" that in its third year will make every Arizonan's tax rate 2.5 percent. It sounds like a good deal until you remember that the tax rate for low-income Arizonans was already 2.59 percent. So they got almost no tax cut at all. The real winners were the wealthy. The Arizona Center for Economic Progress calculated that 75 percent of the tax law's benefits will go to the top 5 percent of earners, those making more than $224,000 a year. Meanwhile, the law was projected to cost the state $1.9 million in revenue over three years.

But what about Proposition 208? The GOP cut it off at the knees with a piece of legislation known as Senate Bill 1783, which set up a mechanism for many wealthy taxpayers to be exempt from the 3.5 percent surcharge tied to education funding. It did this by establishing an alternative tax-filing system for income derived from business profits, capital gains, estates, interest, and dividends—that is, all the ways that many wealthy people make their money. It was projected that the legislation would cut the $827 million in annual school funding by up to $378 million and, overall, cost the state budget $1 billion. In signing the legislation, Ducey ingeniously couched the legislation as a windfall for small businesses. "This tax cut will keep Arizona competitive for small businesses already operating here and new businesses flocking here every day," he said. But the Center for Economic Progress counseled Arizonans to see through that: "Don't let the bill's title mislead you; this legislation provides no benefit for local 'mom and pop' small businesses. . . . The only people who would want to use the 'alternative tax filing' method provided by this bill are rich and very high-income individuals who want to exclude the profits from their businesses, trusts, and estates so they don't have to pay their fair share in taxes to support Arizona public schools."

The tax package has set the stage for an epic battle between the far right, with its billionaire backers in the Koch network, and the progressives who are exerting new muscle in Arizona politics. Many of the same people who were behind Prop 208 formed a new group in the summer of 2021, Invest in Arizona, and collected enough signatures for a measure on the November 2022 ballot that would repeal Senate Bill 1783 and restore the education surcharge. Of course, the GOP once again feared putting any questions about taxes before the voters and in January 2022 was planning to repeal the $1 billion tax cut and replace it with similar legislation, a barely concealed end run around the referendum.

It promised to be a watershed election for Arizona. Ducey was term limited so he could not run again. And Arizona's popular secretary of state, Democrat Katie Hobbs, announced herself as a candidate. Hobbs, a former social worker, is a supporter of traditional public schools and has gotten national exposure with her attacks on the Cyber Ninja election audit. Henry Olsen, a conservative columnist for the *Washington Post*, predicted that Ducey's tax cuts would attract more fiscally conservative migrants from other states and bring suburban Phoenix voters back into the Republican fold. "It won't take many new Republicans to paint Arizona red again," he wrote. But the young professionals flocking to Arizona may not be the voters Olsen wants. They are not likely to be enamored of the Republican legislature's bizarre assault on democracy in the election audit, the blatant corruption in the state's charter school industry, or the state's disgraceful system of public education. Progressive Arizonans, including those in the increasingly active Hispanic community, have found their voice after decades in the wilderness. 2022 may be their year.

Part III

The Road Ahead

7

Clearing the Waters: Progress in the Blue States, at Long Last

THERE WAS A TIME WHEN STEVE ZAIDMAN COULDN'T have imagined it. He couldn't have pictured himself with his feet in the surf and seagulls shrieking and whirling in the sky and the smell of brine and the children splashing in the blue and clear waters. But here he was on Constitution Beach in East Boston, old enough to remember a time when you didn't sit on this beach because you'd smell sewage instead of brine and you wouldn't get your feet near the water. The beach sits on a meandering inlet so forlorn it doesn't even have a name. Other parts of Boston Harbor are on the nautical charts as Moon Head or Broad Sound or Fort Point Channel because they open to the sea or bring mariners somewhere they'd want to go. This is the inlet to nowhere. It was once shaped like a leg wearing a boot, bent at the knee, as if it were about to kick something. But the inlet is so silted over now half the boot is gone. The southern bank is made up entirely of Logan International Airport, a couple of thousand feet from where Zaidman was sitting. Beachgoers have a clear view of the aircraft queuing up, and they hear the roar of each one when it takes off. The western bank, mostly silt, is the edge of an industrial neighborhood that gives way after a few blocks to a field of chemical storage tanks. This nameless body of water has no current and no outlet, which forms a perfect catch basin for sewage or industrial wastes that could come from a thousand places in this crowded and clamorous district of Boston.

And yet people come to this beach like it's Wellfleet or Hilton Head. Zaidman, who lived for decades in nearby Winthrop, resides now amid the forest of high-rises in Boston's West End, retired from his job as youth services director for the town of Wellesley. He could spend summer afternoons on the magnificent Charles River Esplanade near his home or go swimming at Walden Pond, in the northwestern suburbs, not far from where he had worked. But he comes to Constitution Beach, maybe out of nostalgia or maybe because of his sheer amazement that it is clean enough to swim. The sand is bleached white, and though the grass in the park is parched and yellowed by late summer, there is a healthy stand of trees and a playground and bathhouse. It's a far cry from the eighties and nineties, when the area's beaches were usually closed due to sewage overflow. "I remember in Winthrop you'd walk in just up to your ankles and you couldn't see the bottom," he said. "In the forty years I lived there, I think I went to the beach two dozen times. I didn't want to swim there. But people did when it wasn't closed."

Winthrop is a few blocks away from Constitution Beach, on the other side of Belle Isle Inlet. Bill Penwarden, white-bearded and sunburned, sat on a bridge over the inlet with a fishing line dangling into waters emerald and clear to the bottom. He said it was a good spot for striped bass, which can grow to five feet in length. He also can recollect a different time on Boston Harbor, when the fish you caught could be ridden with tumors or fin rot. His childhood was spent in Boston's Dorchester section, near Wollaston Beach in Quincy, where the water was flecked with feces every time it rained. "Wollaston Beach was a joke," Penwarden said. "There were signs up saying 'Beach Closed' all the time. They had a sewage treatment plant and it would overflow every time there was a thunderstorm. When they told you not to swim there because of sewage, they weren't joking, trust me."

The cleanup of Boston Harbor, achieved over three decades at a cost of billions of dollars, is one of the nation's great feats of environmental engineering and civic purpose. It was once considered a natural state of affairs that every urban harbor in America was a dead zone—beaches where no one swam, rivers devoid of fish, clams and oyster beds a distant memory. Up through the 1980s, Massachusetts had been as negligent as any other state in caring for its waters. The harbor was quite literally an open sewer: antiquated, overburdened, and mismanaged sewage treatment plants allowed the wastes of a great metropolis to be flushed straight into its bays and rivers. The state had to be dragged into the enormous and historic task of cleaning up its harbor by lawsuits and political pressure from its own citizens. But once they set themselves to the task, city and state officials working together accomplished it on time, under budget, and with a level of success that stands as a monumental achievement in American civil engineering. It is also a testament to what a state can accomplish when elected officials are dedicated to the betterment of its citizens rather than the interests of the wealthiest donors.

In many blue states, citizens' voices are finally being heard. State governments—in the last two decades, but particularly since 2016—are responding to issues that have long festered due to federal inaction, political gridlock in the state legislatures, and corruption on the part of state leaders now swept from office. New York and New Jersey officials have mounted their own decades-long cleanup of the region surrounding New York Harbor, perhaps not as spectacularly as their counterparts in Massachusetts, but enough to restore beauty and recreation to most of the bays and rivers. San Francisco Bay is no longer a dumping ground for sewage and industrial waste. The water quality has improved so much that harbor porpoises have returned to the bay after disappearing in the World War II era.

But it doesn't stop with the environment. The most activist blue states, tired of waiting on the federal government, have been harnessing the public sector for investments in an array of programs aimed at improving the lives of their citizenry. They have poured

money into green-energy development, pre-K education, job training, public schools, and health care. They have raised taxes on
millionaires and capital gains, cracked down on police miscon-
duct, and raised minimum wages, or at least stopped blocking
municipalities from doing so. Maine and California have begun
offering free lunch to all public school students, not just the poor.
Connecticut's "Baby Bonds" initiative sets aside $3,200 for every
child born to a family that qualifies for Medicaid. Maryland enacted a law preventing police from buying surplus military equipment such as aircraft, drones, silencers, and grenade launchers.
Colorado no longer allows admission preferences for children of
alumni at state universities. Oregon Governor Kate Brown championed campaign finance reform to end her state's distinction as
the only place in the country without limits on political contributions. Voters overwhelmingly approved a constitutional amendment in 2020 that allows state and local officials to regulate
political donations, and limits are now in place for the first time in
the city of Portland. Bills to set donation caps at the state level
died without a floor vote in the 2021 legislative session, but now
that voters have approved the constitutional amendment, the field
is open for campaign-reform proposals in future sessions or on the
November 2022 ballot.

In May 2019, Washington State Governor Jay Inslee signed
legislation that made his state the first in the nation to offer a
"public option" in its health care market. Inslee also reversed his
previous support for capital punishment and ordered a halt to
any further executions. He stood up to Trump's demonization of
political refugees, ultimately settling more of them than any state
except Texas. He launched an initiative, Career Connect Washington, to give people without college degrees an entrée into job
training and high-paying jobs. In the health care realm, Inslee expanded abortion rights, established a guaranteed long-term care
benefit for seniors that will contribute some $36,000 a year to help
with nursing home costs, and put in place a program to protect

schoolchildren from chronic diseases as adults. His did all this while his state boasted the nation's second highest growth in GDP in 2021 and maintained a reputation for being one of the best places in the country to do business.

Former Connecticut governor Dannel Malloy made criminal justice innovations a centerpiece of his administration, taking key steps to roll back the harsh law-and-order measures that his state embraced in the post-Reagan era. He visited prisons twenty-six times in his two terms in office—probably a record for any governor—and enacted policies to make sure fewer people were in them. He raised the age at which people can be tried as adults for most crimes from sixteen to eighteen, decriminalized possession of small amounts of cannabis, and erased tough penalties for nonviolent drug crimes. He also abolished the death penalty and made it easier for inmates to be paroled. From 2012 to 2016, Connecticut saw a 20 percent decrease in its violent crime rate, the sharpest drop in the country, and the inmate population dropped by 33 percent from 2009 to 2019.

With his state's Republicans grudgingly accepting the success of Malloy's initiatives, his Democratic successor, Ned Lamont, continued the reforms. He met with representatives from the Connecticut ACLU's Smart Justice project during his campaign and committed to pursue some of their objectives. Early in his first term, Connecticut became the first state requiring prosecutors to collect data on criminal dispositions in their offices to make sure minorities are not treated more harshly in charging decisions.

In the second half of his governorship, Andrew Cuomo put forth an agenda of public investments as ambitious as anything ever undertaken by the Empire State. In 2017, Cuomo signed legislation that made New York the first state in the country to offer free tuition at four-year public colleges and universities. Students from families that make $125,000 or less are promised free tuition if they head to college straight from high school, attend full-time, and meet other requirements. The plan does not contain everything sought by education advocates, but it put the state in the forefront of the effort to make higher education more affordable. Cuomo and the legislature have also launched an effort to rid the state of virtually all greenhouse gas emissions by 2050, which would mean massive state expenditures to support green-energy infrastructure. The state also earmarked hundreds of millions of dollars to help upstate New York communities harmed by industrial pollution.

Under Governor Gavin Newsom, California has made considerable progress in solving the state's affordable housing and homelessness crises and the existential threats posed by wildfires and water shortages—all while maintaining a surplus in the state's budget. His predecessor, Jerry Brown, began construction of a high-speed rail line linking San Francisco with Los Angeles. The project has been plagued by delays and cost overruns but promises to spur economic development and sharply reduce automobile exhaust emissions. There is also a proposal for a high-speed rail link between Dallas and Houston, except that it has to be built entirely with private funds and investment by the government of Japan. Governor Abbott won't support it, although he has no problem supporting the 430-mile Permian Highway Pipeline, which will carry natural gas from the West Texas oil fields to the Gulf of Mexico. Major government initiatives are now part of the progressive agenda in California, Massachusetts, Washington State, and other swaths of blue-state America. But wherever Republicans control the state government, the public's interest is not even on the political map.

* * * *

THE BOSTON HARBOR cleanup can be seen as presaging a new era in blue-state government activism. What became one of the nation's greatest environmental success stories began almost by happenstance, when a principled man went for a jog on Wollaston Beach on a summer morning in 1982 and didn't like what he saw. Bill Golden was a native of Massachusetts's South Shore who had the region's maritime tradition in his bones. His father was a longtime Coast Guard officer, and from his boyhood home in Cohasset, the younger Golden could see ships lumbering across Massachusetts Bay and mist shrouding the famed lighthouse on Minot's Ledge. Years later, after he became a wealthy attorney, Golden's romance with the harbor would move him and his wife to buy a nineteenth-century lightship, the *Nantucket*, rather than see it end up in a scrapyard. But in the summer of 1982, Golden was in his midthirties and serving as the city solicitor in Quincy. He had a habit of taking a morning run before reporting for work and, on this particular day, found himself jumping over brown clumps of matter as he ran along the packed sand at the edge of the surf. He assumed it was seaweed and jellyfish. When he looked closer, he realized to his horror that it was a mixture of grease and human feces. As he stood there looking down at the gelatinous mass covering his running shoes, an indignation arose in his breast that would have fateful consequences for the entire region. "As I realized what I stepped in, I felt nauseous," he said. "Then I got angry." He didn't need to be an engineer to know where it was coming from: the Nut Island sewage treatment plant, which sits on a spit of land reaching into Quincy Bay from the city's Houghs Neck neighborhood.

Besides being devoted to Boston Harbor, Golden is possessed of a moral stubbornness that is the birthright of any New Englander. It was that rigid sense of purpose, not gladhanding on the rubber-chicken circuit, that would be the hallmark of his later careers as state legislator, high-powered attorney, and environmental activist. Still in his sweaty shorts, his running shoes caked with sand, the young city solicitor strode through the Greek Revival edifice of Quincy's City Hall and into the office of Mayor Francis McCauley. He told McCauley what he had seen and, to his eternal credit, the mayor responded, "What do you want to do about it?" From that simple meeting arose a lawsuit in Massachusetts Superior Court against the Metropolitan District Commission

(MDC), a sprawling state agency whose functions included sewage treatment in communities surrounding Boston Harbor.

The lawsuit faced strong headwinds, even if federal and state laws were clearly on Quincy's side. The Clean Water Act of 1972 made it illegal to discharge pollutants into navigable waters without a legally justifiable permit, and mandated primary and secondary sewage treatment for the nation's metropolitan areas. Of more interest to Golden were state laws, including the Massachusetts Clean Waters Act, that similarly mandated proper sewage treatment. But having laws in place was one thing. Convincing a judge to order a huge metropolitan area to spend billions to correct a problem that had defied solutions for decades was quite another.

Boston Harbor, which covers fifty square miles, is one of the largest harbors of any big city in the country. It includes fifteen islands and thousands of acres of marshes and tidelands. It is potentially a recreational gem, with sandy beaches within sight of Boston's downtown skyline, beds of oysters and clams, and legendary fishing grounds. The waters off Houghs Neck were once known as the "flounder capital of the world" because of the size of its daily catches. But Massachusetts had been dumping raw sewage into that beautiful and historic waterway since the colonial era.

The Bay State launched its first systemic attempt at handling sewage in the 1880s, prompted in part by a cholera epidemic that ravaged Boston in 1865. The newly built system consisted primarily of collecting waste from the communities lining the Charles and Mystic rivers, storing it on Moon Island, and releasing it untreated into the harbor twice a day with the outgoing tides. The MDC, created in 1893, improved on that system by building treatment plants at Nut Island and Deer Island after World War II. But the commission also operated parks, skating rinks, swimming pools, a zoo, and roadways, and was never able to secure sufficient funding from the legislature for upgrades to the treatment plants.

As a result, the plants were overwhelmed by postwar growth in the Boston area. They were understaffed, poorly maintained, and prone to breakdown. Even if they worked as intended, the sludge separated from the wastewater was still released into the outgoing tides, a procedure that was outlawed under federal law in the 1970s but nonetheless continued. On top of that, Boston was one of hundreds of cities around the country with antiquated sewer systems in which stormwater flowed into the same pipes as sewage. Every time it rained, the system would be overwhelmed and stormwater, sewage, and industrial waste would bypass the treatment plants and be released from outfall pipes directly into the harbor, a deliberate process known as "combined sewer overflows," or CSOs. By the time Quincy filed its lawsuit at the end of 1982, the sewage flow into the harbor amounted to hundreds of thousands of gallons a day and no one had a plan to stop it. A 1968 study by the federal government found that 30 percent of the harbor was severely polluted, with the peak of illegal discharges in the 1980s still to come. The treatment system was so antiquated that the Smithsonian requested that Boston donate one of its sewage pumps in East Boston to the museum because it was the last of its kind, dating to 1895. But the city couldn't part with it because it was still in use.

Golden was not a complete novice when it came to environmental law. After his graduation from Yale University in 1970, he served on President Nixon's Advisory Council on Executive Organization and helped draft the legislation creating the Environmental Protection Agency. He later earned a law degree from Boston University and a master's from Harvard. Still, he was under no illusion about his prospects when he appeared before Superior Court Judge Paul Garrity. Garrity was considered a judicial activist who had previously placed the Boston Housing Authority in receivership and had little patience when bureaucrats failed the public. "The easiest way to achieve control is to have people realize that if they get out of line, you'll nuke them," he once told a reporter. But even Garrity was taken aback by what Quincy was asking him to do: break up the MDC, replace it with a new sewer agency, and order a moratorium on new sewer hookups until the pollution was brought under control. "Garrity was laughing at us, just howling," Golden said years later in an interview with the *Patriot Ledger* of Quincy.

Garrity admitted in later comments to the media that he thought Golden was being naive. "I remember how quick he talked, because he was rightly concerned I was going to throw him out on his ear." But Garrity, who had grown up in a triple-decker in a working-class section of Boston's Jamaica Plain, remembered being sickened as a child after swimming at the city's beaches. Golden got his attention when he put on a pair of yellow rubber gloves, reached into a box marked with a skull and crossbones and the word "Dangerous," and pulled out two beakers with specimens from Wollaston Beach. One was filled with brown harbor water and the other with a mixture of sand, human feces, and sanitary napkins. "This is what Quincy kids are forced to swim in when they go to Wollaston Beach," he told the judge. Despite protests from the MDC's lawyer, Garrity decided to hear the case.

Golden and Peter Koff, an environmental lawyer who Quincy hired as co-counsel, had filed the lawsuit in state court for a reason. U.S. District Judge Arthur Garrity (no relation to Paul) had only eight years earlier ignited enormous controversy in Boston by ordering the city to desegregate public schools with busing. They feared the federal courts would be gun-shy about undertaking another act of social engineering so soon after. They waited until Paul Garrity rotated into the Superior Court district that covered Quincy before filing the suit, because they wanted him as their judge. They essentially were judge shopping, and their strategy paid off. When all the facts were in about how MDC officials had managed sewage treatment in the Boston area, Garrity "nuked them."

Garrity became so personally involved in the harbor cleanup that he became known as the "sludge judge," but he had no intention of going it alone. He knew that a solution to the harbor pollution would not only involve complex matters of law and public policy, but would also mean navigating the treacherous shoals of Massachusetts politics if the state's elected officials were going to be brought to the table. The plaintiff's attorneys had in their favor that the progressive technocrat Michael Dukakis was governor and had gone on record promising to make the harbor cleanup a priority, after having failed to do so in an earlier term. But they also needed to win over the powerful senate president, William Bulger, a South Boston clubhouse politician who was not known for his green agenda. Garrity knew just the right man to assist in negotiating such terrain. He appointed as special master Harvard law professor Charles Haar, who was one of his mentors and known as much for political savvy as he was for his legal acumen. Haar would not only weigh evidence and propose engineering strategies but also play a hands-on role in selling it to the politicians on Beacon Hill. "He was really taking the pulse of the legislature," Garrity would say later. "That's what he likes to do. He's a political junkie."

After months of political brinkmanship and threats from Garrity to place the sewage system in receivership, Dukakis signed legislation on December 19, 1984, that created the Massachusetts Water Resources Authority (MWRA) to handle sewage treatment and the supply of drinking water in the Boston area. That was the easy part. The gargantuan task of rebuilding a metropolitan area's sewage-treatment system lay ahead. In 1983, the Conservation Law Foundation, a nonprofit advocacy group shocked by what Quincy's lawsuit had revealed about the harbor's pollution, filed its own suit in U.S. District Court, naming the MDC and the EPA as defendants. The Quincy lawsuit had led to the creation of the MWRA, but it would be up to the federal lawsuit, in which the EPA was eventually dropped as a defendant and became a plaintiff in 1985, to establish the blueprint and schedule for the harbor cleanup.

U.S. District Judge David Mazzone issued an order on May 8, 1986, that committed the MWRA to an engineering project astounding in its scope. The Nut Island treatment plant would be decommissioned and the Deer Island plant demolished and replaced with a new facility that could handle primary and secondary treatment of 1.3 billion gallons of wastewater per day, making it the second largest such plant in the country. The plan further required construction of a 5-mile tunnel from Nut Island that would link South Shore sewage to Deer Island, and a 9.5-mile tunnel—twenty-four feet in diameter—that would carry the fully treated effluent from Deer Island to the middle of Massachusetts Bay, where dilution was expected to render it harmless. Finally, Mazzone ordered the construction of tunnels that would carry runoff from eighty-eight CSOs on the Charles, Mystic, and Neponset rivers to the Deer Island plant. Perhaps most gratifying of all for environmentalists, sludge would no longer be dumped in the harbor but rather, by the end of 1991, pumped to a Quincy facility and refined into fertilizer pellets.

It's ironic that Dukakis and his state were well on their way to a dramatic environmental victory when George H.W. Bush chose to make Boston Harbor an issue in the 1988 presidential campaign. Bush and his chief campaign strategist, Lee Atwater, were merciless in their attacks on Dukakis, the Democratic nominee. Most were exaggerated or downright groundless, but Atwater was making good on his promise to "rip the bark off the little bastard." In what the *New York Times* called "rich political theater," Bush took reporters on a boat ride out of Boston on September 1, 1988, and called it the "harbor of shame," a phrase repeated in the media for many years. At that moment, Massachusetts was doing far more to clean up its waters than has been done to this day in Texas, where Bush got his start in politics and his son would become governor.

The federal court ended its supervision of the harbor cleanup in 2016, thirty-three years after Quincy had filed its first lawsuit. The project cost $4.7 billion, less than the $6 billion price that some projected in the 1980s. It was partly paid for by a near quintupling of residents' water and sewer bills between 1986 and 2002, which did not sit well in the city's working-class neighborhoods. The dramatic rate hikes produced a number of protests, including one in the city of Chelsea in 1993 in which three hundred residents burned copies of their MWRA bills.

But what they got for their money was the most successful environmental cleanup in the nation's history. Boston Harbor, once a cesspool that no one wanted to go near, was transformed into a shimmering recreational and commercial oasis. Beaches are now crowded all summer. Clamming and lobstering are back. By 2004, bacterial counts had declined by two-thirds, and in 2018 the Woods Hole Oceanographic Institution on Cape Cod reported that Boston Harbor flounder had been tumor-free for fourteen consecutive years. The same institute released a study in December 2018 that credited the cleanup with unleashing $30 to $100 billion in commercial development in the region. The cleanup is a work in progress. The state still had a few dozen CSOs to close up in the summer of 2021, as did hundreds of other cities around the country. But Massachusetts was way ahead of the pack.

There is much to learn from the Boston Harbor story. There was no quick fix for such extensive and ongoing contamination, and no single entity could have gotten the job done, not even a swashbuckling "sludge judge." Dukakis and his successors could have dragged out the court battle for a decade before the project even got underway. The legislature could have impeded and underfunded the effort. But the state's leaders chose to do what was right for society, even though they knew the project would take so long they'd never get the credit. It took the judiciary, the state's executive and legislative branches, universities, advocacy groups, the business community, and the purse strings of the federal government to give the people back their harbor.

* * * *

NEW YORK AND NEW JERSEY have also made impressive strides in cleaning up their waterways, despite challenges even more formidable than Massachusetts faced in Boston Harbor. Up through the 1970s, Hudson River pollution—a toxic blend of sewage, industrial waste, and trash—was enough to break the hearts of naturalists and ordinary citizens. The shorelines were littered with everything from shopping carts and wrecked boats to abandoned cars. "Bureaucratic indifference to the river has been the order of the day," *Sports Illustrated* writer and fisherman Robert Boyle wrote in 1969, noting that the Army Corps of Engineers, which claimed jurisdiction over the river, ignored blatant violations of state and federal environmental laws, including oil flowing "for years" from the Penn Central railroad's diesel and electric shops in Croton-on-Hudson, New York, thirty-four miles upriver from the Battery.

> The oil gushes from a pipe which is three feet in diameter and bears the date of 1929. It empties into the Hudson on the south side of Croton Point adjacent to the mouth of the Croton River. The oil discharges have been so heavy that ducks have drowned there. It takes only a few drops of oil to destroy the natural waterproofing of the feathers. . . . Fish and crabs caught in the area are deemed inedible.

The Clean Water Act of 1972 made a bigger difference than any other public policy in the salvation of the river. It outlawed the discharge of any pollutant from a point source into navigable waters without a permit, which included not only industrial discharges but also untreated sewage from municipalities. It also gave states responsibility for its enforcement. The law set the rather lofty goal of making all of the country's navigable waters swimmable and fishable by the mid-1980s. But as was the case with Boston Harbor, no law in itself would bring about the restoration of the Hudson River. It would take the cooperation of state and local officials, businesses, advocacy groups, and citizens themselves.

The EPA filed its first lawsuit against New York City under the Clean Water Act the very year the law was enacted, finding that even though 80 percent of its sewage was treated, there were still 350 million gallons of raw sewage entering New York Harbor every day. The lawsuit led to a 1977 consent decree between the federal government, the New York State Department of Environmental Conservation, and the city to end the sewage discharges, essentially forming a partnership to clean up the harbor. But it took a while. There were still 145 million gallons of daily raw sewage discharges on April 22, 1986, when the city opened the North River treatment plant on the shore of uptown Manhattan, putting in place the last piece of the city's system and ending centuries of dry-weather sewage dumping in the harbor. Another victory for naturalists came in 1991, when the same plant began secondary treatment, so that not only solids but liquid pollutants would be separated from the wastewater. Under constant pressure from environmental groups like Riverkeeper, whose boats have spent decades cruising the Hudson and sampling its water, New York State has taken other steps to cut back on pollution, including the shuttering of the Indian Point nuclear plant in April 2021. New York's environmental scientists estimated that a billion fish, eggs, and larvae were killed in the power plant's intakes every year, a number the plant's operator, Entergy Corporation, protested was no higher than 687 million.

Even Riverkeeper acknowledges that five decades of cleanup efforts have given a new life to the Hudson. Dissolved oxygen levels have increased significantly and fecal bacteria levels have plummeted. The river, even off Manhattan, is now a place of kayaking, sailing, and swimming competitions. Studies have documented the return of species of wildlife not seen in decades. Researchers from the University of Delaware documented a population of 450 Atlantic sturgeon off Hyde Park in Dutchess County in June 2018, including one measuring fourteen feet. A humpback whale was spotted swimming off Manhattan in the winter of 2020.

New York is hardly done with the cleanup. In 2020 it still had 460 combined sewer overflow outfalls on its shores, which release untreated wastewater every time it rains, to the tune of twenty billion gallons a year. Hundreds of cities across the country with antiquated sewer system have the same problem, and most of them—like New York—are under federal consent decrees to do something about it. But there are no easy solutions. New York's latest plan for plugging up the outfalls, put forth in 2020, was scoffed at by environmental groups as falling woefully short of what is needed.

But there is a bigger problem, which ensures that a full restoration of the river may never be achieved, not in a decade or even a century. The largest federal Superfund site in the country is a two-hundred-mile corridor of the river where two General Electric capacitor manufacturing plants, in Fort Edward and Hudson Falls, discharged an estimated 1.3 million pounds of polychlorinated biphenyls, or PCBs, over a thirty-year period ending in 1977. The chemical lays in the sediment of the river and shows up in the tissue of fish, making them unsafe to eat above small amounts. The Hudson River is a major spawning area for striped bass. If a striper is caught off Montauk or the coast of Delaware, it may have spawned in the Hudson and have PCBs in its flesh.

General Electric and the EPA signed a consent decree in 2005 that committed the company to dredging 2.5 million cubic yards of sediment from a forty-acre stretch of the river between the Troy Dam and Fort Edward. But when the EPA allowed the company to declare its work done during the Trump administration, New York State officials protested that 136 acres of the river above Albany were still contaminated. The state pointed to studies by the National Oceanic and Atmospheric Administration showing that the health of fish in the Lower Hudson had not recovered as much as expected. But a federal lawsuit by the state to compel the EPA to order new dredging was thrown out. As far as the federal courts and GE are concerned, the remaining PCBs are staying there.

New York Harbor may not ever achieve the level of cleanliness that environmentalists are fighting for and citizens deserve, but state and city officials have fought for the health of its bays and rivers in ways that their counterparts in most red states have not. While Texas reduces funding to its environmental agency, the Houston Ship Channel and Galveston Bay are as muddy and polluted as ever, sullied by toxic chemicals and untreated sewage from the region's overburdened, damaged, and poorly maintained treatment system. Sewage doesn't just seep into the water; it bubbles up into the city's streets.

Many rivers in Indiana, including the Grand Calumet River, which flows through Gary and into Lake Michigan, are cesspools of sewage and toxic waste that get little attention from the state's government. As recently as 2007, the EPA had to intervene to prevent Indiana from weakening the water discharge permit of U.S. Steel Gary Works, the lake's biggest polluter. In 2019, the ArcelorMittal steel mill released a plume of cyanide and ammonia that flowed into the Little Calumet River. The company kept quiet about it for four days until thousands of dead fish floated past a popular marina.

* * * *

EARLY IN ANDREW CUOMO'S governorship, he invited the Pulitzer Prize–winning historian Robert Caro to Albany so he could pick his brain about Robert Moses, the twentieth-century planning official credited with transforming the urban landscape of New York State. Caro had written a famous biography of Moses, and Cuomo's staff was deferential in its invitation, saying the governor wanted to learn from him. Cuomo actually learned nothing. Instead, he pelted Caro with a nearly two-hour dissertation on his plans for a massive buildout of New York infrastructure, à la Moses. He then abruptly ended the meeting. "It was an arrogant and angering thing to do," Caro later told the *New York Times*. "To think I had given a day of my life for him to lecture me."

Andrew Cuomo is not a likable man. He blustered and bullied his way through his ten years as governor, strong-arming the legislature and intimidating anyone who stood in the way of his ambitions. He oversold his accomplishments and covered up his failures. He closed down a commission he set up to investigate state corruption when it got too close to his allies. His campaigns were flush with dark money. He hid the true number of nursing home residents who died of Covid. He used his staff to help in the writing of a biography that extolled his accomplishments in fighting the virus. And, in a scandal that finally brought about his resignation in August 2021, he was accused by eleven women of sexual harassment, including one who said she was groped. Ethically and temperamentally, he was a nightmare.

But it is undeniable that Cuomo left behind a legacy of public investment unmatched in the modern history of New York State. With help from the federal government, he built new terminals at LaGuardia and Kennedy airports, the massive Moynihan Train Hall in Midtown Manhattan, subway extensions, a new Kosciuszko Bridge connecting Brooklyn and Queens, and a new Tappan Zee Bridge, which he renamed after his father, former governor Mario Cuomo, a move even his brother, CNN anchor Chris Cuomo, thought lacked judgment. There is in fact something to criticize in everything Cuomo did. And yet, at a time when four decades of political gridlock in Washington and budget-cutting fervor in the states had diminished America's public sector, Cuomo built and he built big. He built in a way that should be a paradigm for fast-growing states like Texas and Florida that have been miserly in their public investment but profligate in their corporate tax giveaways. U.S. Senator Rick Scott has bragged in multiple interviews that he spent $85 billion in his two terms as Florida governor on roads, bridges, airports, and seaports. Compare that to Cuomo's announcement in early 2021 that New York, which has a smaller population than Florida, would spend $306 billion on infrastructure in coming years, much of it on climate-friendly transportation projects. Scott prefers highways to climate-friendly transportation. One of the first things he did as governor was reject $2.4 billion in federal money for a high-speed rail link between Tampa and Orlando.

Andrew Cuomo lacked his father's progressivism, his moral rectitude, his oratorical skills, and his ability to inspire others. He came into office in 2010 as a so-called Clinton Democrat with enmity toward big government and public sector unions. In his first year in office, he convinced the legislature to trim funding for health care and education by $2 billion and blocked passage of a millionaire's tax. He kept a lid on taxes for most of his governorship, maintaining corporate tax rates well below those of California, New Jersey, Massachusetts, and even Pennsylvania. Cuomo and the left of his party were always mutually antagonistic. As Nick Paumgarten wrote in the *New Yorker* in October 2020, "It may be hard for someone outside the hothouse of New York politics to understand how much Cuomo is resented by the progressive wing of his party, which his staffers disdainfully call the 'professional left'—to whom he, in turn, is Quid Pro Quo Cuomo."

The governor's fiscal conservatism was in tune with Albany while the Republicans controlled the state senate in the first two years of his tenure. The Democrats gained the majority in 2012, but a group of the party's conservative lawmakers, the Independent Democratic Conference, allied themselves with Republicans and blocked the emergence of a progressive agenda—all with Cuomo's encouragement. But after the 2018 elections swept away the IDC and put progressive Democrats firmly in control of the legislature, Cuomo had no choice but to veer left. In 2021, after pandemic spending put the state's budget in deficit, the governor reluctantly supported a corporate tax hike and an increase in the personal income tax rate from 8.82 percent to 9.65 percent. New York City's top earners, who also pay a local tax of 3.88 percent, ended up with a top marginal rate of 14.8 percent, the highest state income tax in the nation, surpassing California's rate of 13.3 percent. With New York Harbor filled with yachts and apartments going for tens of millions, progressives had been issuing calls to tax the rich for many years. And for good reason. The tax increase was part of a budget deal that brought badly needed assistance to a state struggling with the ravages of coronavirus, including a record $29.5 billion for schools and billions more for rent relief, aid to small businesses and undocumented immigrants, and funding for arts groups. But Cuomo continued to fear that the new tax structure would cause the rich to flee the state.

Despite his conservative impulses, Cuomo was impelled by the accumulated force of his state's public opinion—by the revulsion over Trumpism and the despair of the pandemic—to enact an agenda that was arguably the most progressive and ambitious in the nation. Paumgarten wrote:

> Cuomo has said, and his people insist, that he is a great progressive. They cite the accomplishments: gay marriage, marijuana decriminalization, gun control, a minimum-wage increase, paid family leave. "Every time you set up the government for failure, you're aiding and abetting the conservatives," Cuomo told me. "I'm looking at an original poster: 'Re-elect F.D.R. for Progressive Government.' It's not a new word, a new concept. It was F.D.R. and Al Smith. They were the progressives. F.D.R. was all about you get done what you can get done." Cuomo likes to say that, under his watch, New York has the most progressive record of any state in America, and believes that history will say so. "The right decision ultimately outs," he continued. "If you don't believe that the truth wins, you can't do the job. You have to believe that the right thing gets appreciated in the long run. Only the long run matters."

* * * *

THE LONG RUN: the quest for a sustainable economy and a more equitable society, which can only be achieved with public investment, and will not bear fruit this year or next, or even in time for the next election. That is what the most activist blue states have embraced at long last. They have done so haltingly and imperfectly, with constant harrying from the monied interests. As was the case with Massachusetts and the cleanup of its harbor, Democratic politicians have pursued a forward-looking agenda only after being bludgeoned by progressive organizing, lawsuits from public interest groups, and the mounting evidence—the screaming evidence obvious to all but the most obtuse among us—that solutions can be deferred no longer.

Most blue states have followed California and New York in adopting schedules to make renewable energy 100 percent of their states' power supply by the middle of the century. Washington Governor Jay Inslee made climate change the central issue in his 2020 presidential campaign, even though some political commentators felt his green politics failed to set him apart from his rivals and that his real selling point should have been his record on health care. But Inslee responded that every other political issue had to take a back seat to global warming. "Those (other issues) become relatively moot if the entire ecosystem collapses upon which human life depends," he told *Politico*. "This is a unique issue. It is a unique issue because our survival literally depends on it." How different that is from the views of Rick Scott, whose environmental appointees while he was Florida governor were forbidden to use the term "climate change" or "global warming." In his administration, as with Republican-controlled state governments across America, corporate profits were a higher priority than the needs of humanity.

8

Which Model—California
or Texas?

ONE OF THE BIGGEST CANARDS OF THE TRUMP
era, swallowed whole by many journalists, is that the California
Dream is dead and progressive governance is what killed it. It became almost a rote narrative in the media by 2021 that slowing population growth in California and the "exodus" from the state during
the pandemic had humiliated its long-standing claim to be a model
for America. How could it be a model when its out-of-control housing prices were driving people out of the state and fueling a homelessness crisis, when its schools were underfunded, when millions of
its acres were engulfed every year in wildfires, and when its water
supply was almost tapped out? For journalists and politicos unwilling to let data and context get in the way of a shiny, made-for-TV
narrative, the answer was simple. "The California Dream Is Dying,"
blared a headline in *The Atlantic* in the summer of 2021. The article's author, Conor Friedersdorf, a conservative-leaning California
native, wrote that restrictive zoning, substandard public schools,
and onerous regulation were putting a damper on economic opportunity in his state. "The Democrats who run the state fail all but its
most fortunate residents in the realms of housing, education, and
economic opportunity," Friedersdorf wrote, claiming that members
of the state's privileged classes are "poised to take the California
Dream to their graves by betraying a promise the state offered from
the start." He was hardly alone in predicting the state's eclipse. "Cal-

ifornia Doom: Staggering $54 Billion Budget Deficit Looms" was the headline of a piece in the Associated Press in 2020. "California Burns for Better Leaders," wrote the *Wall Street Journal*'s editorial page. Or, as a team of reporters at the *Washington Post* put it: "California has become a warming, burning, epidemic-challenged and expensive state, with many who live in sophisticated cities, idyllic oceanfront towns and windblown mountain communities thinking hard about the viability of a place they have called home forever. For the first time in a decade, more people left California last year for other states than arrived."

The deluge of bad news for California is good news for the Republican Party, which harbors a special contempt for progressives in the Golden State. California's very existence is an affront to the GOP's philosophy of limited government and social conservativism. It's a state with an activist government, strong social and economic regulation, high taxes, and a welcome mat for immigrants and sexual minorities, and yet it outperforms every red state economically. Anything that suggests the state's inclusive, social democratic model is faltering, that this thorn in the side of conservatism can finally be removed, becomes a rallying cry for the right. On the first night of the Republican presidential convention in 2020, Kimberly Guilfoyle, once married to Gavin Newsom when he was mayor of San Francisco but by then dating Donald Trump Jr., fired up the internet with her condemnation of her home state. "If you want to see the socialist Biden-Harris future for our country, just take a look at California," she said. "It is a place of immense wealth, immeasurable innovation, an immaculate environment, and the Democrats turned it into a land of discarded heroin needles in parks, riots in streets and blackouts in homes."

More than any other blue state, California provokes apoplexy in the Republican ranks. Its every disaster is seen as a political opportunity, its suffering a cause for delight. Thus Texas Senator Ted Cruz could hardly contain his glee when a massive California heat wave in 2019 caused power outages in thirty of its fifty-eight counties. "California is now unable to perform even basic functions of civilization, like having reliable electricity," he tweeted. "Hope you don't like air conditioning!" At the height of the pandemic, a time when the nation should have been pulling together, Texas Governor Greg Abbott fired off a warning on Twitter to the Californians he imagined stampeding to his state: "Remember those high taxes, burdensome regulations, & socialist agenda advanced in CA? We don't believe in that."

And it is in fact Texas that many in the media have crowned as the new exemplar of where America should be headed. The Lone Star State is portrayed as the new land of dreams for the young and enterprising, tomorrow's leaders of finance, technology, film, and music. "You can make a case that the U.S. state with the brightest long-term economic future is Texas," wrote columnist David Leonhardt of the *New York Times* in the winter of 2021. "As California was in the twentieth century, Texas today looks like a state that can embody and shape the country's future." Leonhardt cited the usual litany as evidence that Texas is an economic marvel—its growth by four million people in a decade, its "thriving cultural scene," and the decision by Hewlett-Packard, Oracle, and Tesla to move to the state. He even dug up a study by the Urban Institute showing that the reading and math performance of Texas's elementary and middle school students is above the national average, when test scores are adjusted to account for "demographic differences across students in each state." Forget that the institute's findings are inconsistent with the conclusions of most other highly reputable sources, such as *Education Week*, whose annual school reports cards—which also weigh a variety of metrics, not just test scores—invariably show the quality of Texas schools below that of most other states. The bigger problem with Leonhardt's article is that it ignores the larger context of Texas's disregard for the well-being of its citizens, particularly the less fortunate, as if a society can be measured solely on the level of its economic growth. There is nothing necessarily inaccurate about Leonhardt's piece. Texas may well loom large in the nation's future. The more salient question is what kind future it will be. Will Texas be a sustainable and inclusive society where the majority's interests prevail, or a ghastly environmental wasteland where the profits of distant corporations dictate public policy?

Several chapters of this book have laid bare the huge adverse consequences arising from Texas's backward politics and lack of public investment—polluted rivers and bays, skies blighted by industrial emissions, substandard health care, poorly funded secondary and higher education, political corruption, the now notorious denial of reproductive rights, and the flagrant willingness of its Republican leadership to overthrow the state's democratic institutions so the voices of its most marginalized citizens can be silenced. Much of what is impressive about Texas's economy, its technology sector and "cultural scene," have arisen in the Austin metro area, a progressive region that is despised and frequently undermined by the state's leadership. As noted in chapter 3, Texas is an economic powerhouse in large part because it sits on vast reserves of oil and natural gas. It also is home to a booming technology sector that grew out of higher-education funding and public-private partnerships in the Austin area that were fostered by an earlier generation of state leaders—innovations that never would have happened in the political climate of today's Texas.

Leonhardt pointed out that the central contradiction of the Texas economy is that it rests heavily on an oil and gas sector that is contributing to climate change. That is an understatement. An estimated 35 percent of the state's economic output comes from fossil fuels, which every responsible government on the planet is committed to ridding from the earth over the next several decades. Coping with the loss of an industry that accounts for more than a third of its economy—and an even larger percentage of its blue-collar jobs—will require Texas to launch a vast effort in the public and private sectors to retrain its workforce to meet the needs of a post-carbon economy. It already has a head start in the shift to renewable energy; it's the largest producer of wind energy in the country by far. But giving the public sector a role in guiding Texas toward a future of renewable energy is anathema to the belief system of the state's Republican leaders, who accept millions in campaign contributions from oil and gas companies. Their priority is not a post-carbon future but the construction of hundreds of miles of pipelines to transport natural gas to export facilities on the Gulf of Mexico. Oil and natural gas infrastructure is transforming the physical environment of the Gulf region, upending ways of life and contaminating the state's precious natural resources, all to accommodate industries that need to be eliminated as quickly as possible for the planet to survive. How does *that* make Texas a model for the nation's future?

* * * *

YOU WON'T HEAR IT ON FOX NEWS, or on CNN or MSNBC for that matter, but the state whose policy makers have been the most visionary in preparing their region and the nation for responsible global leadership is not Texas but most decidedly California. Under the stewardship of Governor Jerry Brown and his successor, Gavin Newsom, the Golden State has embarked on a program of social and economic renewal that is arguably more ambitious than anything ever undertaken by a state in the nation's history. It has been underway for less than a decade—Brown first had to overcome a post-recession crisis in the state's finances—and has not come near to solving the state's enormous problems, but the blueprint is clear and the achievements substantial. And the public's support is evidenced by the success of tax-increase referendums, the overwhelming support for Newsom in the 2021 recall election, and the enormous popularity of Brown throughout his latter two terms. If California is the portrait of catastrophe painted by the Republican Party, somebody forgot to tell the voters. Brown assumed the governorship at a time when the state was on the brink of insolvency, but he went on to preside over a major program of public investment—including new outlays for schools, environmental protection, and highway construction—and left his successor with a healthy budget surplus, a feat that prompted Todd Purdum in *The Atlantic* to call Brown "perhaps the most successful politician in contemporary America." A Brown biographer, Jim Newton, longtime reporter and editor at the *Los Angeles Times*, went further: "At the end of the Brown years, California stood apart from and ahead of much of the nation that contained it. California in 2019 was more prosperous and more protective of the environment, more welcoming of immigrants, and more generous with its protections and benefits than most parts of the United States. It demonstrated that a place—a very big and diverse place—could be all those things at once."

The California "exodus" has been grossly mischaracterized. In May 2021, California's finance department reported that the state's population had declined by 0.46 percent in 2020, the first year of negative growth since the state began keeping records in 1900. Census data also showed that 6.1 million Californians had left for other states between 2010 and 2020 and only 4.9 million had arrived from other parts of the country—a net outflow that had accelerated in the last two years of the decade. Taken together, these two sets of data were seen by conservatives as bolstering their claim that progressivism was destroying the Golden State.

It is true that for quite a number of years—three decades, in fact—more people have been leaving California than coming from other states. However, these are not affluent people being driven out by high marginal income taxes, as conservatives claim. The people migrating to the state are mostly young, affluent, and well educated, while those leaving tend to be low-income or middle-class residents who struggle with housing costs. This is in one sense a problem that most states would love to have, an influx of college graduates with skills to compete in the global economy. The problem is that it creates a cycle of inequality in which affluent migrants exert upward pressure on housing costs, which in turn puts more pressure on people of moderate means to leave. As for the population loss of 2020, that is easy to explain. California's growth over the last decade has been due almost entirely to immigration, mostly from Latin America and Asia. Travel restrictions imposed during the pandemic, coupled with the Trump administration's clampdown on immigration, brought the flow of people from other countries almost to a halt. When you also subtract from the population more than fifty thousand excess deaths due to coronavirus, a year of population loss is neither surprising nor likely to continue.

There is an irony to all the predictions of doom for California that have gushed from the mainstream media, all the claims that the dream was over: California emerged from the pandemic stronger economically than any other state. The state everyone said was unfriendly to business added 1.3 million people to its non-farm payrolls between April 2020 and April 2021, more than Texas or New York. Its total personal income surged by $118 billion over the twelve-month period beginning in the second quarter of 2020, more than those two other states combined. California has forever outpaced Texas in economic growth. Between 2014 and 2019, before the onset of the pandemic, real gross domestic product grew by 21 percent in California, compared with 16 percent in Texas. And yet, David Byler in the *Washington Post* applauded Texas's "sturdy economic growth engine" and described California as "languishing." As the pandemic began receding in early 2021, Matthew Winkler, former editor and chief of Bloomberg News, was one of the few national financial journalists who noticed how wrong the pack had been about California: "No one," he wrote, "anticipated the latest data readout showing the Golden State has no peers among developed economies for expanding GDP, creating jobs, raising household income, manufacturing growth, investment in innovation, producing clean energy and unprecedented wealth through its stocks and bonds. All of which underlines Governor Gavin Newsom's announcement last month of the biggest state tax rebate in American history."

Despite numbers like these, it is not hard to find surveys ranking California as the worst state in the country to do business. One came from *Chief Executive* magazine, whose annual "Best and Worst States for Business" survey in April 2021 placed California dead last and Texas and Florida at the top. As pointed out by Michael Hiltzik, a *Los Angeles Times* business columnist, the magazine even made a joke of the state's ranking, asking in its headline for readers to "just guess" which state came up as the worst. "And once again—yawn—California, New York, Illinois and Massachusetts pile up at the bottom of our rankings," the magazine wrote. This is a survey of corporate CEOs. Think about *that* for a second. What has recent history shown to be corporate CEOs' top priority? Answer: their own compensation. It is hardly a surprise, then, that they would rate as most "business friendly" the two biggest states with no personal income tax and relegate the state with the highest personal income tax to the bottom. They are also likely to have an ideological bias against states with strong regulations. Researchers at Harvard Law School published a study showing that corporate CEOs' donations heavily favor the Republican Party, with only 18 percent giving to Democrats. Hiltzik noted that the surveys of best states for business invariably rank California toward the bottom while the indicators of economic growth put it at the top. "How can we reconcile these contradictory facts?" he wrote. "The answer isn't hard to find. It's that these surveys don't actually measure a state's business climate or economic potential. Rather, they're concerned with a state's conformity to right-wing shibboleths about what makes a business-friendly environment."

There is no doubt that California, with its vast land mass, 840 miles of coastline, and an economy larger than all but four countries, is highly regulated. But is it overregulated? A 2020 study by the Mercatus Center at George Mason University found that California had 395,608 regulations, more than any other state. Interestingly, the five most regulated states were all among the most populous states in the country. Texas, supposedly the business-friendly state par excellence, was ranked fifth in the number of regulations, with 263,369. The gross domestic product in Texas was 63 percent that of California in 2019; the number of regulations in Texas was 67 percent of California's. Although the proper number of regulations should not necessarily be directly proportionate to GDP, it is not taking a leap to suggest that a bigger and more complex economy requires greater scrutiny of business activities, especially in a state whose citizens value health issues and environmental protection. Besides, pitting one state against another in the number of regulations plays into the hands of corporately funded think tanks (like Mercatus) that have turned out endless studies since the Reagan era trying to convince policy makers and citizens that regulations harm the economy. In fact, more studies, without the taint of corporate sponsorship, show that the economic benefits of regulation far outweigh the costs. The huge cost to the economy exacted by nitrate pollution, described in chapter 4, is only one depressing example. Perhaps no one ever put it better than the historian Richard Hofstadter, who in the 1950s surveyed the societal benefits of the forty-hour work week, child-labor prohibition, health and safety protections, and other government regulations: "Without this sustained tradition, the American system would have been nothing but a jungle ... and probably would have failed to develop into the remarkable system of production and distribution that it is." California has been vigilant in staving off the jungle, and other states should be as well.

* * * *

CALIFORNIA WASN'T ALWAYS a paragon of progress. In his four-decade journey from fiscal conservative to progressive icon, Jerry Brown personified the dramatic evolution of California and other blue states from standard-bearers of Reaganism to exemplars of social progress. When he began his first eight-year stint as governor in 1975, California was by almost anyone's definition a conservative state. San Francisco may have been a Democratic stronghold, with its aggressive labor contingent, but Southern California and wide swaths of the Central Valley and the Sierra foothills were Republican country. The 1958 election of Brown's father, Pat Brown, a beloved progressive who presided over an expansion of highways, state universities, and the state's water system, was an anomaly in the history of California politics. Prior to his election, there had been only one other Democrat elected governor in the twentieth century. The state went for every Republican presidential candidate between 1952 and 1988, with the exception of Barry Goldwater, who lost everywhere except in the Deep South and his own state of Arizona.

Brown, elected on the strength of his father's reputation, came into office with the instincts of a progressive, promising a governorship that was transparent and incorruptible, a promise that he largely kept. But his style was markedly different than his father's. He did not possess the warmth and gregariousness that were the elder Brown's stock-in-trade. Whereas his father genuinely enjoyed political dinners and ribbon cuttings, his son's idea of relaxation was quiet time at the Tassajara Zen Center or a Trappist monetary in Northern California. He also had little use for the regal trappings of the governorship, canceling the inaugural ball, banning the receipt of gifts, even from the most well-meaning citizens, driving his own blue Plymouth Satellite rather than the state-provided Cadillac limousine, and refusing to live in the governor's mansion that his predecessor, Ronald Reagan, had the state build in suburban Sacramento. Instead, the bachelor and former seminary student rented a $250-a-month flat across the street from the Capitol, where he slept on a mattress and box spring on the floor. He came into office mostly unburdened by political promises and detailed policy prescriptions, espousing instead a movement of spiritual renewal for the nation, a sort of New Age vision of government that fit into the West Coast ethos of the 1970s.

As it turned out, his progressive instincts were hemmed in by the political climate of the mid-1970s. The New Deal liberalism that had held sway since the end of the war, culminating in the enormous social investment of Johnson's Great Society, was about to give way to a new parsimony on the part of elected officials. This was the era of the Vietnam debacle and the OPEC oil embargo, which caused oil prices to quadruple between 1973 and 1974. The nation was in the grips of a new economic malady known as stagflation, with slack demand and high inflation, once considered mutually exclusive, now galloping in unison. The nation's elected officials in both parties, at least in the mainstream, had little appetite for big government. Brown's disdain for profligacy in his personal life perfectly suited him to the era, and he made one of the recurrent themes of his speeches the need for sacrifice and lowered expectations, including limits on public spending. (He famously stated that University of California professors should settle for lesser pay raises because they derived "psychic income.") He pursued some liberal policies, like championing the environment and the United Farm Workers and appointing hundreds of women and minorities to judgeships and high-ranking positions in his administration. But he kept a lid on state spending, accumulating a budget surplus of $5 billion by 1978.

It was an astute reading of the electorate's mood. Toward the end of his first term, in June 1978, California voters overwhelmingly approved Proposition 13, a landmark initiative that amended the state's constitution to limit the tax on real property—residential or commercial—to 1 percent of assessed value. The measure also mandated that assessed value could only increase by 2 percent annually, except in cases where property was sold or substantially renovated, and it rolled back the value of properties to what they were in 1975–76. Overnight, the aggregate of municipal property tax revenues in California was slashed by 53 percent. This historic sundering of municipal finances may have been alleviated somewhat had the state been able to raise taxes and come fully to the rescue of local governments. But the measure also required that any tax increase at the *state level* be approved by two-thirds of both houses in the legislature or two-thirds of the voters, both impossible reaches in that era. California was fitted with a fiscal straitjacket that would impede its progress for generations, and as a matter of political survival, Brown had no choice but to go along. He had strongly opposed Proposition 13, calling the measure "consumer fraud, a rip-off, a legal morass and ... in reality a long-term tax increase, not a reduction." But once it was approved by nearly two-thirds of the voters and Brown watched his popularity plummet in the middle of his reelection campaign, he labeled himself "a born-again tax cutter" and embraced the draconian cuts in government spending that the amendment made unavoidable.

The state's first order of business was to use $4 billion of its surplus to bail out municipal governments, which otherwise would have been have been plunged into a full-scale fiscal emergency. In a special session of the legislature two days after the passage of Proposition 13, Brown also proposed $300 million in spending cuts. "The message is that property tax must be sharply curtailed, and that government spending, wherever it is, must be held in check," he told the lawmakers. "We must look forward to lean and frugal budgets. It's a great challenge, and we will meet it." Brown's about-face on the tax measure was so dramatic, to the consternation of some of his liberal supporters, that it even won over Howard Jarvis, the Los Angeles businessman and political gadfly who had led the state's tax revolt. Jarvis did a television spot for Brown's re-election bid, saying he "knew Gov. Brown was the man who could make it work." By 1980, the state budget surplus that Brown had so proudly amassed was gone.

Conservatives view Jarvis and the tax revolt he spearheaded in a sacred light. It set off movements for property tax reduction in many other states, including Proposition 2½ in Massachusetts, and helped lay the ground for the supply-side economics of the Reagan era. But there can be no doubt that Proposition 13 dimmed the fires of social progress in America's most populous state. As the longtime California journalist Miriam Pawel wrote, "By 1990, a decade of living under Proposition 13 had left overcrowded schools, broken-down parks, and crumbling roads." The deprivation was felt most dramatically in the realm of public education. California once ranked among the states with the highest per-pupil spending, but overnight plummeted to the bottom of the list and never recovered. In 2015–16, the state ranked forty-first in the nation in per-pupil outlays when states' cost of living are taken into account. By 2021, New York was spending $24,000 per pupil, Connecticut and New Jersey were each spending about $20,000, and California was only spending $12,000.

For decades, public education in California, as in most other states, had been funded primarily by local governments. But Proposition 13 shifted the funding to the state, which was now severely limited by the two-thirds provision in funneling needed state monies for education. Four years after the passage of the measure, many urban school districts were still starved of resources and were offering substantially less to their students than they had before 1978. Phil Linscomb, the assistant superintendent for instruction, told a *Los Angeles Times* education reporter in 1982 that many schools had eliminated the sixth period of instruction for eleventh- and twelve-graders, which resulted in many students doing without electives like music, industrial arts, journalism, and typing. Michael Kirst, a Stanford University professor who had previously been head of the State Board of Education, reported that he had researched a puzzling drop in California's SAT scores in the early 1980s and found that students were taking fewer courses in English, math, history, and science.

The diminution of educational resources has continued over the decades. In 2017–18, the average class size for high schools in California was eighteen students, compared with eleven in Massachusetts, New Jersey, and Maryland, ten in Rhode Island, and twelve in New York. California's number had improved from a decade earlier, when it was twenty-two, but the state's classes were still much more crowded in comparison to other progressive states. Proposition 13 was one in an endless number of corrosive legacies that the Great Inflation wreaked on American society in the 1970s. California's property values—and property tax bills—escalated so dramatically because of inflation that a tax revolt was hardly surprising. But the unintended consequences of the measure have been enormous. Starved of property tax revenue, municipalities across the state began courting commercial rather than residential development, so they could reap sales taxes from retail establishments. This in turn aggravated the state's housing shortage and blighted the landscape with superfluous commercial sprawl. But the greater tragedy is the incalculable amounts of money that have been denied municipal governments for schools and other services that could have made a difference in their citizens' lives. When conservatives mock California for its lackluster schools or pitted roadways, they forget that it was a right-wing tax revolt that precipitated its neglect of public services.

Some of the inequities in California's patchwork of property taxes are mind-boggling. The *Los Angeles Times* reported that the high-tech giant Intel, because it bought the land for its Santa Clara headquarters in the 1970s, was paying only $227,000 an acre in property taxes in 2018. Compare that with the San Jose property Adobe Systems bought in 2018, with a tax bill of $27 million an acre. Billionaire investor Warren Buffett pointed out the absurdity of California's municipal tax structure in a 2003 interview with the *Wall Street Journal*. In comments that later elicited a rebuke from the *Journal*'s conservative editorial page because they dared to question the sanctity of tax relief, the Berkshire Hathaway chairman said his annual taxes on a $500,000 home in Omaha, Nebraska, were more than $14,000, while he only paid $2,300 for a $4 million home in Laguna Beach, California. "In effect," Buffett told the paper, "it makes no sense."

Sensical or not, Brown made his piece with Proposition 13 and completed his first eight-year tenure as governor without any meaningful public investment. He chose not to seek reelection and, his popularity waning, lost to Pete Wilson, San Diego's Republican mayor, in his 1982 bid to become a U.S. senator. With the Reagan Revolution now in full flower, California was not done thrashing about in the morass of far-right politics. The state that would one day be an international symbol of social progress was more notable in the 1980s and 1990s for prison building, harsh criminal justice policies, and intolerance toward racial minorities and immigrants. Between 1983 and 2015, the number of inmates in California's prisons and local jails more than doubled, going from 81,000 to 204,000. Brown's two immediate successors as governor, Republicans George Deukmejian and Pete Wilson, presided over law-and-order governorships that redounded to the state's shame. Deukmejian campaigned successfully for the voters' recall of three of Brown's liberal appointees to the California Supreme Court, including the controversial Rose Bird, who served as chief justice and the first woman appointed to the court. He also championed passage of harsher sentencing laws and, in 1989, opened the notorious Pelican Bay Prison, where more than a thousand inmates were held in complete isolation in small windowless cells twenty-three to twenty-four hours a day, some for more than two decades. The Center for Constitutional Rights alleged that such conditions amounted to torture and called Pelican Bay "an outlier in this country and in the civilized world."

Pete Wilson was no less assiduous in pandering to the law-and-order constituency, endorsing the ballot initiative in 1994 that created the nation's most stringent "three-strikes" law, under which an inmate with two previous felony convictions would automatically get twenty-five years to life for a third offense, no matter how minor. Thus a twenty-seven-year-old Compton warehouse employee received a sentence of twenty-five years to life in 1995 for stealing a slice of pepperoni pizza from children on the Redondo Beach Pier. Another defendant, a twenty-three-year-old with bipolar disorder and an IQ of 70, got thirty years to life for stealing a video recorder and coin collection from his neighbors. The injustices of the three-strikes law and other extreme law enforcement measures fell disproportionately on minorities, which didn't exactly generate public outrage. For it was also in the Wilson years—again with his endorsement—that voters backed Proposition 209, which outlawed any preferential treatment for minorities in public employment, public contracts, and state university admissions. The measure had the predictable effect of reducing the percentages of Black and Hispanics admitted to California's top state universities, hardly to the state's advantage. In 2017, Blacks made up 3.4 percent of students admitted to UC Berkeley, a figure lower than it was in 1972.

But the aspect of Wilson legacy most to his discredit, and with the widest ramifications for the future, was his strong support for Proposition 187, a successful 1994 voter initiative that outlawed the provision of any public services to undocumented immigrants, including education. It is hard to imagine a measure more mean-spirited and detrimental to the state's future—and to the future of the Republican Party in California. Later found to be unconstitutional, Proposition 187 woke up a sleeping giant, galvanizing the growing numbers of Hispanic voters to become more active in state politics. Even the conservative Cato Institute described it later as sounding a death knell for the state's GOP. Frank del Olmo, a Mexican-born deputy editorial page editor at the *Los Angeles Times*, predicted as much in 1994. Dissenting from the paper's endorsement of Wilson in 1994, del Olmo wrote that the governor had scapegoated undocumented immigrants for the state's economic problems and that Hispanic voters would have long memories. "By aligning himself with the immigration issue in its most bigoted form, he has given legitimacy to an ugly streak of bigotry in California," he wrote. "And Latinos everywhere will never forgive him for that. . . . Wilson's pro-187 campaign will stick in our craws for generations." In 1990, Wilson had picked up nearly 50 percent of the Hispanic vote; eight years later, the Republican candidate, Dan Lungren, got the support of less than 20 percent of Hispanics, and lost the race to Democrat Gray Davis by twenty points. That daunting arithmetic for the GOP would only get worse as the Hispanic population continued to grow over the next two decades, reaching 39 percent of the state's population in 2020.

By the time Jerry Brown announced his plans for a second act as governor, after stints as Oakland mayor and state attorney general, California was no longer the same state politically and Brown himself had undergone a personal intellectual odyssey. The GOP was pretty much washed up as a viable force in the state's politics. In 2008, the state went for Barack Obama by twenty-four points, and the re-election of Governor Arnold Schwarzenegger and the nod given to State Insurance Commissioner Steve Poizner, both in 2006, would be the last time, as of this writing, that any Republicans ascended to statewide office in California. On the campaign trail in 2010, Brown still positioned himself as a fiscal conservative, vowing not to raise personal or corporate income taxes without the assent of the voters. But he was unabashed in expressing misgivings about some of the conservative positions he took in his first stint as governor. He was particularly contrite about his $94 million prison-building plan and his support for determinate sentencing, which mandated minimum penalties for different types of crimes and removed the ability of judges and parole officials to grant leniency.

Brown had boasted in 1982 that nineteen thousand people would go to prison that year, double the number locked up when he first took office. He would come to regret such enthusiasm for the imprisonment of his fellow citizens, as the prison-building tab rose to $3 billion under his successor, new and harsher sentencing laws proliferated, and the prison population grew more than sevenfold between 1980 and 2006. Even though the state opened twenty-one new prisons in that period, overcrowding became so dire by 2010 that inmates were forced to triple-bunk in gymnasiums, in some instances fifty-four inmates shared a single toilet, the prison suicide rate was 80 percent higher than the national average, and health care was so bad the state averaged a preventable inmate death every week—conditions that prompted the U.S. Supreme Court to order a sharp reduction in the state's inmate population. Meanwhile, mass incarceration proved to be ineffective in controlling crime. "What [did] we do to them?" Brown asked the author Jim Newton in his later years, as he reflected on the human toll of the state's penal system. "Locking someone in a cage and having guards who are not allowed to be familiar, very mechanistic, lockdowns and gang members, crazy people yelling and screaming, dope being smuggled in, tobacco being sold, people being prostituted, people being raped. Is that a good thing? It doesn't sound like it, does it?"

Having helped California lead the nation toward a grim carceral network in his first governorship, Brown used his political comeback to spearhead criminal justice reforms that would be just as influential in the other direction. He put forth a corrections "realignment" in California that moved tens of thousands of nonviolent inmates from state prisons to county jails, with the idea that county sheriffs and probation departments would be better equipped to supervise their eventual release at the local level. While the program drew criticism that state officials were merely transferring the burden of the correctional system to local governments—prompting a new boom in the construction of correctional facilities, this time in the form of county jails—realignment gradually led to the accelerated release of nonviolent inmates. Brown also pushed successfully for voters to support initiatives that changed many nonviolent drug and property crimes from felonies to misdemeanors, restored discretion to sentencing judges and parole officials, and reformed the three-strikes law so that the third strike had to be a serious or violent offense.

The initiatives had a pronounced impact. California's prison population had increased from 50,000 in 1985 to a peak of 173,000 in 2006. It stood at more than 160,000 when Brown was elected to his third term in 2010; but by the time he left office at the end of 2018, the number had fallen to 128,000, a decline of 26 percent from its peak. The governor had undergone a philosophical metamorphosis from his days as law-and-order zealot, and he was unafraid to admit it. "We are all sinners," he told a criminal justice forum in San Diego. "Every one of you people. We all do bad things. A little humility in the face of people who do bad things is called for." He was forthright in claiming his share of the blame for the travesty of the state's prison overcrowding. "I helped screw things up," he said, "and I helped unscrew things." California's criminal justice reforms have continued since Brown left office. When the pandemic forced states around the country to reduce their inmate populations in 2020, California's number went below 100,000 for the first time in thirty years.

The Jerry Brown who returned to the governorship office in 2011 had, in some respects, more in common with his father than the young and cocksure politician who took office in 1975 as a disciple of lowered expectations for state government. He now set his sights on the kind of big infrastructure projects that his father had used to lay the groundwork for the state's explosive growth in the postwar era. In particular, he wanted to shepherd the construction of a high-speed train between San Francisco and Los Angeles—and ultimately tying in San Diego and Sacramento—which he was convinced would reduce vehicle emissions, promote economic development, and spur the creation of high-wage construction jobs. He also wanted to tackle one of California's most existential threats—the depletion of its water supply—with a $19 billion plan to construct two massive tunnels under the Sacramento–San Joaquin River Delta to help convey water to parched agricultural regions and big cities in Southern California. But standing in the way of these massive projects and other key initiatives, such as shoring up the finances of the University of California and K-12 education, was the continued legacy of Proposition 13 and Brown's own pledge that he would not seek any tax increases without the assent of the voters.

Brown's predecessor, Arnold Schwarzenegger, had left him with a financial catastrophe. California's budget is heavily reliant on state income tax revenue, more than half of which comes from wealthy households whose earnings are often subject to the boom-and-bust cycles of Wall Street. The 2008 financial crisis was the biggest bust since the Great Depression, and it cut deeply into California's revenue. Faced with a $42 million budget hole, Schwarzenegger and legislative leaders managed to secure a two-thirds supermajority for a package that included a temporary increase for all income tax brackets of 0.25 percent and a 1 percent sales tax hike, coupled with spending cuts. But with those increases expiring at the end of 2010, Brown came into office with a $26.6 billion budget deficit and a Republican minority unwilling to toss him the lifeline they had willingly given to Schwarzenegger. GOP lawmakers rebuffed Brown's proposal that an extension of the 2009 tax increases be put before the voters. Their rationale was that any new taxes would stifle business investment in the state, as if a financial default or a catastrophic reduction in funding for education and other services would not. Rather than hand Brown any kind of political victory, they would opt for fiscal Armageddon. It was this impending financial disaster—which posed a real threat of bankruptcy for the state—that prompted the original round of media accounts predicting an apocalypse for the Golden State, including a March 2010 headline in *Business Insider* claiming that "California Is Doomed."

But California was not doomed, and neither was Brown's governorship. Unable to win the support of Republican legislators, Brown and his supporters collected enough signatures to put the tax question directly to the voters in the fall of 2011, and they won by a comfortable margin. It was like the planets were knocked out of their orbits—voters in California, the land of the tax revolt, where Proposition 13 was still sacrosanct, chose to raise their own taxes. Even more amazing, 63 percent of the voters agreed in 2016 to maintain those taxes for at least another twelve years. California had achieved fiscal stability and a mandate for public investment for the first time since 1978. Funding flowed into schools, roadways, and higher education, and when Brown left office in 2019, his state had a comfortable budget surplus.

Besides restoring the financial health of his state, Brown could point to a host of other accomplishments during his comeback years. Under his leadership, the state established an earned-income tax credit for the poor, became the first in the country to phase in a $15 minimum wage, and, after the passage of Obamacare, aggressively expanded the state's Medi-Cal program, reducing the portion of uninsured from 20 to 7 percent. He also overhauled K-12 funding and helped restore the reputation of the University of California, to the point that its campuses were nationally recognized for providing affordable education to poor and middle-class students.

Like any governor, Brown did have his setbacks. He never achieved the most important goals of his infrastructure plan. The high-speed rail was saddled with huge cost overruns, mismanagement, difficulties in acquiring land, and declining public support, the latter arising in part because of a Republican effort to denigrate the project. Newsom, newly elected, made conflicting statements about whether he supported the project, and as of early 2022, construction was limited to a 119-mile stretch in the Central Valley. Brown's vision for a San Francisco–Los Angeles connection seemed to have receded to the backwaters of the state's priorities. Brown's plan for two water tunnels beneath the Sacramento–San Joaquin River Delta fared no better, scaled down to a single tunnel after it ran into opposition from environmentalists and communities in Northern California who resented what they saw as a potential raid on their water supplies by powerful business and agricultural interests in the southern part of the state.

In the end, Brown will probably be best remembered, in this country and around the world, for his passionate defense of the planet. As the leader of a state with the fifth largest economy in the world and an outsized influence on national environmental policy, he became a globe-trotting spokesman for the effort to confront climate change. "Human civilization is on the chopping block," he told legislators in Stuttgart, Germany, on a four-country tour in 2017 aimed at building support for the eradication of fossil fuels. "We have to wake up Europe, and wake up America, and wake up the whole world to realize that we have a common destiny and what's at stake." Being an international ambassador for climate issues meant leading the blue-state resistance to the Trump administration's destructive environmental policies, and Brown took on that role with relish. He once called climate skeptics "troglodytes," and when Trump, the chief skeptic, threatened to deactivate the NASA satellites collecting climate data, he blustered: "If Trump turns off the satellites, we'll launch our own damn satellites." During Trump's four years in office, California Attorney General Xavier Becerra filed more than a hundred lawsuits against federal agencies involved in environmental issues.

Brown made sure to back up his eloquence on the world stage with action in his own backyard. One of the reasons he picked up the nickname "Governor Moonbeam" was his advocacy for wind and solar power in the 1970s, long before it was fashionable, and he tackled the issue with renewed vigor in his second governorship. He signed executive orders committing the state to reduce greenhouse gas emissions 40 percent below 1990 levels by 2030, have all electricity carbon-free by 2045, and have the state's entire economy carbon neutral by 2045. He also set a goal of five million electric cars on California roadways by 2030. The signing of executive orders is no guarantee the goals will be achieved in the long term, but he created substantial likelihood of major greenhouse gas reductions by convincing the necessary two-thirds of the legislature to extend the "cap-and-trade" legislation that Schwarzenegger signed in 2013. The program allows polluters to trade carbon-emission rights with others companies, bringing about overall reductions. The program has already generated billions in state revenue from the auction of those rights, money that must be used for carbon-reduction programs. Under the legislation, which Brown signed into law in 2017, 35 percent of the auction revenue must be set aside for programs in environmentally disadvantaged and low-income neighborhoods.

Amid the usual Republican obstructionism, winning reauthorization of the program was a battle that required not a little horse trading on Brown's part, including the promise of favors for key legislators at the district level in exchange for their support. But Brown's passion in selling the measure also didn't hurt. The day before the vote, he made a rare appearance before a legislative committee to appeal for votes. He told them that he, at seventy-nine years old, would not be around to witness the dire consequences of a failure to confront climate change, but that many of them would. "When I look out here," he said, "a lot of people are going to be alive. And you'll be alive in a horrible situation. You are going to see mass migrations, vector diseases, forest fires, Southern California burning up. That's real, guys. That's what the scientists of the world are saying. I'm not here about some cockamamie legacy the people talk about. This isn't for me. I'm going to be dead. It's for you. It's for you, and it's damn real."

* * * *

JERRY BROWN MAY have left his successor a budget surplus, a reformed criminal justice system, and a blueprint for limiting greenhouse gas emissions, but Gavin Newsome came into office staring at a virtual policy void on an issue of profound importance to the state. Along with wildfires and water, the biggest threat to the state's future growth at the outset of Newsom's governorship was the soaring cost of housing. In July 2021, the California Association of Realtors pegged the median sale price of a single-family home at an astounding $811,000, up from $666,000 a year earlier. It was the highest median value in the country, with the exception of Hawaii. In the San Francisco Bay Area, the median price was $1.3 million. Other states that are magnets for wealthy buyers have also seen skyrocketing values for single-family homes—especially while the pandemic was driving affluent city dwellers to the suburbs. In September 2021, the *Boston Globe* reported that a one-room, 251-square-foot home facing a highway in the affluent suburb of Newton was on the market for $449,000. But California's real estate is in a class by itself. The high cost of housing tears at the social fabric of California, not only driving people out of the state but helping to deepen the poverty rate for those who remain. In the Census Bureau's official poverty measure for the years 2017 to 2019, California's rate of 11.4 percent was the twentieth-highest in the nation. But in the supplemental poverty measure, which takes into account housing costs and government assistance and is viewed by most experts as a more meaningful gauge of economic distress, California's rate was 17.2 percent, the highest of any state.

The Golden State is still a place of dreams for the affluent, but it has become a landscape of inequality and dislocation for the poor and working class. In coastal cities like Los Angeles and San Francisco, soaring housing prices have unleashed tides of gentrification in formerly low-rent districts as young middle-class professionals seek affordable places to live. This in turn forces the poor, predominantly people of color, into more crowded and sometimes unsafe housing situations, where they pay an ever-increasing share of their income for rent. One study in 2017 found that more than half of the low-income occupants in rented California housing were paying more than half of their income to their landlords. Faced with that kind of economic pressure, many families have left the cities and moved inland, driving up prices there and creating an economic divide between affluent coastal areas and the more modest communities of the interior. Others cannot leave their employment behind and are forced into extreme deprivation. A depressing number end up living in their cars or motor homes, to the point where several communities in Santa Clara County, including San Jose, have set up special zones where workers sleeping in their vehicles are permitted to park overnight.

If that was the entirety of the state's housing crisis, it would be bad enough. But for too many Californians, a home inside a vehicle would be a luxury. Estimates in 2020 put the average census of homeless people in the state at more than 150,000. Granted, it is nearly impossible to gauge how much of this is due to mental illness or substance abuse as opposed to evictions from a brutal housing market. An academic study funded by Zillow found that communities in which people spend more than 32 percent of their income on rent also see an uptick in homelessness. But you don't have to be a sociologist to know that out-of-control housing prices bear at least some of the blame for California's notorious homeless encampments. Entire blocks of Los Angeles, San Francisco, and elsewhere have been transformed into tent cities reminiscent of the Hoovervilles of the 1930s. Sidewalks smeared with human feces and drug addicts openly shooting up in broad daylight are images that put even the most diehard boosters of California on the defensive. Such a tableau of human indignity is not just a national shame but an international embarrassment. Leilani Farha, the United Nations special rapporteur on adequate housing, included the Bay Area in a tour of homeless encampments worldwide—all the rest of her stops were in developing nations— and was so shocked by what she saw in Oakland and San Francisco that her report found California guilty of human rights violations. "I'm sorry," she told the SFGate website. "California is a rich state, by any measures, the United States is a rich country, and to see these deplorable conditions that the government is allowing, by international human rights standards, is unacceptable."

California's housing crisis is a product of long-standing resistance in local communities to the construction of multi-family housing. In leafy suburbs and in some residential districts of big cities like San Francisco, Los Angeles, and San Diego, homeowners have a well-grounded fear that lifting the single-family zoning that prevails in their neighborhoods would lead to overdevelopment, add traffic, and change the character of their communities. Their resistance could be seen as an act of civic self-preservation in a state whose population exploded in the twentieth century, going from 2 million in 1900 to 34 million in 2000. If it sometimes seemed that everyone on the planet wanted to be in California, it is perhaps understandable that some who got there first wanted to close the door. Local elected officials have accommodated their constituents' NIMBYism by erecting a Hadrian's Wall of regulations that make it impossible to build even duplexes—let alone apartment buildings—in many neighborhoods. And it is not just a case of upper and middle classes seeking to ward off an influx of Black and Hispanic renters. Residents in low-income neighborhoods fear that liberalized zoning regulations would open the door for luxury apartment buildings, drive up rents, and further displace poor families. "Housing politics in California is a hornets' nest of powerful interest groups," Matt Levin wrote on the CalMatters news site. "Developers, realtors, big tech, cities, counties, environmental groups, landlords, anti-gentrification advocates and homeowner groups all lobby lawmakers and the governor one way or the other. It's part of the reason inertia is the default state of things." According to Levin, even the powerful State Building and Construction Trades Council is an impediment to zoning change because it sees expedited review in the construction of low-income housing as a threat to union-level wages and other labor protections.

All these competing interests are why past proposals to give the state power to override local zonings restrictions never made it out of the legislature, defeated by Democrats and Republicans alike. When a Democratic state senator, Scott Wiener, proposed a bill in 2018 (Senate Bill 827) that would have allowed eight-story buildings near transit stops—whether or not municipalities approved them—even the state chapter of the Sierra Club, long an opponent of suburban sprawl, objected to the legislation, arguing that it was so "heavy handed" voters would be turned off on mass transit. Wiener tried again in 2019 with similar legislation, Senate Bill 50, but it also went down in defeat, after attacks from a coalition, Livable California, that included both suburban homeowners and inner-city opponents of gentrification. These may be civic-minded activists who genuinely care about their neighborhoods, but the result of such obstructionism is that the state's housing supply has failed disastrously to keep pace with population growth. A 2016 study by the McKinsey Global Institute found that California needed to build 3.5 million homes by 2025 to meet its housing needs. The study found that the affordability crisis was as acute in rural communities like Salinas and Watsonville as it was in coastal cities and that, overall, Californians were paying $50 billion more in housing costs annually than they were able to afford. "We learned that 50 percent of California's households cannot afford the cost of housing in their local market," the study's authors wrote. "Virtually none of California's low-income and very-low-income households can afford the local cost of housing." They also concluded that the housing shortage was costing the state $140 billion a year in lost economic output.

In his 2018 campaign, Newsom pledged that he would launch a "Marshall Plan" to build 3.5 million homes by 2025—adopting the McKinsey Global Institute's recommendation—and promised an assault on the homelessness problem. It was the hubris of a candidate whose bold ideas had never brought him anything but success in his political career, but he soon had cause to regret such lofty promises. The goal of millions of new homes in such a short period of time was widely criticized as an impossibility, especially after the onslaught of the pandemic impeded new construction. Indeed, the pace of new home construction actually slackened in 2019 and 2020. Newsom quietly backed away from his pledge once in office—by the end of 2019 he was referring to it awkwardly as a "stretch goal." He also declined to join the politically perilous debate over zoning reform, giving only tepid support—never an outright endorsement—to Senate Bills 827 and 50.

That is not to say Newsom was feckless in the face of the housing crisis during the first part of his governorship. Under his predecessor, California had already begun passing a series of laws that gave many single-family homeowners the right to build accessory dwelling units, or ADUs, in their backyards, and to add another unit of up to 500 square feet within their homes as junior accessory dwelling units, or JADUs, which together have spurred the development of tens of thousands of new units, often at below-market rates. Newsom propelled the ADU innovation forward by removing certain regulatory barriers and by providing funding for construction. He also poured billions in new initiatives to provide low- and medium-income housing units, including many geared toward sheltering the homeless. Most significantly, he began vigorous state enforcement of an existing law, enacted in 1967, that required municipalities to plan and set aside land for new housing construction. The law had almost never been enforced in the half-century after its adoption, but the Newsom administration dusted it off and, shortly after the governor's inauguration, filed a lawsuit against the city of Huntington Beach, accusing it of failing to meet its obligation. The state's Department of Housing and Community Development followed up with hundreds of letters warning municipalities to revise their planning codes to accommodate new housing.

But with data showing no increase in housing starts in Newsom's first two years in office, many began to wonder what happened to the Newsom Marshall Plan. "It seems like a pretty meaningful failure," Michael Lens, a professor of urban planning and public policy at UCLA, told the *Los Angeles Times*. "Either a failure of commitment or a failure of effort." What began to look like the governor's housing flop became fodder in the 2021 recall campaign, with Larry Elder, the Trump-like radio personality who was the Republican most likely to succeed Newsom if he lost, declaring that he would issue a state emergency declaration over homelessness. With the recall hanging over him, Newsom became gun-shy about signing any legislation that might prove divisive. Hundreds of bills piled up on his desk, including many pieces of legislation geared toward easing the shortage of affordable housing.

Great conflagrations, like wars or pestilence, have a way of upending societies. They prod somnolent politicians to action, causing them to heed the call of the public and rethink their opposition to programs that once may have seemed too risky. Moderates can become firebrands, as was the case with Franklin Roosevelt and Robert Kennedy. The pandemic was one of those events, and in California it posed an existential threat in a way that it did not in other places. The pandemic freed many white-collar employees—tech workers, software designers, financial consultants, and anyone else whose workspace is essentially a computer screen—from having to report to an office, perhaps ever again. Suddenly they had no need to pay some of the highest housing prices in the country. They could move to Idaho, Texas, or Montana and not only escape crushing rents and mortgages, but also traffic jams, wildfires, and sidewalks cluttered with the homeless. At the end of 2020, media were reporting that tens of thousands of households—one estimate put the number at eighty-nine thousand—had left San Francisco alone since the pandemic had begun. It later became clear that the talk of exodus was overblown and that many were temporary relocations. But the pandemic drove home to many Californians, especially those in elected office, that fifty years of inaction on the mounting housing crisis could no longer be sustained if the state were not to become a hideously unequal society. History may well show that it was a transformative moment for Gavin Newsom, just as the Depression was for Roosevelt and the Vietnam War, inner-city riots, and the assassination of his brother were for RFK. After winning the recall vote by a wide margin, Newsom emerged with a new mandate to take bold action on homelessness and housing affordability, with both the state's economic future and his own political career hanging in the balance.

On September 16, 2021, two days after the recall election, Newsom signed two pieces of housing legislation that could mark a historic—and deeply controversial—reversal of the political stasis that has long stood in the way of solving the affordability crisis. Senate Bill 9, introduced by the state's senate president, Toni Atkins, outlawed single-family zoning statewide, except under limited circumstances, such as historic districts and fire-hazard areas, giving any homeowner the right to convert a one-unit home into a duplex or, if the property is large enough, to subdivide and build two duplexes. Senate Bill 10, introduced by the indefatigable Scott Wiener, allows municipalities—if they so choose—to easily rezone neighborhoods near rapid-transit stations, and on parcels made up of vacant urban land, to accommodate buildings with up to ten units. One provision of the bill gave municipalities the right to opt out of rezoning, which was designed to mollify critics of 2019's failed Senate Bill 50, which would have forced municipalities to accept multi-family zoning in certain districts.

The fight over the two pieces of legislation did not end with Newsom's signature. Within days a Los Angeles nonprofit, AIDS Healthcare Foundation, filed a lawsuit claiming S.B. 10 was unconstitutional because it allowed cities to override zoning laws created by voter initiatives. Michael Lawson, president of the Los Angeles Urban League, complained that it would lead to gentrification rather than affordable housing. "It's a birthday present to the developers," he said. "It will decimate our communities." Others opposed the two bills because of what they saw as their potential to set back efforts at historic preservation, especially a provision in S.B. 10 that allows municipalities, in approving rezoning, to bypass review under the California Environmental Quality Act, a 1970 law that—among many other provisions—has helped preservationists defeat development proposals based on their community impact. "S.B. 10 establishes enabling legislation where jurisdictions can choose to opt in or not, yet there are no safeguards for historic resources once adopted," the Los Angeles Conservancy wrote in an overview of the laws. "It will allow communities to upzone parcels and override existing zoning with little public input or review." Even before Newsom put his signature on the two bills, a group called Californians for Community Planning began collecting signatures to put the issue of local control over zoning on the November 2022 ballot.

Rarely have so many progressive groups been at loggerheads over legislative action. The opponents of the two bills are not hastily formed nonprofits acting as front groups for corporate interests. They are citizens standing up for voter initiatives, historic preservation, and the fight against gentrification, all issues that progressives would normally get behind. The overarching lesson is that there is no easy solution to California's housing crisis. Every special interest, even the most salutary, must give up something to stave off disaster for the state. And California is hardly alone. Affluent cities across the country, from Boston and Seattle to Washington, DC, are facing the same affordability crisis. A restaurant owner in the Outer Banks of North Carolina told the author that the lack of affordable housing in the affluent beach community is part of what is driving the local labor shortage. As the *Los Angeles Times* wrote in an editorial endorsing S.B. 9 and 10, zoning reform is a reckoning that the entire country must soon face:

> This isn't just a California problem. Across the nation, about 75 percent of residential land is zoned exclusively for single-family homes. Too many communities make it too hard to build a diverse housing stock. They prioritize the construction and preservation of single-family homes, at the exclusion of apartments, condos and townhomes that would be more affordable to middle and lower-income renters and buyers. That is fueling a housing shortage; the U.S. needs 3.8 million more homes to meet the demand of household growth and to provide

enough inventory that prices stabilize. . . . Ending single-family zoning is not the silver bullet to end California's housing crisis. But it is an important piece of a larger effort in the state—and the nation—to fix failed policies and misplaced priorities that have led to a broken housing market and woefully inadequate housing safety net.

An analysis by the Terner Center for Housing Innovation at UC Berkeley concluded that S.B. 9—if it survived court challenges—would at best allow construction of 410,000 new units on what are now single-family parcels. It found that the majority of the state's 7.5 million single-family homes are not feasible for duplex conversion either because of size limitations or market realities. But if you add 1.8 million new units that could potentially be built as ADUs or JADUs, the number of homes that could be added to the state's housing stock comes to about 2.2 million. No one knows if homeowners will convert at the rate necessary to fulfill this potential or whether an explosion of duplexes would lower rents. But the response to the laws allowing accessory dwelling units has been impressive. Between 2017 and 2019, California cities issued more than 26,000 ADU permits, 11,500 of them in Los Angeles, and that was before the state and some municipalities enacted policies to quicken the pace of construction.

California's housing crisis, decades in the making, was not a product of progressive governance, as right-wing commentators claim. A host of special interests, spanning the ideological spectrum, conspired to keep restrictive single-family zoning in place. But the massive effort to rezone the state and deal with the crisis came from the left and was largely opposed by Republicans. As of August 2021, every GOP candidate seeking to unseat Newsom in the recall pledged to veto S.B. 9 and 10. California has embraced a revolutionary movement to shift the power over local zoning from municipal governments to the state, which is likely to embolden similar experimentation in other states with burgeoning housing crises. It has been a long time coming, but the Golden State is embarked on aggressive efforts to solve problems that had been neglected through the decades of right-wing leadership.

* * * *

IT IS IMPOSSIBLE to imagine Texas Governor Greg Abbott standing before an international forum and speaking passionately about a threat to humanity. Or to picture him taking responsibility for the wrongs his state has done to it poorest citizens and trying to set them right. Jerry Brown did these things. But it is simply not in the nature of Abbott to look beyond his own political career and the interests of the corporate donors who make that career possible—and that is the tragedy that overlays the governance of America's second most populous state. To conceive of Texas's current leaders as models for the country is to care little about the fate of the poor and the middle class, about racial and gender equality, about the health of the planet, about democracy, about our place in the community of civilized nations.

The problems that beset the working people of Texas have been festering for years and have only been exacerbated by the state's enormous population growth. The low-cost housing that has proved to be such a lure for migrants from California and other states may soon be a thing of the past. Rents are rising fast in cities like San Antonio, Houston, and Austin, and the lack of affordable housing is already a crisis. The deficiencies of the state's child welfare system broke out into the open in October 2021, when authorities in western Harris County found three abandoned children living in a home with no power, along with the skeletal remains of their long-dead sibling stuffed in a closet. The discovery came a decade after a federal court ordered Texas to repair its child welfare agencies and sixteen months after court-appointed monitors described a "disjointed and dangerous child-protection system . . . where harm to children is at times overlooked, ignored or forgotten." A *Houston Chronicle* investigation found in early

2021 that the state's mental health system was severely over-burdened, with waitlists for beds of up to a year. "The state's lack of oversight is so extreme that officials were unable to say which private hospitals received state funds for bed space to help reduce the waitlist," the report said. The state would not provide the newspaper details on a hundred people who died in mental hospitals between 2014 and 2019. Texas's failure to properly regulate its power grid left it defenseless against freezing temperatures in the winter of 2021 that led to two hundred deaths and a loss of power to millions of homes. The Texas legislature responded by passing a law ordering natural gas facilities to weatherize their equipment, but left loopholes that allow many companies to ignore the requirement. As winter approached in 2021, independent experts found that the industry was doing little to avoid a repeat of the disaster. A state with an abundance of natural resources and a booming private sector has the highest percentage of people without medical insurance, the highest number of shuttered rural hospitals, and rural counties with almost no doctors. It ranks toward the bottom of the fifty states in the quality of schools, in the number of people living in poverty, in the number who die of preventable illnesses, and in the amount of toxic chemicals released into the air and water.

In the face of such mounting problems, what are the priorities of the state's governor and legislature? It only takes a cursory review of Texas headlines to arrive at the answer. After Donald Trump's electoral defeat, Abbott announced that Texas would step in to help complete his border wall and dispatch state troopers and Texas Rangers to arrest asylum applicants on legally questionable state trespassing charges. The policy is manifestly counter to Texas's economic interests. The state's oil and gas industry relies on foreign-born workers and is going to need a lot more of them. A recent study by a multinational professional services company found that U.S. oil and gas companies will be short forty thousand qualified employees by the year 2025. The absurdity of Abbott's border initiative doesn't stop there. Innumerable immigration experts, including at the conservative Cato Institute, have found that border barriers are ineffective at controlling illegal migration and drug smuggling. But Abbott's move was not about effective policy or economic efficacy. It was all about politics. The governor was facing a far-right primary challenge in 2022 from Dallas businessman Don Huffines and wanted to throw some red meat to his conservative base.

Abbott was already more conservative than any previous Texas governor, but Huffines has helped pull him even more to the right. Abbott has issued orders outlawing mask mandates in Texas public schools and prohibiting companies from requiring employees to be vaccinated against COVID-19. After the international outrage provoked by photographs of Border Patrol agents on horseback rounding up terrified Haitian migrants, Abbott offered to hire any agents that federal authorities fired over the incident. The governor signed a voter-suppression bill so extreme it prompted a lawsuit by the U.S. Justice Department. He signed another bill, which most legal experts say is blatantly unconstitutional, that had the effect—at least in the short term—of shutting down every abortion clinic in the state. When Huffines raised a fuss about a section of the state child welfare agency website that linked to resources for LGBTQ youth, including suicide prevention, the state closed the section down. Less than nine hours after Trump publicly demanded that Texas conduct an audit of the state's 2020 presidential balloting—even though he won the state by five points—the Texas secretary of state's office announced a comprehensive audit of four counties.

The question hovering over Abbott's frenzy of right-wing policymaking is what any of it had to do with bettering the lives of Texans. California has embarked on vast new programs aimed at coping with the state's enormous challenges. Some may fail and some may succeed. But the state's goal is to create a better world not only for Californians, but for all of humanity. What has Texas done for humanity? Even China and Russia—the latter hugely dependent on its oil and natural gas sectors—have put forth plans to reduce emissions of greenhouse gases, the greatest threat to the health of the planet. Texas's leadership not only has no plan for the reduction of emissions but has not even adopted a strategy for responding to the effects of a heating planet. This in a state that is already coping with heat waves, droughts, hurricanes, floods, wildfires, and widespread power outages that scientists link to climate change. In a visit to the West Texas oil fields in January 2021, Abbott announced he had directed his state agencies to use "all lawful powers and tools" to block any moves by the Biden administration that threaten the state's energy sector. "I am in Midland," he said, "to make clear that Texas is going to protect the oil and gas industry from any type of hostile attack from Washington, D.C." That is not leadership. It is malfeasance. The question whether California or Texas stands as a model for the nation is one that answers itself.

9

Progressive Federalism

IN THE EVENT OF A REPUBLICAN RESURGENCE IN-
side the Beltway, blue states and blue cities will be thrust into the
role of sentinels. They will be alone in continuing to espouse the ide-
als of democracy and enlightenment that were the founding principles of the United States but have been jettisoned by GOP state
leaders across the country. Only they will be capable of mounting a
reliable bulwark against the threat of national backslide, a reversion
to the politics of crony capitalism and social inequality—or worse,
the emergence of an authoritarian regime in Washington. But they
will do so successfully only if they work together in combining and
weaponizing their superior economic and cultural resources.

Conservatives have long owned the concept of federalism, the
founders' belief that states should be free to tailor their government policies to local traditions and circumstances. They have
used federalism as an intellectual cudgel to justify neutering the
federal government, denying minority rights, and restoring sover-
eignty to state governments more easily manipulated by corporate
interests. What they never anticipated was the emergence of what
Yale law professor Heather Gerken has termed "progressive federalism," wherein states that account for an outsized share of the nation's economic and cultural output—namely, the blue states—turn
their weapon against them. That kind of federalism became a real

political force in the blue-state rebellion against the Trump admin-istration, and its further potential as an incubator of social and eco-nomic progress is enormous.

The threat of reversion to far-right national leadership hovers over America. While the Biden administration has made impressive strides toward restoring a federal commitment to public investment and social uplift, unified Republican opposition and the apostasy of two conservative Democratic senators, Joe Manchin and Kyrsten Sinema, blocked the full implementation of programs that enjoyed wide public support. With inflation raging and Biden's popularity having plummeted at the end of 2021, a Republican resurgence in the 2022 and 2024 national elections and the evisceration of many Biden programs loomed as a real possibility. As of this writing, the Republicans have state legislative majorities in twenty-eight states and, in most of them, were in a position to redraw congressional maps after the 2020 census to favor GOP candidates and pick up the five seats needed to regain a majority in the House. To this arithmetic add the voter-suppression tactics that most Republican-controlled states have enshrined in their laws since the 2020 elections—and the darker possibility that they may use such legislation to overturn unfa-vorable state election results—and what remain are dim prospects for a near-term progressive consensus in Washington.

But much has changed since conservatives held such sway over the nation in the decades following the Reagan Revolution. In the 1980s and 1990s, leaders of what are now considered blue states tended to walk in lockstep with right-leaning policies in Washing-ton, favoring budget austerity, deregulation, low taxes, and law-and-order regimes. Today's Democratic states have evolved into regional centers of progressivism that would be defiant of a national right-wing resurgence, maybe even more so than in the Trump era. And the economic power they could bring to this resistance—especially if it is combined with Democratic majorities in the biggest cities of the red states—is formidable.

Imagine the two big clusters of progressive states, on the Pacific coast and the top half of the Eastern Seaboard, as a political bloc whose members work in unison to influence the direction of the country. That hypothetical coalition would be made up of eleven states—the "Ocean Eleven," if you will—that went for Biden in the 2020 election and whose state leadership fully upholds progressive values. These eleven—Maryland, Delaware, New Jersey, New York, Connecticut, Rhode Island, Massachusetts, and Maine in the east, and California, Oregon, and Washington in the west—comprise only 12 percent of the country's square mileage and yet account for more than a third of its gross domestic product, a level of economic output that exceeds all but three of the world's nations. Their combined state budget expenditures make up nearly 39 percent of the nation's total. When the District of Columbia is included, they boast all of the Ivy league universities, most of the top technical schools and regional technology hubs, the bulk of the financial industry, all of the important publishers and media outlets, the federal bureaucracy in Washington, and the entertainment capitals of Los Angeles and New York.

But the blue *states* are only part of the economic resources that would come with a progressive coalition. Virtually all of the important centers of economic growth, technical expertise, and culture in the red states—Houston, Dallas–Fort Worth, Austin, San Antonio, Phoenix, Tucson, Charlotte, Raleigh-Durham, Atlanta, Miami, Memphis, Nashville, northern Virginia, just to name a few—are in metropolitan areas that are led by Democrats and supported Joe Biden. The combined populations of the Houston, Dallas–Fort Worth, Austin, and San Antonio metro areas make up 67 percent of the Texas population. The metro areas of Phoenix and Tucson alone account for 82 percent of Arizona's population. Those metropolitan areas are the economic engines of their states, the source of most of their important commerce and cultural production. Researchers at the Brookings Institution found in 2016 that the 472 counties carried by Hillary Clinton in the 2016 election, only 15 percent of the nation's total and mostly in metropolitan areas, accounted for 64 percent of the nation's economic output. Another study found that just twenty metropolitan areas generate 52 percent of the nation's GDP, with Phoenix alone accounting for 70 percent of Arizona's economic output. The tax money generated by the Democrat-led Phoenix area is why Doug Ducey can afford to funnel dollars to his cronies in the charter school industry. The liberal-leaning metropolitan areas of Texas pay for stunningly irrational schemes cooked up by Governor Greg Abbott, like using state funds to help build a border wall that would not stem the flow of drugs or migrants into his state. Most red-state governments, which would acquiesce in the destruction of green-energy projects, outlaw abortion, and suppress their citizens' right to vote, are sustained fiscally by metropolitan areas whose electoral majorities support none of those policies.

Red-state leaders have statutory means of ensuring that their most productive and creative citizens, the majorities in their metropolitan areas, continue turning over the biggest share of tax dollars for state government operations while having little say over policy. It is enshrined in most state constitutions that cities are "creatures of the state," prohibited from levying taxes or establishing regulations locally if they are proscribed at the state level. This has enabled red states to thwart the growing power and assertiveness of Democrat-led cities by enacting laws of "preemption" that block local government from taking actions to better the lives of their citizens or protect the environment, if the methods run afoul of conservative principles. Such laws have been on the books for many years, California's Proposition 13 being the most famous example. However, since the hard-right takeover of state legislatures beginning in the 2010s, GOP states have stepped up the use of preemption as a means of imposing ideological conformity on cities, with the help of model legislation developed by the corporate-backed American Legislative Exchange Council.

For instance, when Austin passed an ordinance that would prohibit the supply of natural gas to new buildings as of 2030, the local gas company, Texas Gas Service, successfully lobbied the state for a new law that barred local governments from discriminating against any source of energy. Likewise, when Austin and Travis County sought to impede the spread of Covid by stopping restaurants from allowing inside dining after 10:30 p.m. on weekends, Governor Greg Abbott issued an executive order overturning the regulation. The Economic Policy Institute in 2019 counted twenty-six states that had passed laws blocking local government from enacting minimum-wage requirements and a similar number of states that had put up barriers to paid leave, fair work scheduling, prevailing wages, and gig-worker protections. Florida Governor Ron DeSantis has been on a preemption rampage. He not only famously banned municipalities from setting Covid restrictions but also signed legislation in May 2021 that required local governments to pay damages of up to $100,000 if they enact gun regulations exceeding those set at the state level—this despite mass shootings at the Pulse nightclub in Orlando in 2016 and Marjory Stoneman Douglas High School in Parkland in 2018. Integrity Florida, a nonprofit research group, counted forty-two proposed bills in the 2020 legislative session that sought in some way to preempt local governments. "Preemption moves government action away from the entity closest to the people," wrote the report's authors, Alan Stonecipher and Ben Wilcox. "It can be used to block local ordinances that reflect a community's will to help women, people of color, LGBTQ people and those in poverty."

In a democratic nation that cast off the yoke of Great Britain with cries against "taxation without representation," it defies comprehension that our wealthiest, most productive, and most creative citizens—those who pay a disproportionate share of taxes—have allowed themselves to be disenfranchised. Progressives have the best minds and the deepest pockets at their disposal; they have the examples of other developed countries

moving ahead of America in so many realms of social and economic policy; and yet they allow U.S. public policy to be dictated
from the backwaters. The left has been less effective than its conservative counterparts at the state level because its activism is
disjointed and has not effectively emphasized bread-and-butter
issues that can lure swing voters away from the GOP. There is no
corporately funded legislative exchange council pushing model
state laws to help working people. To be sure, there are progressive billionaires like Tom Steyer and George Soros pouring
money into liberal causes, and grassroots organizing networks
like Indivisible, but not enough activists and lobbyists laboring
nonstop in the state and local legislatures, as groups associated
with the Koch brothers and other deep-pocketed conservatives
have been doing for years.

The most effective means for blue states to confront paralysis in
Washington—or a return to full Republican dominance—is for
them to band together in a movement of progressive federalism.
There is a wide array of tools that state leaders can use to influence
or even thwart federal policies, a morally legitimate exercise of power
when one of the two major parties is intent on upending democracy.
Washington depends on state and local governments to administer
a huge portion of its policies. As of 2021, the federal government
had 2.1 million civilian employees, compared with combined state
and local payrolls of nearly 20 million. "Washington can't go it
alone," Heather Gerken wrote in *Democracy Journal*. "When Congress makes a law, it often lacks the resources to enforce it. Instead,
it relies on states and localities to carry out its policies. Without
those local actors, the feds cannot enforce immigration law, implement environmental policy, build infrastructure, or prosecute drug
offenses. Changing policies in these areas—and many more—is
possible only if cities and states lend a hand. This arrangement creates opportunities for federal-state cooperation. But it also allows
for 'uncooperative federalism': State and local officials can use their
leverage over the feds to shape national policy."

More than mere obstructionism, states can enact regulations that go beyond those of the federal government, which in the case of the largest states can have the effect of creating national policy. The classic case is California's establishment of fuel efficiency standards for automobiles that exceeded those of the federal government and, because of the state's huge market, prompted automakers to adhere to those requirements for the entire nation. The same effect on the national market could arise from California's requirement that gas-powered lawn equipment be phased out by 2024. California is on the cutting edge of progressive federalism, an incubator of imaginative ideas for exploiting the power of federal laws even when Washington is not enforcing them. As Gerken pointed out, California law prohibits businesses from engaging in "unlawful, unfair or fraudulent" activities, which the state attorney's office takes to mean that corporations can be sued by the state if they violate federal laws. It also has deputized counties and large cities to file lawsuits under the same law. Thus empowered, the San Francisco City Attorney's Office has brought suit against tax preparers, mortgage lenders, and pharmaceutical companies for violations of *federal* law.

There is no reason other blue states cannot be as audacious as California in filling the void left by federal inaction. The New York State Attorney General's Office and the Manhattan District Attorney's Office were aggressive in prosecuting corrupt Wall Street firms when the feds failed to do the job under George W. Bush's administration. Those two offices were widely reported at the time of this writing to be joined in a criminal investigation of possible tax fraud on the part of Donald Trump, and Attorney General Letitia James filed a lawsuit in 2020 against the National Rifle Association, alleging financial impropriety by its executives and seeking the group's dissolution as a nonprofit.

But a real movement of progressive federalism would go beyond criminal and regulatory enforcement and not depend on one state or another deciding on its own to defy the federal government. It would be perfectly within the bounds of the law, though something of a political hurdle, for the progressive coastal states to form a coalition that would act in unison not only in business regulation but also in other aspects of governance traditionally under the purview of the federal government. A coalition of states with a bigger GDP than all but three countries could carve out swaths of the nation with their own coordinated systems of health care, higher education, labor relations, housing assistance, environmental enforcement, and even industrial policy. Republicans have set a precedent for such coalition building with their embrace, in state after state, of ALEC's model legislation, and the lawsuits, signed by almost every Republican attorney general, seeking to outlaw the Affordable Care Act and overturn the result of the 2020 presidential election. It would mean blue-state governors and legislative leaders setting aside their state's narrow interests—leaving behind the "race to the bottom" to attract business investment—and focusing on the good of the nation, the health of the planet, and the welfare of working people no matter where they live.

Interstate compacts and similar forms of cooperation have a long history. New York, New Jersey, and Connecticut have maintained the Interstate Environmental Commission for some eighty years to regulate their shared waterways and exchange ideas on the preservation of natural resources. At least forty-two states have cooperated in setting standards for the licensing of professionals ranging from physicians and nurses to speech therapists. There are scores of other compacts between states, for the operation of bridges and tunnels, the handling of child custody cases, and many other societal functions. In the 1990s, several northeastern states whose environments were damaged by acid rain joined a successful federal lawsuit to compel Midwestern power companies to curtail their emissions.

Such compacts could go much further. The blue states must join forces across a broader range of issues. With Republicans moving ahead in unison with partisan gerrymandering, a new landscape of voter suppression, the politicization of once-independent election authorities, attacks on abortion rights, attacks on public education, and opposition to climate initiatives, it is past time for a progressive coalition to set a national and international example of good governance and help steer America away from its path toward mediocrity. Instead of ALEC-sponsored bills to weaken worker protections and preempt municipal minimum-wage laws, there could be uniform legislation across the blue states to ban the use of plastic bags and single-use containers, create paid family leave, or allow multi-family zoning in neighborhoods where there is an affordability crisis.

Blue states could strike a blow against dark money in political campaigns if they all agreed to model legislation that would place restrictions on super PACs and other independent groups that have eclipsed political parties in influencing state elections, with no requirement that they disclose donors' identities. Progressives have been stymied in winning passage for such reforms at the federal level, even with Biden as president, but they are achievable at the state level. The problem is that some Democratic state leaders benefit from dark money as much as Republicans, and have slow-walked reform. For example, New Direction New Jersey, a non-profit raising money for Governor Phil Murphy, initially reneged on its promise in 2019 to disclose its donors, prompting the passage of legislation that mandated such disclosure. Murphy signed the law reluctantly, and when a federal judge found the law unconstitutional, he was not quick to help create a replacement bill that would survive judicial review. A coalition of states with some members supporting such reforms—California has a law requiring disclosure—would put pressure on those who are not so enthusiastic.

If the coalition were formalized and officials from the various states met regularly and held press conferences to announce joint initiatives, such as making community college free in all of the participating states, for example, it would garner national attention and expose the venality of states that are failing their citizens by taking marching orders from corporate interests. And those corporate interests would begin paying attention. It was notable how skittish corporations became when Georgia passed its controversial elections law, when North Carolina restricted transgendered citizens from using bathrooms of their choice, and when Texas passed a law that could have the effect of outlawing abortion. In September 2021, more than fifty national companies signed a letter protesting the Texas abortion law. Many were companies that might be expected to support progressive causes, like Netflix and Ben & Jerry's. But the Democratic Party's opposition research division, Corporate Accountability Action, paid for television and digital ads highlighting bigger companies that had donated to the Texas lawmakers behind the abortion bill, including AT&T, Time Warner Cable/Charter Communications, and NBC Universal—which together had given more than $1 million to the law's sponsors. Imagine the governors of states that account for more than a third of the nation's GDP holding a joint press conference announcing that their governments would divest pension funds from and refuse to do business with companies that bankroll the Republican assault on democracy. Such a move has clear precedent. Some thirty states, including some led by Democrats, like New York, New Jersey, and California, have passed laws or issued executive orders that withhold pension investments or other business dealing with companies that have boycotted Israel because of its treatment of Palestinians in the Occupied Territories. Would Democrat-led states not feel the same kind of moral repugnance at dealing with companies helping to upend the Constitution and destroy American democracy?

America's economy has evolved in such a way as to obviate the barriers that once prevented states and cities from following their own paths in the regulation of business and the provision of social justice to their citizens. The conventional literature of federalism in the twentieth century assumed that the federal government would collect the revenue, handle the funding, and oversee the administration of social welfare programs, while leaving the states free to compete for business. Any state that departed from that paradigm would risk the exodus of jobs and businesses to places with a lower tax and regulatory burden. But this process of sorting has been replaced by what Richard Schragger, a University of Virginia law professor, has termed "agglomeration"—the tendency of corporations in a postindustrial era dominated by technology and finance to cluster in urban locales where "specialized knowledge is transmitted easily within and across industries through face-to-face contact."

> [The] picture of salutary subnational, inter-jurisdictional competition . . . does not fit with what economists increasingly appreciate about economic development: that it is clustered in specific places and regions. Economic activity is not evenly distributed across geographical space. Instead, population growth and economic development tend to be path dependent: productive activity and population flows follow existing productive activity and population. This means that even in markets with few jurisdictional barriers, the location of economic production will likely follow predetermined paths. So too, government policies are not likely to either depress economic activity where it is already inclined to exist nor increase economic activity where it is not.

Texas may still be able to lure some businesses away from California because of low real-estate costs and the knowledge base in the Austin area, but the Bay Area will continue to be a mecca for the technology sector. No matter how many tax incentives and anti-worker provisions Indiana dangles in front of businesses, they are not going to attract an Intel or a Microsoft, even for back offices. This is a form of liberation for any state that wants to raise taxes for investment in the education, training, and social needs of its workforce while embracing a new vision of what their society can become. States need not buckle under corporate blackmail or join the race to the bottom for business. Many state leaders will continue to do so, continue to fight for tax giveaways to corporations, but only because it yields financial rewards for themselves and their cronies.

Democratic states need to take a higher road and induce red states to do so as well. They need to be more involved in political organizing, in winning the hearts and minds not only of their own voters but those of the nation as a whole, in forcing a national conversation about policies that are racist, anti-worker, dangerous to the global environment, or just inimical to democracy. Just as California Governor Jerry Brown defied the federal government in the Trump years and helped lead a global movement to combat climate change, a coalition of blue states could forge international alliances in the fight for social and economic justice.

In an editorial written as the Supreme Court was about to take up a challenge to Mississippi's law banning all abortions after fifteen weeks, the *New York Times* predicted that the majority would not completely overturn *Roe v. Wade*, but would allow states to further curtail reproduction rights. "As the justices are well aware," the *Times* wrote, "categorically eliminating a right that tens of millions of women have counted on, and which, according to a 2019 poll, more than three-quarters of Americans support upholding in some form, would invite an enormous social and political backlash that could end up doing damage to the very causes they hold dear." An *enormous social and political backlash*—that is precisely what blue-state and blue-city governments are capable of unleashing, and not just over the question of abortion rights, if they alight down the path of unity already blazed by the far right. The road to 2024 is filled with both peril and promise for America, and the states will play a major role in determining whether it will be the end of the road for democracy or a pathway to a new era of equality.

Acknowledgments

This book was researched and written over a period of four years, but its real genesis was in a meeting I had in March 2017 with Carl Bromley, who was then editorial director of The New Press. Carl had edited a previous book I had written on Ronald Reagan's legacy for Nation Books, and his enthusiasm for the concept that became *States of Neglect* made the difference in my having the confidence to move ahead with the book. His support continued even after he moved on to Melville House, and for this I owe him a debt of gratitude.

I am also grateful to Diane Wachtell, executive editor and co-founder of The New Press, which has been such an important platform for progressive ideas over the last three decades. She was supportive of the project from day one. I would also like to offer heartfelt thanks to Marc Favreau, the editorial director of The New Press, whose careful and patient editing made this a better book, to Brian Baughan for deft copy editing, and to Emily Albarillo and everyone else in the New Press production team. My former newspaper colleague Guy Sterling was kind enough to read the manuscript and offer thoughtful suggestions. I thank him for being so generous with his time and insight.

States of Neglect could not have been written without the tireless work of numerous investigative reporters at regional newspapers who have continued to hold state leaders accountable even as the resources of those news organizations have dwindled over the last decade and half. They are the unsung heroes of American journalism. There are too many to mention all of them, but I found especially useful the work of Ken Ward Jr. at the *Charleston Gazette-Mail*, Tom Loftus of the Louisville *Courier-Journal*, Kiah Collier of the *Texas Tribune*, and Craig Harris of the *Arizona Republic*. And, of course, no one can seriously research the impact of corporate money on state politics without consulting the work of author and *New Yorker* writer Jane Mayer and Gordon Lafer, a professor of labor studies at the University of Oregon.

I also must thank my friend Michael Dunn, professor of biomedical engineering at Rutgers University, who provided invaluable assistance on questions of statistical analysis, and Janice Ann Reinauer, who gave feedback and emotional support throughout this project and understood its importance even when not always agreeing with its conclusions.

Notes

INTRODUCTION

5 **"one of the biggest policy blunders"**: Patrick McGeehan, "Christie Halts Train Tunnel, Citing Its Cost," *New York Times*, October 7, 2010.

5 **rejected billions in unemployment benefits**: Ben Philpott, "Texas Gov. Under Fire for Rejecting Stimulus Funds," NPR, March 31, 2009.

5 **high-speed rail projects**: David Schaper, "Not So Fast: Future for High-Speed Rail Uncertain," NPR, November 12, 2010.

5 **numerous studies found**: Ben Casselman, "Cutoff of Jobless Benefits Is Found to Get Few Back to Work," *New York Times*, August 20, 2021.

5 **cost red-state economies**: Nicholas Reimann, "States Cutting $300-a-Week Unemployment Benefits Face $12 Billion Economic Hit, Congressional Committee Says," *Forbes*, June 2, 2021.

5 **barred state and local authorities**: Dan Margolies, "Justice Department Says Missouri New 2nd Amendment Law Is 'Legally Invalid,'" St. Louis Public Radio, August 18, 2021, news.stlpublicradio.org/government -politics-issues/2021-08-18/justice-department-says-missouri-new-2nd -amendment-law-is-legally-invalid.

6 **most extreme of nine laws**: Glenn Thrush and Nicholas Bogel-Burroughs, "Why GOP-Led States Are Banning the Police from Enforcing Federal Gun Laws," *New York Times*, June 18, 2021.

6 **"rein in this rogue agency"**: Kate Galbraith, "EPA Shoots Down Texas Pollution Regulations," *Texas Tribune*, June 30, 2010, www.texastribune .org/2010/06/30/epa-states-pollution-permits-dont-meet-federal-law.

6 **"make clear that Texas"**: Patrick Svitek, "Gov. Greg Abbott Says He'll Fight Joe Biden's Energy and Climate Agenda," *Texas Tribune*, January 28, 2021, www.texastribune.org/2021/01/28/abbott-biden-energy.

6 **"I go into the office in the morning"**: Catalina Camia, "Texas Gov. Hopeful Likes to Sue Barack Obama," *USA Today*, July 15, 2013.

6   **delay or defeat federal initiatives** Paul Nolette, "State Litigation During the Obama Administration: Diverging Agendas in an Era of Political Polarization," *Publius: The Journal of Federalism*, Vol. 44, Issue 3, Summer 2014, pp. 451–74, academic.oup.com/publius/article/44/3/451/2760318.

7   **"The mutability of the laws":** Letter from James Madison to Thomas Jefferson, *The Debate on the Constitution* (New York: Library of America, 1993), pp. 198–99.

7   **An ABC News / Ipsos poll:** Brittany Shepherd, "Majority of Americans Think January 6 Attack Threatened Democracy: Poll," ABC News, January 2, 2022.

8   **had passed thirty-four laws:** Brennan Center for Justice, "Voting Laws Roundup," December 21, 2021, www.brennancenter.org/our-work/research-reports/voting-laws-roundup-december-2021.

8   **"While none of these bills have become law":** Will Wilder, Derek Tisler, and Wendy Weiser, "The Election Sabotage Scheme and How Congress Can Stop It," Brennan Center for Justice, November 8, 2021, www.brennancenter.org/our-work/research-reports/election-sabotage-scheme-and-how-congress-can-stop-it.

8   **threatened to jail the mayors:** Patrick Marley, "Gableman Seeks to Jail Two Mayors If They Don't Sit for Interviews as Part of His Partisan Election Review," *Milwaukee Journal Sentinel*, December 2, 2021, www.jsonline.com/story/news/politics/2021/12/02/gableman-seeks-jail-mayors-if-they-dont-sit-interviews-election-review/8840663002.

8   **"slow-motion insurrection":** Nicholas Riccardi, "'Slow-Motion Insurrection': How GOP Seizes Election Power," Associated Press, December 30, 2021.

9   **purge the boards of Black Democrats:** James Oliphant and Nathan Layne, "Georgia Republicans Purge Black Democrats from County Election Boards," Reuters, December 9, 2021.

9   **"make elections more difficult to administer":** Protect Democracy, "A Democracy Crisis in the Making: How State Legislatures Are Politicizing, Criminalizing, and Interfering with Elections," April 2021, updated June 2021, protectdemocracy.org/project/democracy-crisis-in-the-making/#.

9   **"an insidious and pervasive evil":** *South Carolina v. Katzenbach*, U.S. Supreme Court, 383 U.S. 301(1966), March 7, 1966.

10   **reinstate a strict voter ID law:** "The Effects of Shelby County v. Holder," Brennan Center for Justice, August 6, 2018, www.brennancenter.org/our-work/policy-solutions/effects-shelby-county-v-holder.

10   **"with almost surgical precision":** Ibid.

11   **frozen 53,000 voter registrations:** Ben Nadler, "Voting Rights Become a Flashpoint in Georgia Governor's Race," Associated Press, October 9, 2018.

11   **pared 1.4 million voters:** Ibid.

11 **"a remarkable architect of voter suppression":** P.R. Lockhart, "Georgia, 2018's Most Prominent Voting Rights Battleground, Explained," *Vox*, November 6, 2018.

11 **so many polling places were closed:** Stephen Fowler, "Why Do Nonwhite Georgia Voters Have to Wait in Line for Hours? Too Few Polling Places," NPR, October 17, 2020.

11 **reduced the amount of time voters:** Nick Corasaniti and Reid J. Epstein. "What Georgia's Voting Law Really Does," *New York Times*, April 2, 2021.

11 **get rid of voting by mail:** Amy Gardner and Mike DeBonis, "How the Corporate Backlash to Georgia's New Voting Law Is Shaping Other Fights Around the Country over Access to the Polls," *Washington Post*, April 12, 2021.

11 **no significant issues of fraud in the election:** David Wickert, "Five Fraud Claims: What Investigators Found," *Atlanta Journal-Constitution*, December 30, 2021, www.ajc.com/politics/election/five-fraud-claims-what-investigators-found/ISF2NV2RKBF2TIEI4ULXWJFZNA.

12 **surrounded by six white males:** Will Bunch, "Georgia Governor Signed a Voter Suppression Law Under a Painting of a Slave Plantation," *Philadelphia Inquirer*, March 26, 2021, www.inquirer.com/opinion/georgia-governor-brian-kemp-painting-slave-plantation-20210326.html.

12 **"Jim Crow with a suit and tie":** Ari Berman, "Georgia Republicans Are Doubling Down on Racist Voter Suppression," *Mother Jones*, February 19, 2021.

12 **"Boy, did we screw up":** Charles Koch, *Believe in People: Bottom-Up Solutions for a Top-Down World* (New York: St. Martin's Press, 2020), p. x.

12 **leaders of major corporations:** David Gelles and Andrew Ross Sorkin, "Hundreds of Companies Unite to Oppose Voting Limits, but Others Abstain," *New York Times*, April 14, 2021.

12 **business groups pushing Congress:** Dan Mangan, "Major Business Leaders Tell Congress: Certify Biden Won Electoral College, Trump Lost," CNBC, January 4, 2021.

12 **"woke corporate hypocrites":** David Gelles and Andrew Ross Sorkin, "Hundreds of Companies Unite to Oppose Voting Limits, but Others Abstain," *New York Times*, April 14, 2021.

12 **"stay out of politics":** Lisa Mascaro, "After New Law, McConnell Warns CEOs: 'Stay Out of Politics,'" Associated Press, April 5, 2021.

13 **eleven states flipped:** Gordon Lafer, *The One-Percent Solution: How Corporations Are Remaking America One State at a Time* (Ithaca, NY: Cornell University Press, 2017), p. 2.

14 **"This includes not only restrictions":** Ibid., p. 3.

14 **Within five years of *Citizens United*:** Ibid.

14 **described the enormous influence:** Jane Mayer, *Dark Money: The Hidden History of the Billionaires Behind the Rise of the Radical Right* (New York: Doubleday, 2016).

15   **block the creation of public transit systems:** Hiroko Tabuchi, "How the Koch Brothers Are Killing Public Transit Projects Around the Country," *New York Times*, June 19, 2018.

16   **derailed Tennessee's plan for Medicaid expansion:** Lafer, *The One-Percent Solution*, p. 1.

16   **"handed the keys to the governor's office":** Annie Gowen, "In Kansas, Gov. Sam Brownback Puts Tea Party Tenets into Action with Sharp Cuts," *Washington Post*, December 21, 2011.

16   **cost the state budget $4.5 billion:** Michael Mazerov, "Kansas Provides Compelling Evidence of Failure of 'Supply-Side' Tax Cuts," Center on Budget and Policy Priorities, January 22, 2018, www.cbpp.org/research/state -budget-and-tax/kansas-provides-compelling-evidence-of-failure-of -supply-side-tax.

16   **three credit downgrades:** Russell Berman, "Kansas Republicans Sour on Their Tax-Cut Experiment," *The Atlantic*, February 24, 2017.

16   **weaker than all of its neighboring states:** Mazerov, "Kansas Provides Compelling Evidence of Failure."

17   **regretted the role he played:** Douglas Belkin, "Charles Koch Says His Partisanship Was a Mistake," *Wall Street Journal*, November 13, 2020.

17   **"large, very large, chunk of conservatives":** Jane Mayer, "Inside the Koch-Backed Effort to Block the Largest Election-Reform Bill in Half a Century," *New Yorker*, March 29, 2021.

17   **more than a hundred ALEC-drafted pieces of legislation:** Lafer, *The One-Percent Solution*, p. 13.

18   **scores of well-known corporations:** Ibid., pp. 13–14.

18   **"If it's voter ID, it's ALEC":** Nancy Scola, "Exposing ALEC: How Conservative-Backed State Laws Are All Connected," *The Atlantic*, April 14, 2012.

18   **More than half of the sixty-two Voter ID laws:** Alexander Hertel-Fernandez, *State Capture: How Conservative Activists, Big Businesses, and Wealthy Donors Reshaped the American States—and the Nation* (New York: Oxford University Press, 2019), pp. 2–3.

19   **states with the highest personal income tax rates:** Institute on Taxation and Economic Policy, *Trickle-Down Dries Up: States Without Personal Income Taxes Lag Behind States with the Highest Top Tax Rates*, October 26, 2017, itep.org/trickle-down-dries-up.

19   **using broken laptops:** Josephine Sedgwick, "25-Year-Old Textbooks and Holes in the Ceiling: Inside America's Public Schools," *New York Times*, April 16, 2018.

19   **cut funding for public colleges:** Michael Mitchell, Michael Leachman, and Matt Saenz, "State Higher Education Funding Cuts Have Pushed Costs to Students, Worsened Inequality," Center for Budget and Policy Priorities, October 24, 2019, www.cbpp.org/research/state-budget-and-tax /state-higher-education-funding-cuts-have-pushed-costs-to-students.

19   **paid lobbyist for natural-gas companies:** Ken Ward and Kate Mishkin, "Speaker's Gas Ties Put Ethics in Focus," *Charleston Gazette-Mail*, December 6, 2018, www.wvgazettemail.com.

19   **pushed state broadband contracts:** Eric Eyre, "Internet Access, Not Just Speed; Highest-Need Areas to Get Funding First in Revised Senate Bill," *Charleston Gazette*, April 11, 2013, www.wvgazettemail.com.

19   **makes no secret of fighting for its interests:** Ken Ward Jr., "A Coal Company Owned by This Billionaire Governor Has Pledged to Stop Breaking Pollution Laws," ProPublica, December 4, 2020, www.propublica.org /article/a-coal-company-owned-by-this-billionaire-governor-has-pledged -to-stop-breaking-pollution-laws; "Justice Signs Bill Lowering Coal Severance Tax," MetroNews, March 27, 2019, wvmetronews.com/2019/03/27 /justice-signs-bill-lowering-coal-severance-tax/; Mike Tony, "Justice Signs Fossil Fuel-Friendly Bills into Law, Lets Solar-Friendly Bill Become Law Without Signature," *Charleston Gazette-Mail*, May 3, 2021, www.wvgaz ettemail.com.

20   **enacted laws banning or restricting:** Leticia Miranda, "How States Are Fighting to Keep Towns from Offering Their Own Broadband," ProPublica, June 26, 2015, www.propublica.org/article/how-states-are-fight ing-to-keep-towns-from-offering-their-own-broadband.

20   **"one of the most brazen efforts":** Michael Corkery, "States Erase Interest Rate Laws That Protected Poor Borrowers," *New York Times*, October 21, 2014.

20   **lower per-capita economic growth:** "Per Capita Real Gross Domestic Product (GDP) of the United States in 2019, by State," Statistica, May 17, 2021, www.statista.com/statistics/248063/per-capita-us-real-gross-domes tic-product-gdp-by-state.

20   **higher poverty:** Elliott Davis Jr., "The States with the Highest Poverty Rates," *U.S. News and World Report*, June 25, 2021.

20   **inferior school performance:** "Map: A-F Grades, Rankings for States on School Quality," *Education Week*, September 1, 2020, www.edweek.org /policy-politics/map-a-f-grades-rankings-for-states-on-school-quality /2020/09; Adam McCann, "States with the Best and Worst School Systems," WalletHub, July 26, 2021, wallethub.com.

20   **higher rates of suicide:** National Center for Health Statistics, "Suicide Mortality by State," 2019, www.cdc.gov/nchs/pressroom/sosmap/suicide -mortality/suicide.htm.

20   **greater prevalence of diabetes:** Centers for Disease Control and Prevention, "National and State Diabetes Trends," 2019, www.cdc.gov /diabetes/library/reports/reportcard/national-state-diabetes-trends .html.

20   **higher rates of infant mortality:** National Center for Health Statistics, "Infant Mortality Rates by State," 2017, www.cdc.gov/nchs/pressroom /sosmap/infant_mortality_rates/infant_mortality.htm.

20   **higher rates of teen pregnancy:** National Center for Health Statistics, "Teen Birth Rate by State," www.cdc.gov/nchs/pressroom/sosmap/teen -births/teenbirths.htm.

20   **less effective health care systems:** David C. Radley, Sara R. Collins, and Jesse C. Baumgartner, "2020 Scorecard on State Health System Performance," The Commonwealth Fund, New York, 2020scorecard.common wealthfund.org/rankings.

20   **lower health care spending:** Rhea K. Farberman et al., *The Impact of Chronic Underfunding on America's Public Health System: Trends, Risks, and Recommendations, 2019,* Trust for America's Health, April 24, 2019, www.tfah.org/report-details/2019-funding-report.

20   **Republican-led states are more dependent:** Laura Schultz, "Giving or Getting: New York's Balance of Payments with the Federal Government," Rockefeller Institute of Government, January 2021, rockinst.org /wp-content/uploads/2021/01/2021-Balance-of-Payments-Report-web .pdf.

21   **average life expectancy:** Lenny Bernstein, "U.S. Life Expectancy Declines Again, a Dismal Trend Not Seen Since World War I," *Washington Post,* November 28, 2018.

21   **states with the highest life expectancy:** National Center for Health Statistics, "Life Expectancy at Birth by State," 2018, www.cdc.gov/nchs /pressroom/sosmap/life_expectancy/life_expectancy.htm.

21   **human development index:** Joachim Klement, "Red States, Blue States: Two Economies, One Nation," CFA Institute, blogs.cfainstitute.org /investor/2018/03/13/red-states-blue-states-two-economies-one-nation.

21   **fifty most important scientists:** Jia You, "The Top 50 Science Stars of Twitter," *Science,* September 17, 2014, www.science.org/content/article/top -50-science-stars-twitter.

21   **Statistics on research-and-development expenditures:** Colin Edwards, "Useful Stats: 2020 Higher Ed R&D Expenditures Increased in Most States Despite Pandemic," State Science and Technology Institute, ssti.org /blog/useful-stats-2020-higher-ed-rd-expenditures-increased-most-states -despite-pandemic.

22   **suicide rate per 100,000 people:** World Health Organization, Global Health Observatory Data Repository, published by the World Bank, data .worldbank.org/indicator/SH.STA.SUIC.P5?end=2015&locations=RU -LT-SY-NG-US-IT-AF-GH-EG-AE-IQ&start=2015&view=bar.

22   **infant mortality rate:** European Commission, Eurostat News, "Infant Mortality Halved Between 1997 and 2017," ec.europa.eu/eurostat/web /products-eurostat-news/-/DDN-20190719-1; National Center for Health Statistics, "Infant Mortality Rates by State.

22   **have tended to show:** International Telecommunications Union database, cited by the World Bank, data.worldbank.org/indicator/IT.NET .USER.ZS.

22 **nineteen of twenty states:** Michael Martin, "Computer and Internet Use in the United States: 2018," Census Bureau, American Community Survey Reports, April 2021, www.census.gov/content/dam/Census/library /publications/2021/acs/acs-49.pdf.

23 **less pronounced in many European countries:** Karen Davis, et al., "Mirror, Mirror on the Wall, 2014 Update: How the U.S. Health Care System Compares Internationally," The Commonwealth Fund, June 16, 2014, www.commonwealthfund.org/publications/fund-reports/2014/jun /mirror-mirror-wall-2014-update-how-us-health-care-system.

23 **29 million people were uninsured:** U.S. Census Bureau, American Community Survey Tables for Health Insurance Coverage, 2019, www.census .gov/data/tables/time-series/demo/health-insurance/acs-hi.html.

1. DEAD LAST IN EVERYTHING: PROFILE OF A FAILED STATE

29 **Absorbs their rivulets of acids:** U.S. Environmental Protection Agency, "Metals and pH TMDLs for the Elk River Watershed, West Virginia," September 2001, p. 1-1 dep.wv.gov/WWE/watershed/TMDL/grpb/Docu ments/Elk/2972_WV_ElkRiver_TMDL.pdf.

30 **"It was sickeningly sweet":** Interview with Jeff Ellis, December 12, 2018.

30 **"I thought they might have been fixing a water main":** Interview with Denise Witt, December 12, 2018.

30 **wouldn't tell the public for seven more hours:** U.S. Chemical Safety and Hazard Investigation Board, *Investigation Report: Chemical Spill Contaminates Public Water Supply in Charleston, West Virginia*, May 2017, pp. 7–8, www.csb.gov/assets/1/20/final_freedom_industries_investigation_report _(5-11-2017).pdf?15829.

31 **bubbling "fountain-like":** Ibid.

31 **Just a little odor from a heavy schedule of deliveries:** Ken Ward Jr., "DEP Inspectors Describe Early Scene at Freedom Leak Site," *Charleston Gazette*, January 13, 2014, www.wvgazettemail.com.

31 **"This was a Band-Aid approach":** Ibid.

31 **Hundreds of people reported to emergency rooms:** U.S. Chemical Safety and Hazard Investigation Board, *Investigation Report*, pp. 55–58.

31 **put the spill at more than ten times that amount:** Ibid, p. xi.

31 **polluting water as far as four hundred miles away:** Ibid, p. 12.

32 **"We don't know that the water is not safe":** Trip Gabriel, "Thousands Without Water After Spill in West Virginia," *New York Times*, January 10, 2014.

32 **37 percent of households continued to drink:** U.S. Chemical Safety and Hazard Investigation Board, *Investigation Report*, p. 66.

34 **the first recipients:** Trip Gabriel, "50 Years into the War on Poverty, Hardship Hits Back," *New York Times*, April 20, 2014.

34   **"When I grew up":** Interview with Ted Boettner, June 14, 2018.

34   **directly benefits his business interests:** Ken Ward Jr., "A Coal Company Owned by This Billionaire Governor Has Pledged to Stop Breaking Pollution Laws," ProPublica, December 4, 2020, www.propublica.org/article/a -coal-company-owned-by-this-billionaire-governor-has-pledged-to-stop -breaking-pollution-laws; "Justice Signs Bill Lowering Coal Severance Tax," MetroNews, March 27, 2019, wvmetronews.com/2019/03/27/justice-signs -bill-lowering-coal-severance-tax/; Mike Tony, "Justice Signs Fossil Fuel-Friendly Bills into Law, Lets Solar-Friendly Bill Become Law Without Signature," *Charleston Gazette-Mail*, May 3, 2021, www.wvgazettemail .com.

34   **fighting in the fall of 2021 to weaken any portion:** Coral Davenport, "This Powerful Democrat Linked to Fossil Fuels Will Craft the U.S. Climate Plan," *New York Times*, September 19, 2021.

34   **earned $4.5 million:** Daniel Boguslaw, "Joe Manchin's Dirty Empire," September 3, 2021, *The Intercept*, theintercept.com/2021/09/03/joe -manchin-coal-fossil-fuels-pollution.

34   **more campaign donations from coal:** Davenport, "This Powerful Democrat Linked to Fossil Fuels Will Craft the U.S. Climate Plan."

35   **"There are so many chemicals out there":** Steven Mufson, "New Owner of Freedom Industries Must Face Fallout of West Virginia Chemical Spill," *Washington Post*, January 17, 2014.

35   **safety form's fields were essentially left blank:** Ibid.

35   **ditch the treaty:** Cliff Forrest, "The 'Business Case' for Paris Is Bunk," *Wall Street Journal*, May 29, 2017.

35   **donated $1 million to the president's inauguration:** Paul J. Gough, "Trump's Top Contributors," *Pittsburgh Business Times*, April 20, 2017.

36   **"I will never back down from the EPA":** "Text of Gov. Earl Ray Tomblin's State of the State Address," *Charleston Gazette*, January 8, 2014, www .wvgazettemail.com.

36   **two years cutting the DEP's budget:** Evan Osnos, "Chemical Valley," *New Yorker*, March 31, 2014.

36   **no one from the DEP:** U.S. Chemical Safety and Hazard Investigation Board, *Investigation Report*, p. 66.

36   **no evidence on the premises:** Ibid.

36   **donated more than $1 million:** American Waterworks Company profile, OpenSecrets, www.opensecrets.org/orgs/summary?id=D000031514& cycle=A.

37   **net income for the company:** Macrotrends, "American Water Works Net Income, 2008–2021," www.macrotrends.net/stocks/charts/AWK/ameri can-water-works/net-income.

37   **come under attack across the country:** SourceWatch, American Water Works Company profile, www.sourcewatch.org/index.php/American _Water_Works_Company,_Inc.; see also Violation Tracker, American

Water Works company summary, violationtracker.goodjobsfirst.org/prog
.php?parent=american-water-works, as well as news and legal database
searches.

37 **"Illinois-American Water mistreated its customers":** Illinois Attorney
General Lisa Madigan, "Madigan, Village of Homer Glen File Complaints
with ICC Alleging Pattern of Non-compliance by Water Utility," press release, illinoisattorneygeneral.gov/pressroom/2006_02/20060201.html.

38 **3,752 breaks and leaks:** Andrew Brown, "City Residents Speak Against
Water Rate Increase," *Charleston Gazette-Mail*, October 27, 2015, www
.wvgazettemail.com.

38 **"Our No. 1 resource in West Virginia":** Matt Murphy, "Officials Blast
Water Company," *Charleston Gazette-Mail*, July 1, 2015, www.wvgaz
ettemail.com.

38 **"These companies usually get what they want":** Andrew Brown, "Utilities Ask PSC to Alter Rate Policy," *Charleston Daily Mail*, July 6, 2015,
www.wvgazettemail.com.

38 **only two states that did not order private utilities:** Fred Pace, "West
Virginia Not Lowering Utility Rates," *Herald-Dispatch*, June 26, 2018,
www.herald-dispatch.com.

39 **decided to earmark $4.6 million:** Max Garland, "WV American Water
Settlement Would Lower Customer Rates," *Charleston Gazette-Mail*,
August 18, 2018, www.wvgazettemail.com.

39 **"rebuild the public trust":** Pamela Pritt, "Health Department Official
Offers Post-Spill Suggestions," *Register-Herald*, February 4, 2014, www
.register-herald.com.

39 **responding to the Elk River spill:** Jared Hunt, "Utility to Ask State for a Rate
Increase," *Charleston Daily Mail*, April 2, 2015, www.wvgazettemail.com.

39 **McIntyre later revised:** Paul J. Nyden, "W.Va. American Water Wants a
Rate Increase," *Charleston Gazette*, May 1, 2015, www.wvgazettemail.com.

40 **so geared toward the interests:** West Virginia AFL-CIO, "Anti-worker
Roll Call of the Week," July 6, 2015, www.wvaflcio.org/legislative-and
-political/anti-worker-roll-call-vote-of-the-week.html.

40 **West Virginia is among the three states:** Alexander Hertel-Fernandez,
*State Capture: How Conservative Activists, Big Businesses, and Wealthy Do-
nors Reshaped the American States—and the Nation* (New York: Oxford
University Press, 2019), p. 72.

41 **reduced the number of regulated tanks:** Pamela Pritt, "Several Bills
Passed in Senate Session Saturday," *Register-Herald*, March 1, 2015; Chris
Maher, "West Virginia Rolls Back Tough Rules on Above-Ground Storage
Tanks," *Wall Street Journal*, March 14, 2015.

41 **"most egregious assault":** West Virginia AFL-CIO, "Anti-worker Roll
Call of the Week."

41 **"Almost everything we got done":** Interview with Norm Steenstra,
June 14, 2018.

41   **generates more than $800 million:** Steven Allen Adams, "All Eyes on West Virginia House as Personal Income Tax Phase-Out Stays Alive," *Parkersburg News and Sentinel*, December 13, 2021, www.newsandsentinel .com/news/business/2021/04/all-eyes-on-west-virginia-house-as-personal -income-tax-phase-out-stays-alive.

41   **was the fifth-highest in the country:** U.S. Census Bureau, "Income and Poverty in the United States: 2019," www.census.gov/data/tables/2020 /demo/income-poverty/p60-270.html.

41   **highest rate of overdose deaths:** Centers for Disease Control and Prevention, National Center for Health Statistics, "Drug Overdose Mortality by State," www.cdc.gov/nchs/pressroom/sosmap/drug_poisoning_mortality /drug_poisoning.htm.

41   **third-highest rate of cancer deaths:** Centers for Disease Control and Prevention, National Center for Health Statistics, "Cancer Mortality by State," 2018, www.cdc.gov/nchs/pressroom/sosmap/cancer_mortality /cancer.htm.

41   **lowest life expectancy:** Robert Wood Johnson Foundation and University of Wisconsin Population Health Institute, County Health Rankings and Roadmaps, 2018, www.countyhealthrankings.org/app/texas/2020 /measure/outcomes/147/data.

42   **second-highest rate of obesity:** Centers for Disease Control and Prevention, "Adult Obesity Prevalence Maps," 2019, www.cdc.gov/obesity/data /prevalence-maps.html.

42   **second-highest rate of diabetes:** Centers for Disease Control and Prevention, National Center for Chronic Disease Prevention and Health Promotion, *Diabetes Report Card*, 2019, www.cdc.gov/diabetes/pdfs/library /Diabetes-Report-Card-2019-508.pdf.

42   **highest rate of hepatitis C:** Centers for Disease Control and Prevention, National Notifiable Diseases Surveillance System, "Viral Hepatitis," 2017, www.cdc.gov/hepatitis/statistics/2017surveillance/TablesFigures-HepC .htm#tabs-1-1.

42   **eighth-highest rate of suicide:** Centers for Disease Control and Prevention, National Center for Health Statistics, "Suicide Mortality by State," 2018, www.cdc.gov/nchs/pressroom/sosmap/suicide-mortality/suicide.htm.

42   **sixth-highest rate of teen pregnancy:** Centers for Disease Control and Prevention, National Center for Health Statistics, "Teen Birth Rate by State," 2018, www.cdc.gov/nchs/pressroom/sosmap/teen-births/teenbirths .htm.

42   **sixth-highest infant mortality:** Centers for Disease Control and Prevention, National Center for Health Statistics, "Infant Mortality Rates by State," 2018, www.cdc.gov/nchs/pressroom/sosmap/infant_mortality _rates/infant_mortality.htm.

42   **highest rate of accidental deaths:** Centers for Disease Control and Prevention, National Center for Health Statistics, "Accident Mortality by

State," 2018, www.cdc.gov/nchs/pressroom/sosmap/accident_mortality
/accident.htm.

42   **highest rate of people collecting Supplemental Security Income:** Social
Security Administration, Research, Statistics, and Policy Analysis, "SSI
Recipients by State and County," 2019, www.ssa.gov/policy/docs/statcomps
/ssi_sc.

42   **third-lowest median household income:** U.S. Census Bureau, American
Community Survey, S1901: Income in the Past 12 Months (in 2018
Inflation-Adjusted Dollars), 2018, data.census.gov; "List of U.S. State and
Territories by Income," Wikipedia, en.wikipedia.org/wiki/List_of_U.S.
_states_and_territories_by_income#States_and_territories_ranked_by
_median_household_income.

42   **third-highest unemployment rate:** U.S. Bureau of Labor Statistics, "Local Area Unemployment Statistics," 2019, www.bls.gov/lau/lastrk19.htm.

42   **West Virginia ranked dead last:** Federal Reserve Bank of St. Louis, Economic Research, "Labor Force Participation Rate," 2019, fred.stlouisfed.org
/release/tables?rid=446&eid=784070.

42   **male life expectancy of sixty-four years:** Charles Boothe, "Deadly Distinction: Life Expectancy for Males in McDowell County Lowest in U.S.,"
Bluefield Daily Telegraph, March 27, 2016, www.bdtonline.com; World
Bank, Life Expectancy at Birth by Country, 2018, data.worldbank.org
/indicator/SP.DYN.LE00.IN.

42   **county was reported to have:** "Teen Birth Rates; More Troubling News
for Mercer, McDowell," *Bluefield Daily Telegraph*, February 8, 2013, www
.bdtonline.com; World Bank, Infant Mortality Rate (per 1,000 Live Births)
By Country, data.worldbank.org/indicator/SP.DYN.IMRT.IN.

42   **state's general fund is shrinking:** Ted Boettner, "Yes, State Government
and Taxes Are Shrinking," West Virginia Center on Budget and Policy
blog, July 5, 2017, wvpolicy.org/yes-state-government-and-taxes-are
-shrinking.

42   **"What many of these lawmakers neglected to mention":** Ibid.

43   **last place among the fifty states:** "List of U.S. States and Territories by
Educational Attainment," Wikipedia, en.wikipedia.org/wiki/List_of_U.S.
_states_and_territories_by_educational_attainment.

43   **still found the public resources:** Jerry Bruce Thomas, *An Appalachian
New Deal: West Virginia in the Great Depression* (Morgantown, WV: West
Virginia University Press, 2010), p. 7.

44   **"most pro-growth tax reform":** Sean O'Leary, "Will Tax Reform Work
This Time?," West Virginia Center on Budget and Policy blog, April 14,
2015, wvpolicy.org/will-tax-reform-work-this-time.

45   **"The business tax cuts blew a huge hole":** Ibid.

45   **"bunch of political you-know-what":** Ben Kamisar, "West Virginia Governor Reveals Platter of Bull Dung to Slam State Budget," *The Hill*,
April 14, 2017.

45   **owed more than $2 million in federal fines:** Howard Berkes, Anna Boiko-Weyrauch, and Robert Benincasa, "Billionaire Spent Millions in Charity, but Avoided Mine Fines," National Public Radio, November 15, 2015.

46   **"He's a major figure":** Ibid.

46   **pointed out that the coal subsidy:** Christopher Ingraham, "West Virginia Governor Wants to Sell Trump on a $4.5 Billion Coal Bailout by Calling It 'Homeland Security Initiative,'" *Washington Post*, August 10, 2017.

46   **he made Larry Puccio:** Andrew Brown, "Puccio to Lobby for Justice's Businesses," *Charleston Gazette-Mail*, January 21, 2017, www.wvgazettemail.com.

47   **"The Broadband Council should focus":** Eric Eyre, "Internet Access, Not Just Speed; Highest-Need Areas to Get Funding First in Revised Senate Bill," *Charleston Gazette*, April 11, 2013, www.wvgazettemail.com.

47   **forty-seventh among fifty states:** Eric Eyre, "Speed Matters; 45 Percent of West Virginians Have Internet Speeds Below the Federal Standard," *Charleston Gazette*, December 26, 2010, www.wvgazettemail.com.

47   **high-speed network that solely benefited:** Eric Eyre, "Audit Shut Down; Tomblin Halted Review in 2011 When Frontier Responded to Issues," *Charleston Gazette*, May 28, 2013, www.wvgazettemail.com.

48   **"It takes what is a private enterprise":** Joel Ebert, "Debate Continues on W.Va. Broadband Bill; Measure Would Create Fiber Network to Improve Access Throughout State," *Charleston Daily Mail*, www.wvgazettemail.com.

48   **an unseemly bidding war:** Eric Eyre, "Carmichael Leaves Citynet, Returns to Frontier," *Charleston Gazette-Mail*, August 2, 2016, www.wvgazettemail.com.

48   **A possible answer was provided:** Eric Eyre, "Citynet Hires Ex-Frontier Exec, Senate President," *Charleston-Gazette Mail*, September 6, 2017, www .wvgazettemail.com.

48   **prime mover of the bill:** Ken Ward and Kate Mishkin, "Speaker's Gas Ties Put Ethics in Focus," *Charleston Gazette-Mail*, December 6, 2018, www .wvgazettemail.com.

48   **There are more than a dozen other legislators:** Ibid.

49   **"Save your vote for the general election":** "Presidential Candidate Donald Trump Rally in Charleston, West Virginia," C-SPAN, May 5, 2016, www.c-span.org/video/?409094-1/donald-trump-addresses-supporters charleston-west-virginia.

50   **boom times for the U.S. coal industry:** U.S. Energy Information Administration, "Annual Coal Report," www.eia.gov/coal/annual/; Trevor Houser, Jason Bordoff, and Peter Marsters, *Can Coal Make a Comeback?*, Columbia University Center on Global Energy Policy, April 2017, energypolicy.columbia.edu/sites/default/files/Center%20on%20Global%20 Energy%20Policy%20Can%20Coal%20Make%20a%20Comeback%20 April%202017.pdf.

51   **coal industry was in virtual collapse:** Clifford Krauss, "Coal Production Plummets to Lowest Level in 35 Years," *New York Times*, June 10, 2016.

51   **only 1.4 percent of the state's workers:** Jim Gaines, "Coal Job Losses to Keep Hurting Appalachia, Beyond," *Knoxville News-Sentinel*, February 4, 2018, www.knoxnews.com/story/money/business/2018/02/04/study-coal -job-losses-appalachia-impact-study-tennessee-west-virginia/1083544001.

51   **rebounded to nearly fourteen thousand:** "Coal Mining Employment in West Virginia from 2010 to 2019, by Mine Type," Statista, www.statista .com/statistics/215786/coal-mining-employment-in-west-virginia.

52   **drowning 125 people in a tsunami of toxic sludge:** *The Buffalo Creek Flood and Disaster: Official Report from the Governor's Ad Hoc Commission of Inquiry, 1973*, accessed through the West Virginia Department of Arts, Culture and History, 129.71.204.160//history/disasters/buffcreekgovreport.html.

52   **had led directly to the accident:** U.S. Department of Labor, Mine Safety and Health Administration, *Report of Investigation, Upper Big Branch Mine Explosion*, April 5, 2010, www.msha.gov/sites/default/files/Data _Reports/Fatals/Coal/Upper Big Branch/FTL10c0331noappx_0.pdf.

52   **calculated that five hundred mountains had been blown apart:** Appalachian Voices, "Mountaintop Removal 101," appvoices.org/end-mount aintop-removal/mtr101.

52   **40 percent flatter than before the advent of mountaintop removal:** *Duke Today* Staff, "Central Appalachia Flatter due to Mountaintop Mining," *Duke Today*, February 5, 2016, today.duke.edu/2016/02/mountain topmining.

53   **"If a rock this big hits you":** Shirley Stewart Burns, *Bringing Down the Mountains: The Impact of Mountain Removal Surface Coal Mining on Southern West Virginia Communities, 1970 to 2004* (Morgantown: University of West Virginia Press, 2007), p. 71.

53   **dumping of blasting debris into "valley fills":** Earthjustice, "Studies for the Draft Environmental Impact Statement Demonstrate That the Environmental Harm from Mountaintop Removal Coal Mining and Valley Fills Is Substantial and Irreversible," earthjustice.org/sites/default/files /library/policy_factsheets/EIS_fact_sheet.pdf.

53   **"There was blasting dust being peppered down on us":** Interview with Junior Walk, October 17, 2017.

54   **"When twenty-year-old nonsmokers start coming down with lung cancer":** Interview with Debbie Jarrell, June 13, 2018.

54   **killed a higher percentage of people:** Centers for Disease Control and Prevention, "Drug Overdose Mortality by State."

54   **saw a spike in deaths:** West Virginia Department of Health and Human Services, "West Virginia Experiences Increase in Overdose Deaths; Health Officials Emphasize Resources," April 23, 2021, dhhr.wv.gov/News/2021 /Pages/West-Virginia-Experiences-Increase-in-Overdose-Deaths;-Health -Officials-Emphasize-Resources.aspx.

54   **shipped 39,000 pain pills:** Eric Eyre, "Records of Pill Shipments Un-
      sealed; Documents Show Nation's Largest Drug Firms Supplied 'Pill
      Mills' in Poor, Rural Parts of State," *Charleston Gazette-Mail*, May 24,
      2016, www.wvgazettemail.com.
55   **"vast amounts of narcotic medications":** Ibid.
55   **board did nothing with the reports:** Eric Eyre, "Pill Rules Not Enforced;
      'Suspicious' Drug Order Regulation Not on Pharmacy Board's Radar,"
      Charleston Gazette-Mail, December 19, 2016, www.wvgazettemail.com.
55   **previously been a lobbyist:** Eric Eyre, "Despite Recusal, Morrisey Met
      with Drug Firms About Lawsuit," *Charleston Gazette*, October 13, 2013,
      www.wvgazettemail.com.
56   **Morrisey's wife, Denise Henry:** Ibid.
56   **$1.47 million to his wife's Washington lobbying firm:** Eric Eyre, "AG
      Issued Instructions on Drug Firm Lawsuit," *Charleston Gazette-Mail*,
      October 25, 2015, www.wvgazettemail.com.
56   **"I have discussed this with the AG":** Ibid.
57   **"If we hadn't found federal grants":** Interview with Connie Priddy,
      June 12, 2018.
57   **dropped by 86 percent after the ACA became law:** Matt Broaddus, Peggy
      Bailey, and Aviva Aron-Dine, "Medicaid Expansion Dramatically Increased
      Coverage for People with Opioid-Use Disorders, Latest Data Show," Cen-
      ter on Budget and Policy Priorities, February 28, 2018, www.cbpp.org
      /research/health/medicaid-expansion-dramatically-increased-coverage
      -for-people-with-opioid-use.
57   **had driven up health premiums in West Virginia by 160 percent:** Lori
      Kersey, "Gupta: Ruling Could Mean Millions Losing Insurance," *Charles-
      ton Gazette-Mail*, February 7, 2019, www.wvgazettemail.com.
58   **even declined in 2021:** John Holahan, Jessica Banthin, and Erik Wengle,
      Marketplace Premiums and Participation 2021, Urban Institute, May 2021,
      www.urban.org/research/publication/marketplace-premiums-and-parti
      cipation-2021.
58   **well established by nonpartisan experts:** Holahan, Banthin, and Wen-
      gle, *Marketplace Premiums and Insurer Participation 2021*.

2. "A GOOD, HONEST, CHRISTIAN MAN"

59   **It wasn't much of a milestone:** Justin Sayers and Matthew Glowicki, "De-
      quante Was Going to Graduate First Grade This Week; Instead, He Was
      Killed by a Stray Bullet," *Courier-Journal*, May 23, 2017, www.courier-journal
      .com.
59   **Bevin refused to provide details:** Justin Sayers, "Bevin Blasts 'Out of Con-
      trol' Gun Violence; Plans to Meet Next Week with Local Religious Lead-

ers," *Courier-Journal*, May 27, 2017, www.courier-journal.com/story/news /crime/2017/05/26/bevin-blasts-out-control-gun-violence-louisville-plans -meet-religious-leaders/350038001.

60 **And then the plan was unveiled:** Justin Sayers, "Bevin Calls for Prayer Patrols; Governor Outlines Spiritual Plan to Combat West End Violence," *Courier-Journal*, June 2, 2017, www.courier-journal.com.

61 **regarding such violence as a cultural deficiency:** Sayers, "Bevin Blasts 'Out of Control' Gun Violence."

62 **"above suspicion":** Herbert Croly, *The Promise of American Life* (Cambridge, MA: Belknap Press of Harvard University Press, 1965), p. 1. Originally published in 1909 by MacMillan (New York).

62 **usurp the power of local elected officials:** Julie Bosman and Monica Davey, "Anger in Michigan over Appointing Emergency Managers," *New York Times*, January 22, 2016; Representative John Conyers, "Flint Is the Predicted Outcome of Michigan's Long, Dangerous History with 'Emergency Managers,'" *The Nation*, February 17, 2016.

62 **stripped their governorships:** Maggie Astor, "Wisconsin, Limiting Governor, Borrows a Page from North Carolina's Book," *New York Times*, December 5, 2018.

63 **allowed state money to flow into his resort business:** Ken Ward Jr., "Welcome to the Greenbrier, the Governor-Owned Luxury Resort Filled with Conflicts of Interest," *Charleston Gazette-Mail* and ProPublica, October 24, 2019, www.propublica.org/article/west-virginia-greenbrier-gover nor-jim-justice-little-trump.

63 **thirty-four states, almost all Republican:** U.S. Commission on Civil Rights, *An Assessment of Minority Voting Rights Access in the United States: 2018 Statutory Enforcement Report*, www.usccr.gov/pubs/2018/Minority _Voting_Access_2018.pdf.

63 **unprecedented mid-decade redistricting:** Associated Press, "Justices Back Most Parts of G.O.P. Changes to Texas Districts," *New York Times*, June 28, 2006.

63 **"The whole aim of practical politics":** H.L. Mencken, *In Defense of Women* (New York: Alfred A. Knopf, 1922), p. 53.

63 **"strip the bark off the little bastard":** Associated Press, "Gravely Ill, Atwater Offers Apology," *New York Times*, January 13, 1991.

64 **"People who discuss CRT":** Rashawn Ray and Alexandra Gibbons, "Why Are States Banning Critical Race Theory," Brookings Institution, November 2021, www.brookings.edu/blog/fixgov/2021/07/02/why-are-states -banning-critical-race-theory.

64 **"In Florida we are taking a stand":** Official news release, Florida Governor's Office, December 15, 2021, www.flgov.com/2021/12/15/governor -desantis-announces-legislative-proposal-to-stop-w-o-k-e-activism-and-criti cal-race-theory-in-schools-and-corporations.

64   **"If Disney wants to pick a fight":** Brooks Barnes, "Disney to Lose Special Tax Status in Florida Amid 'Don't Say Gay' Clash," *New York Times*, April 21, 2022.

65   **moderate business-oriented Republican:** J. David Goodman, "For Texas Governor, Hard Right Turn Followed a Careful Rise," *New York Times*, December 12, 2021.

65   **caused huge backups:** Maya Yang, "Texas Forced to Reverse Mexican Truck Inspection Plan as Drivers Block Bridges," *The Guardian*, April 16, 2022.

65   **bus and fly migrants:** Emily Hernandez, "Top U.S. Border Official Says Busing Migrants Out of Texas Complicates Federal Officials' Jobs," *Texas Tribune*, April 14, 2022, www.texastribune.org/2022/04/14/texas-migrants-buses-washington-dc.

65   **"arch, arch far-right conservative":** Ibid.

66   **faced so many corruption allegations:** Emma Platoff, "Texas Attorney General Is Back in Hot Water. He's Escaped Before," *Texas Tribune*, November 11, 2020, www.texastribune.org/2020/11/11/texas-ag-ken-paxton-criminal-allegations.

66   **"less to do with individual perfidy":** George Packer, "The Corruption of the Republican Party," *The Atlantic*, December 14, 2018.

67   **purposely exposing his children to chicken pox:** Deborah Yetter and Tom Loftus, "Bevin Exposed His 9 Kids to Chickenpox, Says Vaccine Not for Everyone," *Courier-Journal*, March 20, 2019, www.courier-journal.com/story/news/politics/2019/03/20/matt-bevin-exposed-kids-chickenpox-instead-vaccine/3221848002.

67   **dispatched the Kentucky State Police:** Tom Loftus, "Beshear: Bevin Show of Force Broke Meetings Law," *Courier-Journal*, June 14, 2016, www.courier-journal.com/story/news/politics/ky-governor/2016/06/14/beshear-bevins-police-display-violated-law/85871728.

67   **caught on video:** "Kentucky Governor Matt Bevin Urges Preachers to Ignore Federal Law on Politicking," CBS News, October 5, 2016.

67   **invited Kentuckians to his Facebook:** Phillip M. Bailey and Morgan Watkins, "Gov. Matt Bevin Blocks Hundreds on Twitter and Facebook," *Courier-Journal*, June 15, 2017, www.courier-journal.com/story/news/politics/2017/06/15/kentucky-gov-matt-bevin-blocks-hundreds-twitter-and-facebook/361281001.

67   **legalization of cockfighting:** Joseph Gerth, "Matt Bevin Attended Cockfighting Rally," *Courier-Journal*, April 2, 2014, www.courier-journal.com/story/news/politics/2014/04/02/matt-bevin-attended-cockfighting-rally/7223291.

67   **"If Matt Bevin had moved to a state":** Joseph Gerth, "McConnell's Terse Backing of Bevin Shows Rift?," *Courier-Journal*, May 30, 2015, www.courier-journal.com/story/news/politics/gerth/2015/05/30/terse-endorsement-signals-rift/28220127.

68   **dangling from a Black Hawk helicopter:** Jared Peck, "Truex Hangs On in Overtime in Dominating Quaker State 400 Win," *Lexington Herald-Leader*, July 8, 2017, www.kentucky.com.

68   **"a good, honest, Christian man":** Roger Alford and Bruce Schreiner, "Paul Calls Bevin 'Good, Honest, Christian Man,'" Associated Press, November 15, 2013.

68   **unpopular in his home state:** Curtis Tate, "Poll: McConnell Is the Least Popular Senator in the Chamber He Leads," McClatchy Washington Bureau, September 13, 2016, www.mcclatchydc.com/news/politics-govern ment/congress/article101647842.html.

68   **two million federal employees:** Brad Plumer, "Absolutely Everything You Need to Know About How the Government Shutdown Will Work," *Washington Post*, September 30, 2013.

68   **holding Republicans responsible:** Dan Balz and Scott Clement, "Poll: Major Damage to GOP After Shutdown, and Broad Dissatisfaction with Government," *Washington Post*, October 22, 2013.

68   **"progressive liberal voting record":** Patrick O'Connor, "Kentucky Tea Party Groups Deride McConnell," *Wall Street Journal*, July 22, 2013.

69   **"mudslinging Mitch":** Tom Eblen, "Fancy Farm Shows That McConnell Is in for a Fight," *Lexington Herald-Leader*, August 3, 2013, www.kentucky .com/news/politics-government/election/article44437200.html.

69   **"East Coast con man":** Manu Raju and Kyle Cheney, "How Matt Bevin Learned to Love Mitch McConnell," *Politico*, June 8, 2015.

69   **"You can't punch people in the face":** Ibid.

70   **Heiner was forced to apologize:** Sam Youngman, "Heiner Apologizes to Comer over Campaign's Communication with Controversial Blogger," *Lexington Herald-Leader*, April 29, 2015, www.kentucky.com/news /politics-government/article44596779.html; Joseph Gerth, "College Girlfriend Says James Comer Abused Her," *Courier-Journal*, May 4, 2015, www.courier-journal.com/story/news/politics/elections/kentucky/2015 /05/04/james-comer-domestic-violence/26901137.

70   **"You told me that yourself, Hal":** Karyn Bruggeman, "Bevin: Heiner Spoke of Comer Rumors Months Ago," *National Journal*, May 8, 2015, nationaljournal.com.

70   **fundraising apparatus and a database:** Manu Raju and Kyle Cheney, "How Matt Bevin Learned to Love Mitch McConnell," *Politico*, June 8, 2015.

70   **denunciation of a 2015 Supreme Court decision:** Linda B. Blackford, Jack Brammer, and Kyle Arensdorf, "Emotional Moments Follow Ruling in Kentucky Same-Sex Marriage Case," *Lexington Herald-Leader*, June 26, 2015, www.kentucky.com.

70   **blamed Conway for failing:** Karyn Bruggeman, "Bevin Takes Aim at Conway on Gay Marriage," *National Journal*, June 29, 2015, national journal.com.

70   **stood behind Kim Davis:** Joseph Gerth, "Bevin: Gay Marriage Executive Order Needed," *Courier-Journal*, August 15, 2015, www.courier-journal .com/story/news/politics/elections/2015/08/14/bevin-calls-executive -order-gay-marriage/31745305.

71   **"I will prevent those dollars":** Karyn Bruggeman, "Bevin Pledges to De-fund Planned Parenthood," *National Journal*, August 6, 2015, national journal.com.

71   **attributed to the Kim Davis controversy:** James Mayse, "Conservative Enthusiasm, Support Led to Bevin Victory," *Messenger-Inquirer*, November 5, 2015, www.messenger-inquirer.com.

72   **to hire an Indianapolis law firm:** Tom Loftus, "Bevin Still on Trail of Ex-Foe 3 Years Later," *Courier-Journal* via *Cincinnati Inquirer*, June 29, 2019, /www.cincinnati.com.

72   **no evidence either Steve or Andy Beshear knew:** Ibid.

72   **no criminal charges and no evidence:** Ibid.

73   **"Mutual toleration refers to the idea":** Steven Levitsky and Daniel Ziblatt, *How Democracies Die* (New York: Crown, 2018), p. 102.

73   **"You're the Hunter Biden of Kentucky":** Daniel Desrochers, "Matt Bevin and Andy Beshear Bicker, Battle and Belittle During KET Debate," *Lexington Herald-Leader*, October 28, 2019, www.kentucky.com.

73   **"plenty of time to dance on the grave":** Joseph Gerth, "Matt Bevin Lost Because He's a Jerk. Good Riddance!," *Courier-Journal*, November 7, 2019, www.courier-journal.com/story/news/local/joseph-gerth/2019/11/06 /kentucky-governor-race-matt-bevin-lost-beshear-because-hes-jerk/41763 14002.

74   **Ramsey was a Bevin campaign contributor:** Tom Loftus, "Anchorage, PVA Differ on Bevin Mansion," *Courier-Journal*, June 5, 2017, www.courier -journal.com.

74   **later gave the appraiser's wife:** Tom Loftus, "Wife of Bevin's Appraiser Gets Job; May Lands $90K State-Appointed Post After Raising Her 'Medically-Fragile Son,'" *Courier-Journal*, February 7, 2018, www.courier -journal.com.

74   **barred the county's assessors:** Ibid.

74   **"should exercise restraint":** Levitsky and Ziblatt, *How Democracies Die*, pp. 8–9.

75   **sought the abolishment or reorganization:** Adam Beam, "Kentucky At-torney General Sues GOP Governor for Fourth Time," Associated Press, June 20, 2017.

75   **other governors had exploited that law:** Bruce Schreiner, "Court Hears Arguments in Case Pitting Bevin Against Beshear," Associated Press, April 12, 2019.

75   **dismissing the entire board:** Jack Brammer, "Governor Says He Has 'Ab-solute Authority' to Disband Any State Board," *Lexington Herald-Leader*, June 21, 2016, www.kentucky.com.

75   **"Find entire parts of your campus"**: Bruce Schreiner, "Kentucky Governor: Cut College Programs That Don't Pay Off," Associated Press, September 12, 2017.

75   **4.5 percent budget reduction**: Adam Beam, "Bevin Calls for Spending Cuts in His First Budget Proposal," Associated Press, January 27, 2016.

75   **Another one of his power grabs**: John Cheves and Jack Brammer, "Gov. Matt Bevin Revamps State Board That Oversees Pensions," *Lexington Herald-Leader*, June 17, 2016, www.kentucky.com.

76   **had one of the biggest shortfalls**: Proposed Second Amended Verified Complaint, *Jeffrey C. Mayberry v. KKR & Co.*, Commonwealth of Kentucky, County of Franklin Circuit Court, Case No. 17-CI-1348.

76   **"Starting in the fall of 2009"**: "The Pension Gamble," *Frontline*, PBS, October 23, 2018, www.pbs.org/wgbh/frontline/film/the-pension -gamble.

77   **"Kentucky is not a police state"**: Tom Loftus, "Bevin's Reorganization of Pension Board Upheld," *Courier-Journal*, January 10, 2018, www.courier -journal.com/story/news/politics/2018/01/09/judge-allows-bevin -reorganization-pension-board/1014931001.

77   **block any Syrian refugees**: Adam Beam, "Bevin Opposes Syrian Refugee Settlement in Kentucky," Associated Press, November 16, 2015.

77   **blood might be shed**: Rachel Dicker, "Kentucky Gov. Matt Bevin Says Blood May Need to Be Shed If Hillary Clinton Is Elected," *U.S. News and World Report*, September 13, 2016.

77   **soft on gun rights**: Steve Contorno, "Republican Challenger Matt Bevin Attacks Senate Minority Leader Mitch McConnell's Gun Record," PolitiFact, February 24, 2014, www.politifact.com/factchecks/2014/feb/24 /matt-bevin/republican-challenger-matt-bevin-attacks-senate-mi.

78   **national leader in reducing its uninsured rate**: Dan Witters, "Kentucky, Arkansas Post Largest Drops in Uninsured Rates," Gallup News, February 8, 2017, news.gallup.com/poll/203501/kentucky-arkansas-post-largest -drops-uninsured-rates.aspx.

78   **49 percent of Kentuckians are evangelical**: "Religious Landscape Study: Adults in Kentucky," Pew Research Center, www.pewforum.org/religious -landscape-study/state/kentucky.

78   **Bible literacy courses**: Paul LeBlanc, "Kentucky Public Schools Can Now Offer Bible Literacy Courses," CNN, June 30, 2017.

78   **"Bring Your Bible to School Day"**: Lucas Aulbach, "Bevin Touts 'Bring Your Bible to School Day' to Students," *Courier-Journal*, October 3, 2019, www.courier-journal.com/story/news/politics/2019/10/02/matt-bevin -supports-bring-your-bible-to-school-day-2019/3839618002.

78   **"Year of the Bible"**: Jack Brammer, "Bevin Declares 2017 the 'Year of the Bible' in Kentucky," *Lexington Herald-Leader*, December 21, 2016, www .kentucky.com.

78   **Noah's Ark theme park:** Linda Blackford, "State Awards $18 Million Tax Break to Noah's Ark Theme Park," *Lexington Herald-Leader*, April 26, 2016, www.kentucky.com.

78   **religious freedom bill:** Darcy Costello, "Louisville's Plea Rejected; Calif. Allows No Exemptions from Political Subdivisions," *Courier-Journal*, July 1, 2017, www.courier-journal.com/story/news/politics/2017/06/30 /lexington-denied-exemption-california-state-travel-ban/444432001.

78   **believe abortion should be illegal in all cases:** "Religious Landscape Study: Adults in Kentucky," Pew Research Center, www.pewforum.org /religious-landscape-study/state/kentucky.

79   **"For many in Kentucky":** Matt Jones, *Mitch, Please! How Mitch McConnell Sold Out Kentucky (and America, Too)* (New York: Simon & Schuster, 2020), pp. 40–41, Apple Books.

79   **harassed the state's other abortion provider:** Joe Sonka, "Transition Could Affect Pending State Lawsuits," *Courier-Journal*, December 3, 2019, www.courier-journal.com/story/news/politics/2019/11/21/kentucky -election-beshear-transition-governor-could-upend-lawsuits/42476 85002.

79   **"He has accepted blood money":** Phillip M. Bailey, "Bevin: Beshear Represents 'Life Over Death' in Abortion Fight," *Courier-Journal*, October 13, 2019, www.courier-journal.com.

80   **attracted new business investment:** Kentucky Cabinet for Economic Development, "With Nearly $5.8 Billion in Corporate Investments This Year, Kentucky Shatters All-Time Record," States News Service, May 26, 2017.

80   **"as significant as any economic deal":** Jack Brammer and Daniel Desrochers, "Aluminum Plant Getting Millions in State Incentives to Create Jobs in E. Kentucky," *Lexington Herald-Leader*, April 26, 2017, www.kentucky .com.

80   **company's investors ousted its CEO:** Will Wright, "'I Have My Doubts.' Former Braidy CEO Questions Project Viability Following Firing," *Lexington Herald-Leader*, February 19, 2020, www.kentucky.com.

80   **$200 million from a Russian company:** Morgan Watkins, "Senate Report: Russian Firm Investing in Brady Mill Is Kremlin Proxy," *Courier-Journal*, October 13, 2019, www.courier-journal.com/story/news/2020 /08/19/senate-report-russian-investor-braidy-mill-kremlin-proxy /5607217002.

80   **pace of job growth shrank:** Arizona State University, W.P. Carey School of Business, Seidman Research Institute, Job Growth Database.

81   **would not come to fruition:** Joe Sonka, "A Look at Bevin, Beshear Claims on Job Growth," *Courier-Journal*, October 31, 2019, www.courier-journal .com/story/news/politics/elections/kentucky/2019/10/31/kentucky -election-fact-checking-bevin-beshear-job-growth/2498546001.

81   **official poverty rate:** U.S. Census Bureau, "Historical Poverty Tables: People and Families—1959 to 2020," Table 21. Number of Poor and Pov-

erty Rate by State, www.census.gov/data/tables/time-series/demo/income
-poverty/historical-poverty-people.html.

81   **twenty-third highest in unemployment in 2015:** Federal Reserve
Bank of St. Louis, "Unemployment Rate in Kentucky" (data for all fifty
states compiled from this site by author), fred.stlouisfed.org/series
/KYURN#0.

81   **Democrats were blindsided:** Daniel Desrochers, John Cheves, and Jack
Brammer, "Surprise Pension Bill Wins Final Approval in Kentucky Legislature. Teachers Outraged," *Lexington Herald-Leader*, March 29, 2018,
www.kentucky.com.

82   **"I guarantee you somewhere in Kentucky today":** Daniel Desrochers and
Jack Brammer, "Bevin: 'I Guarantee' a Child Was Sexually Assaulted
Because Teachers Attended Protest," *Lexington Herald-Leader*, April 13,
2018, www.kentucky.com.

82   **No one among the state's punditry:** Ben Tobin, "Rand Paul: 'Teachers'
Anger' Cost Matt Bevin the Kentucky Gubernatorial Election," *Courier-
Journal*, November 11, 2019, www.courier-journal.com/story/news/politics
/rand-paul/2019/11/11/rand-paul-teachers-anger-cost-bevin-kentucky
-governor-election/2560458001.

3. THE MIRAGE OF SUCCESS

83   **"live and raise a family":** "Hickory," TopRetirements.com, www.topre
tirements.com/reviews/North_Carolina/Hickory.html; "Hickory Is Trend-
ing," City of Hickory website, www.hickorync.gov/trending.

83   **written off as one of the nation's biggest losers:** Peter Whoriskey, "Glo-
balization Brings a World of Hurt to One Corner of North Carolina,"
Washington Post, November 10, 2009.

83   **It is almost unimaginable today:** Julie Cunnane, "Catawba County Reinvents Itself as High-Tech Manufacturing Hub," *Business North Carolina*,
April 29, 2019, businessnc.com/catawba-county-reinvents-itself-as-high
-tech-manufacturing-hub.

83   **with the help of low wages and anti-union militancy:** John Mullin, "The
Rise and Sudden Decline of North Carolina Furniture Making," *Econ Focus* (Federal Reserve Bank of Richmond magazine), Fourth Quarter 2020,
www.richmondfed.org/-/media/richmondfedorg/publications/research
/econ_focus/2020/q4/economic_history.pdf.

84   **lost half of its jobs:** Ibid.

84   **loss of some 170,000 jobs:** Brent D. Glass and Kelly Kress, "Decline, Con-
solidation, and the Future of Textiles in the State," NCpedia, State Library of North Carolina, www.ncpedia.org/textiles-part-4-decline.

84   **saw the loss of 45,000 jobs:** Cunnane, "Catawba County Reinvents Itself as High-Tech Manufacturing Hub."

84   **offered the companies generous tax breaks:** Ken Ekins, "$6.4M a Job
for Apple in Maiden: New Data Center Report Questions Economic Value
of Incentives, Tax Rebates, Law Changes," *Charlotte Business Journal*, October 11, 2016, www.bizjournals.com.

85   **brought no more than a few hundred jobs:** Craig Jarvis, "Apple Came to
NC Almost a Decade Ago. Here's How It Changed One Community," *Raleigh News and Observer*, July 8, 2018, www.newsobserver.com/news
/business/article214062219.html.

85   **All it takes is for government to get out of the way:** "Pat McCrory on
the Issues," OnTheIssues.org, www.ontheissues.org/Pat_McCrory.htm.

85   **hundreds of homeless people:** Kevin Griffin, "Number of Homeless
Here Up Sharply Last Two Years," *Hickory Daily Record*, February 2, 2020,
hickoryrecord.com.

86   **adopted a more compassionate and proactive approach:** Kevin Griffin,
"Hickory's Homelessness Point Person Talks Successes, Challenges in First
Year on the Job," *Hickory Daily Record*, November 24, 2020, hickoryrecord
.com.

87   **deplorable conditions in the town's homeless camps:** Gene R. Nichol,
The Faces of Poverty in North Carolina: Stores from Our Invisible Citizens
(Chapel Hill: University of North Carolina Press, 2018), pp. xii–xvii.

87   **"profound impact on impoverished North Carolinians":** Ibid., p. 12.

87   **A Houston business consultant tallied:** "Companies Moving to Texas,"
Decide Consulting, decideconsulting.com/companies-moving-to-texas.

88   **"Are Texas and Florida":** Hillary Hoffower, "Are Texas and Florida the
New California and New York?," *Business Insider*, December 17, 2020,
www.businessinsider.com/pandemic-tech-finance-migration-california
-texas-florida-new-york-2020-12.

88   **a thousand people a day:** Maria Mendez, "Where Is Texas's Growing Population Coming From," *Texas Tribune*, May 8, 2019, www.texastribune
.org/2019/05/08/texas-keeps-growing-where-are-newest-transplants
-coming.

88   **posted a real GDP growth rate:** U.S. Bureau of Economic Analysis, Real
Gross Domestic Product by State, retrieved from FRED, Federal Reserve
Bank of St. Louis, fred.stlouisfed.org.

88   **"13 Mind-Blowing Facts":** Laura McCamy, "13 Mind-Blowing Facts
About Florida's Economy," *Markets Insider*, May 20, 2019, markets
.businessinsider.com/news/stocks/florida-economy-facts-2019-5.

88   **"Why is Texas's population skyrocketing":** David Byler, "Texas Population and Political Power Are Growing. Here's Why," *Washington Post*,
May 3, 2021.

89   **marveled at the exodus of businesses:** "Fareed Zakaria GPS," CNN,
June 27, 2021; Fareed Zakaria, "Democrats Need to Show They Can Be
Trusted with Power," *Washington Post*, June 24, 2021.

89   **"Major cities, such as New York, Los Angeles and San Francisco":** Jack Kelly, "Wall Street Banks and Tech Companies Are Fleeing New York and California," *Forbes*, December 14, 2020.

90   **crime rates exploded in cities:** Jon Hilsenrath, "Homicide Spike Hits Most Large U.S. Cities," *Wall Street Journal*, August 2, 2020.

90   **"The state continues to attract":** Tim Henderson, "Americans Are Moving South, West Again," Pew Charitable Trusts, January 8, 2016, www .pewtrusts.org/en/research-and-analysis/blogs/stateline/2016/01/08 /americans-are-moving-south-west-again?cid=10123.

91   **In early 2020, tech jobs on average:** Conor Dougherty, "Arizona Boom Draws Californians and Changes Political Hue," *New York Times*, March 15, 2020.

91   **100 million square feet of vacant office space:** Alex Williams, "New York Is Dead. Long Live New York," *New York Times*, May 15, 2021.

92   **"Bumper-to-bumper traffic has returned":** Kellen Browning, "Tech Workers Who Swore Off the Bay Area Are Coming Back," *New York Times*, July 15, 2021.

92   **"booster class of bankers, retailers":** Keith Orejel, "Political Power Keeps Shifting from the Rust Belt to the Sun Belt. Here's Why," *Washington Post*, May 20, 2021.

93   **immigrants made up 42 percent:** American Immigration Council, "Immigrants in Texas," www.americanimmigrationcouncil.org/research /immigrants-in-texas.

93   **published a ranking of the best state economies:** Samuel Stebbins and Grant Suneson, "Utah, Idaho Are Among the States with the Best Economies in the U.S., Where Do Other States Fall?," 24/7 Wall Street via *USA Today*, August 27, 2020.

93   **When the states were ranked by per capita GDP:** "Per Capita Real Gross Domestic Product (GDP) of the United States in 2019, by State," Statistica, May 17, 2021, www.statista.com/statistics/248063/per-capita-us-real -gross-domestic-product-gdp-by-state.

94   **two-thirds of U.S. net industrial development:** Daniel Yergin, *The New Map: Energy, Climate, and the Clash of Nations* (New York: Penguin Press, 2020), p. 27.

94   **Texas's exports to Mexico:** Anil Kumar, "Did NAFTA Spur Texas Exports?" Federal Reserve Bank of Dallas, March–April 2006, www.dallasfed .org/~/media/documents/research/swe/2006/swe0602b.pdf.

95   **convinced Democratic Governor Luther Hodges:** Scott Huler, "The Man and Plan Behind Research Triangle Park," *Our State*, August 25, 2014, www.ourstate.com/research-triangle-park.

95   **a similar concern about the state's reliance:** Lisa Hartenberger, Zeynep Tufekci, and Stuart Davis, "A History of High Tech and the Technopolis in Austin," in *Inequity in the Technopolis: Race, Class, Gender, and the*

Digital Divide in Austin, ed. Joseph Straubhaar et al. (Austin: University of Texas Press, 2012), pp. 67–69.

95   **those universities have watched the growth:** Michael Mitchell, Michael Leachman, and Matt Saenz, "State Higher Education Funding Cuts Have Pushed Costs to Students, Worsened Inequality," Center for Budget and Policy Priorities, October 24, 2019, www.cbpp.org/sites/default/files/atoms/files/10-24-19sfp.pdf.

96   **Texas Governor Abbott blasted out a tweet:** Greg Abbott (@Greg-Abbott_TX), Twitter, November 8, 2018, twitter.com/gregabbott_tx/status/1060733755856424960?lang=en.

96   **"You are driving them away":** Nick Reisman, "Florida Governor Says He'd Welcome More New Yorkers," Spectrum News, February 22, 2019, spectrumlocalnews.com/nys/rochester/politics/2019/02/22/florida-governor-says-he-d-welcome-more-new-yorkers.

96   **nine hundred people a day:** Talia Kaplan, "NY, NJ Exodus to Florida Fueled by 'Tax Hell': Official," Fox Business, May 24, 2020.

97   **one of the lowest rates:** Janelle Cammenga, "State Corporate Income Tax Rates and Brackets for 2022," Tax Foundation, January 18, 2022, taxfoundation.org/publications/state-corporate-income-tax-rates-and-brackets.

97   **reported that an estimated 99 percent:** Jason Garcia, "In Florida, 99% of Companies Pay No Corporate Tax—with Lawmakers' Blessing," *Orlando Sentinel*, November 13, 2019, www.orlandosentinel.com/news/os-ne-florida-corporate-tax-avoidance-20191113-sx37z4l3d5b6viugtl4thlqxem-story.html.

97   **one of the most inequitable tax systems:** Meg Wiehe et al., *Who Pays? A Distributional Analysis of the Tax Systems in All 50 States*, Institute on Taxation and Economic Policy, October 2018, itep.sfo2.digitaloceanspaces.com/whopays-ITEP-2018.pdf.

98   **"While the Sunshine State has a reputation":** Esteban Leonardo Santis, "Florida's Sales Tax Holidays Aren't Free," *Tampa Bay Times*, June 26, 2021, www.tampabay.com/opinion/2021/06/26/floridas-sales-tax-holidays-arent-free-column.

98   **even the conservative Tax Foundation:** Justin Ross, "Gross Receipts Taxes: Theory and Recent Evidence," Tax Foundation, October 2016, taxfoundation.org/gross-receipts-taxes-theory-and-recent-evidence.

98   **tossed a bomb in the middle:** Christopher R. Berry, "Reassessing the Property Tax," University of Chicago, Harris School of Public Policy, January 2021, cpb-us-w2.wpmucdn.com/voices.uchicago.edu/dist/6/2330/files/2019/04/Berry-Reassessing-the-Property-Tax-Jan21.pdf.

99   **aired on June 27, 2021:** "Fareed Zakaria GPS," June 27, 2021; Zakaria, "Democrats Need to Show They Can Be Trusted with Power.".

100   **based almost entirely:** Ryan Fazio, "NY and CA Spend Billions More in Taxes Than TX and FL—and Get Worse Results," *New York Post*, February 1, 2020; Steven Malanga, "The Real Problem with the Blue State

Model," *City Journal*, Winter 2019, www.city-journal.org/democrat-states -midterms?wallit_nosession=1.

100   **gave the four top places:** "Map: A-F Grades, Rankings for States on School Quality," *Education Week*, September 1, 2020, www.edweek.org/policy -politics/map-a-f-grades-rankings-for-states-on-school-quality/2020/09.

101   **WalletHub's 2021 rankings:** Adam McCann, "States with the Best and Worst School Systems," WalletHub, July 26, 2021, wallethub.com.

101   **WalletHub ranked Texas:** John S. Kiernan, "Property Taxes by State," WalletHub, February 23, 2021, wallethub.com.

102   **Texas was rated as having the ninth-worst:** David C. Radley, Sara R. Collins, and Jesse C. Baumgartner, "2020 Scorecard on State Health System Performance," The Commonwealth Fund, New York, 2020scorecard .commonwealthfund.org/rankings.

103   **ranked fortieth out of the fifty:** Rhea K. Farberman et al., *The Impact of Chronic Underfunding on America's Public Health System: Trends, Risks, and Recommendations, 2020*, Trust for America's Health, April 2020, www .tfah.org/report-details/publichealthfunding2020.

103   **Thirty-five Texas counties had no physician:** Texas A&M University, Rural and Community Health Institute, in partnership with Episcopal Health Foundation, "What's Next? Practical Suggestions for Rural Communities Facing a Hospital Closure," 2017, architexas.org/news/whats-next -final-rchi.pdf.

103   **provision of mental health services:** Mental Health America, "Ranking the States," 2020, www.mhanational.org/issues/ranking-states#overall-ranking.

103   **They also have higher rates:** State-by-state statistics for suicide, teenage pregnancy, infant mortality, life expectancy, and accidental death were found at the National Center for Health Statistics, "Stats of the States," cdc .gov; crime rates at the Uniform Crime Report, fbi.gov; incarceration rates at the Sentencing Project, "State-by-State Data," www.sentencing project.org/the-facts/#map.

103   **real median household income:** "Real Median Household Income by State, Annual," Federal Reserve Bank of St. Louis, fredstlouisfed.org.

104   **supplemental poverty rates:** U.S. Census Bureau, "The Supplemental Poverty Measure: 2019," September 15, 2020, www.census.gov/library/public ations/2020/demo/p60-272.html.

104   **Florida was also tied:** "Unemployment Benefits by State, 2021," World Population Review, worldpopulationreview.com/state-rankings/unemploy ment-benefits-by-state.

104   **states with the highest personal income tax rates:** Institute on Taxation and Economic Policy, *Trickle-Down Dries Up: States Without Personal Income Taxes Lag Behind States with the Highest Top Tax Rates*, October 26, 2017, itep.org/trickle-down-dries-up.

105   **Abbott's appointees to the commission:** Eric Dexheimer and Jay Root, "'Muzzled and Eviscerated': Critics Say Abbott Appointees Gutted

Enforcement of Texas Grid Rules," *Houston Chronicle*, February 26, 2021, www.houstonchronicle.com/politics/texas/article/critics-abbott-power -grid-rules-texas-deadly-storm-15982421.php.

105   **six major chemical accidents:** U.S. Chemical Safety and Hazard Investigation Board, www.csb.gov/investigations/current-investigations/?Type=1.

105   **Florida's cuts in environmental enforcement:** Lauren Ritchie, "Rick Scott's Disdain for the Environment Means He Owns Algae Mess Plaguing the State," *Orlando Sentinel*, September 14, 2018, www.orlandosentinel .com/news/lake/os-lauren-ritchie-toxic-algae-20180914-story.html.

105   **After a Miami condominium collapsed:** Michael LaForgia, Adam Playford, and Lazaro Gamio, "Law Enforcement Let South Florida Towers Skirt Inspections for Years," *New York Times*, July 4, 2021.

106   **issued a ranking of the best states:** Adam McCann, "Best States to Live In," WalletHub, June 15, 2021, wallethub.com.

106   **"It enjoys a reputation for progressive outlook":** V.O. Key, *Southern Politics in State and Nation* (New York: Alfred A. Knopf, 1949), pp. 205–6.

106   **There was a white backlash:** Rob Christensen, *The Paradox of Tar Heel Politics: The Personalities, Elections, and Events That Shaped Modern North Carolina* (Chapel Hill: University of North Carolina Press, 2008), p. 179.

107   **"It was both the face of the New South":** Jane Mayer, *Dark Money: The Hidden History of the Billionaires Behind the Rise of the Radical Right* (New York: Doubleday, 2016), p. 244.

107   **"In many ways, North Carolina in the early 1960s":** Christensen, *The Paradox of Tar Heel Politics*, p. 191.

108   **arranged $2 million in donations:** Lucille Sherman, "How a Decade of Republican Majorities Reshaped North Carolina," *Raleigh News and Observer*, October 30, 2020, www.newsobserver.com/news/politics-govern ment/election/article246776737.html.

108   **one attack ad after another:** Mayer, *Dark Money*, pp. 261–62.

109   **cost the state $2.8 billion:** "The Cost of Trickle-Down Economics for North Carolina," Institute on Tax and Economic Policy, May 26, 2017, itep .org/the-cost-of-trickle-down-economics-for-north-carolina.

109   **"They've prioritized these corporate tax giveaways":** Sherman, "How a Decade of Republican Majorities Reshaped North Carolina."

110   **North Carolina's supplemental poverty rate:** U.S. Census Bureau, "Supplemental Poverty Measure," 2019, www.census.gov/library/publications /2020/demo/p60-272.html.

110   **concentrated poverty neighborhoods:** Brian Kennedy II, "Special Report: Concentrated Poverty, Segregation on the Rise in NC," NC Policy Watch, April 19, 2018, www.ncpolicywatch.com/2018/04/19/special -report-concentrated-poverty-segregation-on-the-rise-in-nc.

110   **"The study throws a wet blanket"**: Rob Christensen, "What Has Republican Control of NC Done for the Economy? A New Study Has Some Answers," *Raleigh News and Observer*, July 19, 2018, www.newsobserver.com.

110   **"the 2010s were actually a lost decade"**: Mel Umbarger, "The State of North Carolina at the End of a Decade," North Carolina Justice Center, December 10, 2019, www.ncjustice.org/reporter-memo-the-state-of-north -carolina-at-the-end-of-a-decade.

111   **"unforgiving war on poor people"**: Michael A. Cooper Jr., "The War on the War on Poverty," *New Republic*, February 15, 2015.

111   **Rooting out what he sees**: Chris Kromm, "Investigative Series: How Pope Reigns," *Facing South*, January 14, 2011, www.facingsouth.org/2011/01 /investigative-series-how-pope-reigns.html; Sue Sturgis, "How Art Pope's Money Shaped UNC's Toxic Debate over Nikole Hannah-Jones, *Facing South*," July 16, 2021, www.facingsouth.org/2021/07/how-art-popes -money-shaped-uncs-toxic-debate-over-nikole-hannah-jones.

4. THE DEAD ZONES

116   **"sounds like a hard, hard rain"**: Interview with Bill and Shelby Jane Boudreaux, March 7, 2020.

116   **synthetic rubber manufacturing complex**: Will H. Shearon Jr., "Synthetic Rubber Manufacture," *Texas State Historical Association Handbook of Texas*, 1952, www.tshaonline.org/handbook/entries/synthetic-rubber -manufacture; Fact Statement, *Drawhorn vs. Texaco Chemical Company*, Ninth Court of Appeals, Jefferson County, Texas, Case No. 09-93-117 CV.

117   **polluting Port Neches's air and water**: Harry Hurt III, "The Cancer Belt," *Texas Monthly*, May 1981, www.texasmonthly.com/articles/the -cancer-belt.

117   **record fines totaling nearly $10 million**: Dan Wallach, "Huntsman Agrees to Revised Penalties over Port Neches, Texas, Plant Emissions," *Beaumont Enterprise*, May 30, 2003, www.beaumontenterprise.com.

117   **In the midst of its investigation**: Michael May, "The One That Got Away," *Texas Observer*, November 8, 2002, www.texasobserver.org/1134-the-one -that-got-away-polluting-perps-go-down-but-huntsman-walks.

118   **posted its own air monitors**: Dina Cappiello, "Chronicle Cross-County Study Reveals Risky Load of Air Toxics," *Houston Chronicle*, January 16, 2005, www.chron.com/news/article/Chronicle-cross-county-study-reveals -risky-load-1643020.php.

118   **found illegal chemical releases in Texas had doubled**: Luke Metzger et al., *Illegal Air Pollution in Texas*, Environment Texas and Frontier Group, December 2019, environmenttexas.org/sites/environment/files/reports /TX_Pollution_scrn(1).pdf.

118   **spiked to 74,500 pounds:** Environmental Protection Agency, Toxic Release Inventory, edap.epa.gov/public/extensions/TRISearchPlus/TRI SearchPlus.html.

119   **The last federal inspection:** Ibid.

119   **"Clearly there had been a mechanical failure":** Kiah Collier, "Ahead of Explosion, Port Neches Plant Reported an Increase of Rogue Emissions of Explosive Gas," *Texas Tribune*, January 30, 2020, www.texastribune.org /2020/01/30/texas-plant-reported-increasing-rogue-emissions-explosion.

120   **Investigators later found asbestos:** Kaitlin Bain, "Communications After TPC Group Blast Give More Information About Asbestos Discovery, Official Response," *Beaumont Enterprise*, February 23, 2020, www .beaumontenterprise.com/news/article/EXCLUSIVE-Communications -after-TPC-Group-blast-15078676.php.

120   **grabbed his four-year-old daughter:** Kiah Collier, "Texas Regulators Want Stiffer Penalties for Company Whose Port Neches Plant Exploded," *Texas Tribune*, December 18, 2019, www.texastribune.org/2019 /12/18/texas-regulators-want-tougher-penalties-company-after-port-neches -blas.

120   **skyrocketed to 316,000:** Environmental Protection Agency, Toxic Release Inventory.

122   **decimated their programs for environmental enforcement:** Environmental Integrity Project, "The Thin Green Line: Cuts in State Pollution Control Agencies Threaten Public Health," December 5, 2019, environ mentalintegrity.org/wp-content/uploads/2019/12/The-Thin-Green-Line -report-12.5.19.pdf.

122   **went so far as to ban:** Tristram Korten, "In Florida, Office Ban Term 'Climate Change,'" Florida Center for Investigative Reporting via the *Miami Herald*, March 8, 2015, www.miamiherald.com/news/state/florida/article 12983720.html.

122   **"Trojan horse" for liberals:** Katie Glueck, "Bobby Jindal: White House 'Science Deniers,'" *Politico*, September 16, 2014.

122   **the five states whose industries:** Environmental Integrity Project, "The Thin Green Line."

123   **release more toxic chemicals:** Environmental Protection Agency, Toxic Release Inventory.

123   **highest amounts of carbon dioxide and methane:** U.S. Energy Information Administration, Table 5. Per Capita Energy-Related Carbon Dioxide Emissions by State (1990–2017), www.eia.gov/environment/emissions /state/; Johannes Friedrich, Mengpin Ge, and Alexander Tankou, "6 Charts to Understand U.S. State Greenhouse Gas Emissions," World Resources Institute, August 10, 2017, www.wri.org/blog/2017/08/6-charts-under stand-us-state-greenhouse-gas-emissions.

123   **increase in auto emissions:** Nadja Popovich and Denise Lu, "The Most Detailed Map of Auto Emissions in America," *New York Times*, Octo-

ber 10, 2019. The *Times* analyzed Boston University's Database of Road Transportation Emissions, daac.ornl.gov/cgi-bin/dsviewer.pl?ds_id=1735.

123   **burn more coal:** U.S. Energy Information Administration, "State Profiles and Energy Estimates," www.eia.gov/state/seds/data.php?incfile=/state/seds/sep_sum/html/rank_use_source.html&sid=US.

123   **allow more fracking:** Elizabeth Ridlington, Kim Norman, and Rachel Richardson, *Fracking by the Numbers: The Damage to Our Water, Land and Climate from a Decade of Dirty Drilling*, Frontier Group and Environment America Research & Policy Center, April 2016, environmentamerica.org/sites/environment/files/reports/Fracking by the Numbers vUS.pdf.

123   **have more oil and gas pipelines:** U.S. Energy Information Administration, "State Profiles and Energy Estimates."

123   **more contaminated waterways:** Jeff Inglis, Tony Dutzik, and John Rumpler, *Wasting Our Waterways: Toxics Industrial Pollution and Restoring the Promise of the Clean Water Act*, Frontier Group and Environment America Research & Policy Center, June 2014, environmenttexas.org/reports/txe/wasting-our-waterways-0.

123   **more closed beaches:** Gideon Weissman and John Rumpler, *Safe for Swimming? Water Quality at Our Beaches*, Frontier Group and Environment America Research & Policy Center, July 2019, environmenttexas center.org/sites/environment/files/reports/TXE Safe for Swimming Jul19web rev1.pdf.

123   **five other major chemical accidents:** U.S. Chemical Safety and Hazard Investigation Board, "Current Investigations," www.csb.gov/investigations/current-investigations/?Type=1&pg=1.

123   **"When you look at all these facilities":** Kiah Collier, "Port Neches Plant Rocked by Multiple Explosions Has History of Environmental Missteps," *Texas Tribune*, November 27, 2019, www.texastribune.org/2019/11/27/texas-plant-rocked-explosions-mandatory-evacuations-ordered.

123   **not one of the Republican-led states:** Sam Ricketts et al., "States Are Laying a Road Map for Climate Leadership," Center for American Progress, April 30, 2020, cdn.americanprogress.org/content/uploads/2020/04/29135758/StatesClimate-brief.pdf?_ga=2.1428401.1404689193.1607791117-184995117.1607791117.

124   **developed vast "dead zones":** "NOAA Forecasts Very Large 'Dead Zone' for Gulf of Mexico," National Oceanic and Atmospheric Administration, June 12, 2019, www.noaa.gov/media-release/noaa-forecasts-very-large-dead-zone-for-gulf-of-mexico.

124   **only two had done so:** Kris Sigford et al., *Decades of Delay: EPA Leadership Still Lacking in Protecting America's Great River*, Mississippi River Collaborative, November 2016, www.msrivercollab.org/wp-content/uploads/Decades-of-Delay-MRC-Nov-2016.pdf.

125   **"He's got to own this slimy mess":** Lauren Ritchie, "Rick Scott's Disdain for the Environment Means He Owns Algae Mess Plaguing the State,"

Orlando Sentinel, September 14, 2018, www.orlandosentinel.com/news
/lake/os-lauren-ritchie-toxic-algae-20180914-story.html.

125   **"Long-term unsustainable use of the aquifer":** Jeremy Frankel, "Crisis
on the High Plains: The Loss of America's Largest Aquifer—the Ogallala,"
University of Denver Water Law Review, May 17, 2018, duwaterlawreview
.com/crisis-on-the-high-plains-the-loss-of-americas-largest-aquifer-the
-ogallala.

125   **A study by researchers at the University of Kansas:** Rex C. Buchanan
et al., "The High Plains Aquifer," Kansas Geological Survey, Public Information Circular 18, January 2015, www.kgs.ku.edu/Publications/pic18
/index.html.

126   **"We think it's a harsh method":** Karen Dillon, "Ogallala Water Continues to Pour onto Farm Fields Despite Decades of Dire Forecasts," *Lawrence
Journal-World*, September 27, 2014, www2.ljworld.com/news/2014/sep/27
/ogallala-water-continues-pore-farm-fields-despite-.

126   **cut back 20 percent without sacrificing profits:** Frankel, "Crisis on the
High Plains."

126   **Low-lying wetland forests:** "In the U.S. Southeast, Natural Forests Are
Being Felled to Send Fuel Overseas," Natural Resources Defense Council,
October 2015, www.nrdc.org/resources/us-southeast-natural-forests-are
-being-felled-send-fuel-overseas.

127   **In a 1968 essay:** Russell Kirk, "Man, Enemy of Nature," from the "To the
Point" syndicated newspaper column, February 26, 1968, available from the
Russell Kirk Center, kirkcenter.org/environment-nature-conservation
/man-enemy-of-nature.

128   **"The real evil":** Roger Scruton, *How to Think Seriously About the Planet:
The Case for an Environmental Conservatism* (New York: Oxford University Press, 2012), p. 81.

128   **costs the tourism industry:** Environmental Protection Agency,
Nutrient Pollution Fact Sheet, www.epa.gov/nutrientpollution/effects
-economy.

129   **"Crops are stunted or destroyed":** John Kennedy, "Special Message to the
Congress on Improving the Nation's Health," February 7, 1963, Public Pa-
pers of the Presidents of the United States: John F. Kennedy, 1963 (Washington, DC: Office of the Federal Register, National Archives and Records
Service, U.S. Government Printing Office, 1964), 1:141–47.

129   **222 million pounds of toxic chemicals:** Environmental Protection
Agency, Toxic Release Inventory.

129   **emissions of carbon dioxide:** U.S. Energy Information Administration,
Table 5. Per Capita Energy-Related Carbon Dioxide Emissions by State
(1990–2017), www.eia.gov/environment/emissions/state.

130   **"We've got a great union":** Alec MacGillis, "The Permanent Candidate:
What's Driving Rick Perry?," *The Atlantic*, October 20, 2011.

130   **"a sort of Confederate-based":** Ibid.

130 **"I had not one piece of legislation":** R.G. Ratcliffe, "Conservatives Battle for Lieutenant Governor Post; Republican Perry Staying as Close to Gov. Bush's Coattails as Possible," *Houston Chronicle*, October 4, 1998, www.chron.com.

130 **"I'm not sure you can ever ascribe a real philosophy":** MacGillis, "The Permanent Candidate."

131 **sponsored a bill to strip Hightower's department:** Ratcliffe, "Conservatives Battle for Lieutenant Governor Post."

131 **distanced himself from Reagan's positions:** Byron W. Daynes and Glen Sussman, *White House Politics and the Environment: Franklin D. Roosevelt to George W. Bush* (College Station: Texas A&M University Press, 2010), pp. 155–56.

131 **allied him with agribusiness:** James Drew, "In Perry's Texas, It's Hands Off," *Dallas Morning News*, December 22, 2013, www.dallasnews.com.

131 **"American business in general":** Ibid.

132 **accepted a $25,000 contribution:** "A Good Man Is Gone: Benny Preston Fisher, 1942–2002," *Texas Observer*, March 29, 2002, www.texasobserver.org.

132 **"All my life":** Abby Rapoport, "The V.I.P. Room," *Texas Observer*, December 2011, www.texasobserver.org.

132 **eliminated 230 regulations:** Drew, "In Perry's Texas, It's Hands Off."

132 **The details of the tragedy:** U.S. Chemical and Hazard Investigation Board, *West Fertilizer Company Fire and Explosion, Final Report*, January 18, 2016, www.csb.gov/west-fertilizer-explosion-and-fire-.

133 **President Obama signed an executive order:** Ibid., p. 14.

133 **Perry told a news conference:** Dug Begley and Ingrid Lobet, "Theories Emerging on West Explosion, Fire," *Houston Chronicle*, April 23, 2013, www.houstonchronicle.com/news/houston-texas/houston/article/Theories-emerging-on-West-fire-explosion-4454663.php.

133 **stockpiles of the chemical:** Doug J. Swanson and David Tarrant, "It Could Happen Again," *Dallas Morning News*, December 15, 2013, res.dallasnews.com/interactives/2013_December/westretrospective/1215_westretrospective.html.

134 **"In their defense":** Paul J. Weber, "Fire Marshal: 5 Facilities Refused Inspection," Associated Press, August 26, 2013.

134 **"It could happen again":** Swanson and Tarrant, "It Could Happen Again."

134 **"a broken-down Southern state":** Richard Parker, *Lone Star Nation: How Texas Will Transform America* (New York: Pegasus Books, 2014), p. 50.

135 **experimenting since the early 1980s:** Daniel Yergin, *The New Map: Energy, Climate, and the Clash of Nations* (New York: Penguin Press, 2020), pp. 5–8.

135 **paid $3.5 billion:** Ibid., p. 8.

136 **four million barrels of oil:** Clifford Krauss, "The 'Monster' Texas Oil Field That Made the U.S. a Star in the World Market," *New York Times*, February 3, 2019.

136   **net exporter of petroleum:** Bradley Olson, "U.S. Becomes Net Exporter of Oil, Fuels for First Time in Decades," *Wall Street Journal*, December 6, 2018.

136   **world's leading producer of oil and natural gas:** U.S. Energy Information Administration, "The U.S. Leads Global Petroleum and Natural Gas Production with Record Growth in 2018," August 20, 2019, www.eia.gov /todayinenergy/detail.php?id=40973.

137   **two-thirds of U.S. net industrial development:** Yergin, *The New Map*, p. 27.

137   **flare off the gas or let it escape:** Haroko Tabuchi, "Despite Their Promises, Giant Energy Companies Burn Away Vast Amounts of Natural Gas," *New York Times*, October 16, 2019.

138   **"would not unring the bell":** Mary B. Powers, "Court Halts Opponents' Block to Nearly Done $2B Texas Natural Gas Line," *Engineering News-Record*, August 30, 2020, www.enr.com/articles/49947-court-halts-opp onents-block-to-nearly-done-2b-texas-natural-gas-line.

138   **had been given $10.5 million:** J.T. Stepleton, "Oil and Gas Money Gave Rick Perry the Energy to Win in Texas," National Institute on Money in State Politics, January 9, 2017, followthemoney.org.

138   **Since then, Abbott has pulled away:** National Institute on Money in Politics, www.followthemoney.org/show-me?dt=1&f-fc=1,2,3&c-t-eid=1128 1947#[{1|gro=d-cci.

139   **"an act of God":** Peggy Fikac, "Perry Stands By 'Act of God' Remark About Spill," *Houston Chronicle*, May 5, 2010, www.chron.com/business/energy /article/Perry-stands-by-act-of-God-remark-about-spill-1698755.php.

139   **opposed new federal regulation:** Jennifer A. Dlouhy, "Rick Perry Joins Coastal Governors' Energy Coalition to Lobby for Offshore Drilling," *Houston Chronicle*, May 2, 2011, blog.chron.com/txpotomac/2011/05/rick -perry-joins-coastal-governors-energy-coalition-to-lobby-for-offshore -drilling.

139   **overruled decisions by smog-choked cities:** Matthew Tresaugue, "City Rebuffed by State over Refinery Air Permit," *Houston Chronicle*, February 25, 2010, www.chron.com/news/houston-texas/article/City-rebuffed -by-state-over-refinery-air-permit-1699575.php.

139   **"rein in this rogue agency":** "Statement by Gov. Perry Regarding the EPA's Decisions to Disapprove Texas' Air Permitting Program," States News Service, June 30, 2010.

140   **fifteen million gallons of toxin-laced wastewater:** Sam Howe Verhovek, "Shrimpers Voice Fear on Growth of Factory," *New York Times*, June 20, 1993.

140   **$3.4 million penalty:** Ibid.

140   **black coffin draped with a fish net:** Mark Smith, "Environmentalists Put Coffin by Governor's Office," *Houston Chronicle*, August 13, 1993, www .chron.com.

140   **scuttle her fishing boat:** Tony Freemantle, "Shrimper Stages Persistent Fight to Stop Company from Polluting Bays," *Houston Chronicle*, October 7, 2001, www.chron.com/news/houston-texas/article/Shrimper-stages -persistent-fight-to-stop-company-2034803.php.

140   **a goal of "zero discharge":** Christine Keyser, "An Unreasonable Woman," *In These Times*, December 24, 2011.

141   **called Wilson and asked her to meet him:** Lily Moore-Eissenberg, "Nurdles All the Way Down," *Texas Monthly*, October 2019, www.texasmo nthly.com/news/texans-gulf-coast-plastic-pollution.

141   **calling Formosa a "serial offender":** Memorandum and Order, *San Antonio Bay Estuarine Waterkeeper, et al., v. Formosa Plastics Corp., Texas, et al.,* U.S. District Court for the Southern District of Texas, Victoria Division, 6:17-CV-0047, June 27, 2019.

141   **"the government treats petrochemical investment":** Bruce Einhorn and Joe Carroll, "A Plastics Giant That Pollutes Too Much for Taiwan Is Turning to America," *Bloomberg Businessweek*, December 13, 2019, www .bloombergquint.com/businessweek/asian-company-that-pollutes-too -much-at-home-expands-in-america.

142   **"They are not building this in Taiwan":** Ibid.

142   **fined Formosa a meager $121,000:** Environmental Protection Agency, Toxic Release Inventory.

142   **released 13.6 million pounds:** Ibid.

142   **550,000 barrels of crude:** Revised Findings of Fact and Conclusions of Law, *Environment Texas Citizen Lobby, Inc., and Sierra Club v. ExxonMobil Corporation, ExxonMobil Chemical Company, and ExxonMobil Refining and Supply Company,* U.S. District Court for the Southern District of Texas, Houston Division, H-10-4969, April 26, 2017, p. 6.

143   **37 million pounds:** Environmental Protection Agency, Toxic Release Inventory.

143   **described seeing a toxic haze:** Revised Findings, *Environment Texas Citizen Lobby, Inc., and Sierra Club v. ExxonMobil Corporation,* p. 22.

143   **released more than ten million pounds:** Sierra Club Lone Star Chapter, "A Historic Legal Victory Against ExxonMobil," press release, June 22, 2017, www.sierraclub.org/texas/blog/2017/06/historic-legal-victory -against-exxonmobil.

143   **"high-priority" violations of the Clean Air Act:** Environmental Protection Agency, Toxic Release Inventory.

144   **$55 million industry:** Dick Russell, "The Crisis Comes Home: Declining Catches in New England and the Gulf Coast," *Environmental Magazine*, September 1, 1996, dickrussell.org/1996/09/01/the-worlds-fisheries -a-state-of-emergency-part-2.

144   **estimated 1.2 million pounds of mercury:** Lise Olsen and David Hasemyer, "A Sprawling Superfund Site Has Contaminated Lavaca Bay. Now, It's Threatened by Climate Change," joint investigation by *Inside Climate*

News, the *Texas Observer*, and NBC News, September 26, 2020, inside
climatenews.org/news/25092020/superfund-epa-lavaca-bay-climate
-change.

144   **purchased most of the seventy homes:** Naveena Sadasivam, "Company
Town: How Big Business Turned a Gulf Coast Beach Town into an Industrial Zone," *Texas Observer*, May 31, 2016, www.texasobserver.org
/quintana-freeport-lng-company-town.

145   **knocked on the doors:** Ibid.

145   **$25,000 apiece to keep quiet:** Ibid.

146   **"a working person's waterway":** Richard Parker, "Sun, Sand and Tank-
ers? Port Aransas Battles Big Oil and Gas Ambitions," *Houston Chronicle*,
August 22, 2020, www.chron.com/opinion/outlook/article/Opinion-Sun
-sand-and-tankers-Port-Aransas-15506140.php.

5. CODE RED

148   **"She loved to party":** Interview with Makeska Shoemaker, November 19,
2020; Giacomo Bologna, "Mississippi Woman Dies After Rural Hospital
Closes ER," *Clarion-Ledger*, March 12, 2019, www.clarionledger.com.

148   **grown tired of the millions:** Giacomo Bologna, "Rural Hospitals in Crisis; Did Health Care Policy Failure Kill This Mom?," *Clarion-Ledger*,
March 18, 2019, www.clarionledger.com.

148   **the crisis is particularly acute:** Michael Braga et al., "Leaving Billions of
Dollars on the Table: Rural Hospitals Foundering in States That Declined
Obamacare," GateHouse Media, July 28, 2019, stories.usatodaynetwork
.com/ruralhospitals/financialtroubles.

149   **absorbed $3 million:** Bologna, "Rural Hospitals in Crisis."

149   **"They could not keep that emergency room":** Ibid.

149   **"He looked like he was shocked":** Bologna, "Mississippi Woman Dies
After Rural Hospital Closes ER."

149   **lost $182,000 in a year:** Giacomo Bologna, "Is There an Ambulance Avail-
able? Longer Response Times Growing in Rural Mississippi," *Clarion-
Ledger*, March 19, 2019, www.clarionledger.com.

149   **twenty-four minutes after getting the call:** Bologna, "Mississippi Woman
Dies After Rural Hospital Closes ER."

150   **"They could have saved":** Interview with Makeska Shoemaker, November 19, 2020.

150   **"been pushed by a Republican":** Tim Kalich, "Campaign Money May Be
Driving Medicaid Issue," *Northside Sun*, August 8, 2019, www.northsidesun
.com.

150   **have been inflicting deep budget cuts:** Rhea K. Farberman et al., *The Impact of Chronic Underfunding on America's Public Health System: Trends,*

Risks, and Recommendations, 2020, Trust for America's Health, April 2020, www.tfah.org/report-details/publichealthfunding2020.

150 **Mississippi has seen five rural hospitals:** Michael Topchik et al., "The Rural Health Safety Net Under Pressure: Rural Hospital Vulnerability," Chartis Center for Rural Health, February 2020, www.chartis.com/forum /insight/the-rural-health-safety-net-under-pressure-rural-hospital-vulner ability/; Giacomo Bologna, "Is Your Hospital on This List? 31 Mississippi Hospitals at Risk of Closing, Report Says," *Clarion-Ledger,* March 12, 2019, www.clarionledger.com/story/news/politics/2019/03/12/these-rural -mississippi-hospitals-high-financial-risk/3129938002.

151 **study for the National Bureau of Economic Research:** Sarah Miller et al., "Medicaid and Mortality: New Evidence from Linked Survey and Administrative Data," National Bureau of Economic Research working paper, August 2019, www.nber.org/papers/w26081; Matt Broaddus and Aviva Aron-Dine, "Medicaid Expansion Has Saved at Least 19,000 Lives, New Research Finds," Center on Budget and Policy Priorities, Washington, DC, November 6, 2019, www.cbpp.org/sites/default/files/atoms/files /11-6-19health.pdf.

152 **preventable chronic diseases cost the U.S. economy:** Hugh Waters and Marlon Graf, *The Cost of Chronic Disease in the U.S.,* Milken Institute, August 2018, milkeninstitute.org/sites/default/files/reports-pdf/Chronic Diseases-HighRes-FINAL.pdf.

152 **citizens who heckled Democratic lawmakers:** Jane Mayer, *Dark Money: The Hidden History of the Billionaires Behind the Rise of the Radical Right* (New York: Doubleday, 2016), pp. 193–94; Lee Fang, "Right-Wing Harassment Strategy Against Dems Detailed in Memo," *ThinkProgress,* July 31, 2009, archive.thinkprogress.org/right-wing-harassment-strategy-against -dems-detailed-in-memo-yell-stand-up-and-shout-out-rattle-him-94e9 af741078/.

153 **"We packed these town halls":** Eliana Johnson, "Inside the Koch-Funded Ads Giving Dems Fits," *National Review,* March 31, 2014, www .nationalreview.com/2014/03/inside-koch-funded-ads-giving-dems-fits-eli ana-johnson.

153 **pressured elected officials in Republican states:** Mayer, *Dark Money,* p. 351.

153 **demonstrable improvement in their health care systems:** Benjamin D. Sommers, Katherine Baicker, and Arnold M. Epstein, "Mortality and Access to Care Among Adults After State Medicaid Expansions," *New England Journal of Medicine,* September 13, 2012, www.nejm.org/doi/full/10.1056 /NEJMsa1202099#t=articleTop; Rachel West, "Expanding Medicaid in All States Would Save 14,000 Lives Per Year," Center for American Progress, October 24, 2018, www.americanprogress.org/issues/healthcare/reports/2018 /10/24/459676/expanding-medicaid-states-save-14000-lives-per-year.

153   **acknowledged even by many Republicans:** Hunter Field, "Medicaid Expansion Gets Nod as Arkansas House Passes $8.2b Spending Bill," *Arkansas Democrat-Gazette*, March 8, 2018, www.arkansasonline.com/news /2018/mar/08/medicaid-expansion-gets-nod-20180308.

153   **the percentage of uninsured in Arkansas:** Dan Witters, "Arkansas, Kentucky Set Pace in Reducing Uninsured Rate," *Gallup News*, February 4, 2016.

153   **helped shore up struggling rural hospitals:** Joe Thompson, "Arkansas Shows Medicaid Expansion Can Work in Mississippi," *Clarion-Ledger*, August 6, 2019, www.clarionledger.com/story/opinion/columnists/2019/08 /06/arkansas-shows-medicaid-expansion-can-work-mississippi/19313 46001.

153   **In a single fiscal year:** Hunter Field, "Medicaid Expansion Gets Nod as Arkansas House Passed $8.3b Spending Bill," *Arkansas Democrat-Gazette*, March 8, 2018, www.arkansasonline.com/news/2018/mar/08/medicaid -expansion-gets-nod-20180308.

154   **What does Rutledge want:** Max Brantley, "Rutledge Admits She Wants to Kill the Entire Affordable Care Act," *Arkansas Times*, December 20, 2019, arktimes.com/arkansas-blog/2019/12/20/rutledge-admits-she-wants -to-kill-the-entire-affordable-care-act.

154   **"liberal Republicans":** Luke Ramseth, "Legislature Overrides Education Veto," *Clarion-Ledger*, August 12, 2020.

154   **excuse to halt abortions:** Giacomo Bologna and Alissa Zhu, "Mississippi Gov. Tate Reeves: Abortions Must Be Cancelled During Coronavirus Pandemic," *Clarion-Ledger*, March 24, 2020, www.clarionledger.com/story /news/politics/2020/03/24/mississippi-gov-abortions-must-halted-dur ing-coronavirus-pandemic/2909422001.

154   **He leads his state in public prayer:** Reeves's policy pronouncements have been widely reported in the Mississippi media. For examples, see "Tate Reeves on the Issues," OntheIssues.org, www.ontheissues.org/Senate/Tate _Reeves.htm.

155   **quietly been in talks:** Rogelio V. Solis, "Gov. Bryant Quietly in Talks About a Medicaid Expansion Plan for Mississippi," *Mississippi Today*, via Associated Press, December 20, 2018, mississippitoday.org.

155   **"I am opposed to Obamacare expansion in Mississippi":** Luke Ramseth, "Groups Starts Push for Medicaid Expansion," *Clarion-Ledger*, September 24, 2020, www.clarionledger.com.

155   **campaign contributions and other support:** Jerry Mitchell, "School Leaders' Choice: Cutting Public Education," Mississippi Center for Investigative Reporting, February 16, 2019, www.mississippicir.org/news/state -leaders-choice-cutting-public-education.

156   **"Our broad coalition":** Geoff Pender, "Medicaid Expansion Ballot Initiative Officially Halted," *Mississippi Today*, May 19, 2021, mississippito

day.org/2021/05/19/mississippi-medicaid-expansion-ballot-initiative
-halted.

156 **Of the twenty states the group rated:** David C. Radley, Sara R. Collins,
and Jesse C. Baumgartner, "2020 Scorecard on State Health System Performance," The Commonwealth Fund, 2020scorecard.commonwealthfund
.org/rankings.

157 **One team of researchers:** Jonathon P. Leider et al., "Inaccuracy of Official Estimates of Public Health Spending in the United States, 2000–2018,"
American Journal of Public Health, July 2020, ajph.aphapublications.org
/doi/10.2105/AJPH.2020.305709.

157 **One study of 2019 state spending:** Farberman et al., *The Impact of
Chronic Underfunding on America's Public Health System*.

157 **compared the percentage of low-income people:** Kaiser Family Foundation, "Medicaid Fact Sheets," May 27, 2020, www.kff.org/interactive
/medicaid-state-fact-sheets.

158 **"We're approaching Third World care":** Andy Miller, "Official: Approaching Third World Care in Georgia," *Albany Herald*, November 21,
2014.

158 **"A black man in Mississippi":** Olga Khazan, "The States with the Worst
Healthcare Systems," *The Atlantic*, May 1, 2014.

158 **"Racial and ethnic minorities":** Ibid.

159 **What was the state's response?:** Bill Crawford, "Health-Care Budget
Cuts, Job Losses Hurt an Already Bad Situation in Mississippi," *Sun
Herald*, May 7, 2017, www.sunherald.com/opinion/other-voices/article
148927174.html.

159 **cut the state health department budget:** Jerry Mitchell, "UMMC Faces
Unexpected $35M Cut, Possible Layoffs," *Hattiesburg American*, Febru-
ary 24, 2017, www.hattiesburgamerican.com/story/news/local/2017/02
/24/ummc-faces-unexpected-cut-possible-layoffs/98374236.

160 **"Like hardworking Mississippi families":** Geoff Pender, "Bryant Orders
More Emergency Budget Cuts, Dips into Savings," *Clarion-Ledger*,
March 24, 2017, www.clarionledger.com/story/news/politics/2017/03/24
/budget-cuts-bryant/99587290.

160 **Reeves was even less empathetic:** Geoff Pender, "More Mississippi Budget Cuts Proposed; Leaders Unapologetic," *Clarion-Ledger*, November 27,
2017, www.clarionledger.com/story/news/politics/2017/11/27/more-miss
issippi-budget-cuts-proposed-legislature-reeves-gunn/897452001.

160 **pushed through fifty-one tax cuts:** Adam Ganucheau, "How Much Have
Tax Cuts Cost Mississippi? $577M Since 2012," *Mississippi Today*, May 2,
2017, mississippitoday.org/2017/05/02/how-much-have-tax-cuts-cost-mis
sissippi-577m-since-2012.

160 **"Corporate site selection professionals":** Norton Francis, "State Tax Incentives for Economic Development," Tax Policy Center, February 2016,

www.taxpolicycenter.org/sites/default/files/alfresco/publication-pdfs
/2000636-state-tax-incentives-for-economic-development.pdf.

161   **job growth of 0.4 percent:** Arizona State University, W.P. Carey School
of Business, Seidman Research Institute, Job Growth Database.

161   **"people are going to die":** Laura Ungar, Jason Dearen, and Hannah Recht,
"Florida's Cautionary Tale: How Gutting and Muzzling Public Health Fueled COVID Fire," *Kaiser Health News* and Associated Press, August 24,
2020, khn.org/news/floridas-cautionary-tale-how-starving-and-muzzling
-public-health-fueled-covid-fire.

161   **fourteen states with the highest:** Dana Milbank, "How Does Ron De-
Santis Sleep at Night," *Washington Post*, March 14, 2022.

162   **"dismantled to the extent":** Laura Ungar, Jason Dearen, and Hannah
Recht, "Florida's Cautionary Tale: How Gutting and Muzzling Public
Health Fueled COVID Fire," *Kaiser Health News* and Associated Press,
August 24, 2020, khn.org/news/floridas-cautionary-tale-how-starving-and
-muzzling-public-health-fueled-covid-fire.

162   **"making government more efficient":** Ibid.

162   **highest Covid death rates:** Dana Milbank, "How Does Ron DeSantis
Sleep at Night," *Washington Post*, March 14, 2022.

162   **began as an advocate:** Lawrence Mower, Kirby Wilson, and Romy Ellen-
bogen, "DeSantis Signs Vaccine Mandate Bills into Law as Florida Challenges New Rule," *Tampa Bay Times*, November 18, 2021, www.tampabay
.com/news/florida-politics/2021/11/18/desantis-signs-vaccine-mandate
-bills-into-law-as-florida-challenges-new-rule.

163   **"Doesn't impact anyone else?":** "Your 'Personal Choice' Not to Get
Covid Vaccine Is Putting Our 'Healthcare Heroes' at Risk," *Miami Herald*, editorial, September 5, 2021, www.miamiherald.com.

163   **"If anyone was in doubt":** Emily Ramshaw, "Perry: Texas Won't Implement Key Elements of Federal Health Reform," *Texas Tribune*, July 9, 2012,
www.texastribune.org/2012/07/09/perry-tx-wont-implement-key-ele
ments-health-reform.

163   **ranked fortieth out of the fifty states:** Farberman et al., *The Impact of
Chronic Underfunding on America's Public Health System*.

163   **rate of uninsured adults was 29 percent:** Stan Dorn, "The COVID-19
Pandemic and Resulting Economic Crash Have Caused the Greatest
Health Insurance Losses in American History," Families USA, July 13,
2020, www.familiesusa.org/resources/the-covid-19-pandemic-and-resul
ting-economic-crash-have-caused-the-greatest-health-insurance-losses-in
-american-history.

164   **Staffing for local health departments:** Edgar Walters, "How Years of Underfunding Public Health Left Texas Ill Prepared for the Pandemic,"
Texas Tribune, September 17, 2020, www.texastribune.org/2020/09/17
/texas-coronavirus-health-funding.

164   **Hospital Preparedness Program dropped 40 percent:** Ibid.

164   **a golfing buddy made him aware:** Ibid.

165   **number of cases in the Rio Grande Valley:** Sarah R. Champagne, "Ten Out of the 12 Hospitals in Texas' Rio Grande Valley Are Now Full," *Texas Tribune*, July 4, 2020, www.texastribune.org/2020/07/04/texas-coron avirus-rio-grande-valley-hospitals.

165   **"The people themselves are primarily responsible":** Trevor J. Mitchell, "Why Gov. Noem Won't Order a Shelter-in-Place for North Dakotans," *Sioux Falls Argus Leader*, April 1, 2020, www.argusleader.com/story/news /2020/04/01/coronavirus-why-gov-noem-wont-order-shelter-place-south -dakotans/5106939002.

166   **But neighboring Minnesota did:** Centers for Disease Control and Prevention, Morbidity and Mortality Weekly Report, "COVID-19 Outbreak Associated with a 10-Day Motorcycle Rally in a Neighboring State," November 27, 2020, www.cdc.gov/mmwr/volumes/69/wr/mm 6947e1.htm.

167   **construction of about 6,800 medical facilities:** John Henning Schumann, "A Bygone Era: When Bipartisanship Led to Health Care Transformation," Public Radio Tulsa and NPR, October 2, 2016.

167   **"Most of what we knew how to do":** Braga et al., "Leaving Billions of Dollars on the Table."

168   **reduced by 10 percent:** Matt McKillop and Vinu Ilakkuvan, *The Impact of Chronic Underfunding on America's Public Health System: Trends, Risks, and Recommendations, 2019,* Trust for America's Health, April 2019, www.tfah.org/wp-content/uploads/2020/03/TFAH_2019 _PublicHealthFunding_07.pdf.

168   **would exceed $500 billion:** Congressional Budget Office letter to House Speaker John Boehner, July 24, 2012, www.cbo.gov/sites/default/files /112th-congress-2011-2012/costestimate/43471-hr6079_0.pdf.

168   **89 of the 134 rural hospitals:** Hospital Closure Database, University of North Carolina, Cecil G. Sheps Center for Health Services Research, "181 Rural Hospital Closures Since January 2005," www.shepscenter.unc.edu /programs-projects/rural-health/rural-hospital-closures.

168   **A study by the Chartis Center:** "The Rural Health Safety Net Under Pressure: Rural Hospital Vulnerability," Chartis Center for Rural Health, February 2020, www.chartis.com/insights/rural-health-safety-net-under -pressure-rural-hospital-vulnerability.

168   **study of fifty-five rural hospital closings:** Fred C. Eilrich, Gerald A. Doeksen, and Cheryl F. St. Clair, *The Economic Impact of Recent Hospital Closures on Rural Communities,* National Center for Rural Health Works, July 2015, ruralhealthworks.org/wp-content/uploads/2018/04/Impact-of -HospitalClosure-August-2015.pdf.

169   **"hospital closure is a frightening thing":** Braga et al., "Leaving Billions of Dollars on the Table: Rural Hospitals Foundering in States That Declined Obamacare."

169 **drove nearly an hour to Chanute:** Sarah Jane Tribble, "No Mercy: After the Hospital Closes, How Do People Get Emergency Care?," NPR, August 18, 2019.

170 **"didn't know that they could just refuse":** Ibid.

171 **portrayed many of them as medical deserts:** Texas A&M University, Rural and Community Health Institute, in partnership with Episcopal Health Foundation, *What's Next? Practical Suggestions for Rural Communities Facing a Hospital Closure*, 2017, architexas.org/news/whats-next -final-rchi.pdf.

6. Defund the Children

172 **published its annual ranking:** Josh Hafner, "America's Best High Schools in 2018, as Ranked by U.S. News and World Report," *USA Today*, May 9, 2018.

172 **heartfelt essay by a "charter school mom":** Sarah Raybon, "Charter School Mom: BASIS Deserves High Praise," American Federation for Children website, May 11, 2018, medium.com/american-federation-for -children/charter-school-mom-basis-deserves-high-praise-74426270beec.

173 **one of the directors in its Arizona office:** Sarah Raybon LinkedIn profile, www.linkedin.com/in/sarah-raybon-3778378a.

173 **a 92 percent participation rate:** "U.S. News & World Report Releases the 2016 Best High Schools Rankings," *U.S. News and World Report*, April 19, 2016, www.usnews.com/info/blogs/press-room/articles/2016-04-19/us -news-releases-the-2016-best-high-schools-rankings.

173 **In a ranking of Arizona's best high schools:** Angela Gonzalez, "Here Are Arizona's Top 50 High Schools Ranked by SAT Score," *Phoenix Business Journal*, October 16, 2019, www.bizjournals.com.

173 **an average of $100,000 in scholarships:** "The BASIS Charter Schools Story," www.basised.com/who-we-are/basis-story.

173 **frustrated that Arizona schools fell short:** Ibid.

174 **loosest regulations for charter schools:** Bryan C. Hassel and Michelle Godard Terrell, *The Rugged Frontier: A Decade of Public Charter Schools in Arizona*, Progressive Policy Institute, June 2004, files.eric.ed.gov/fulltext /ED491207.pdf.

174 **accounted for 28 percent of its public schools:** Arizona Charter Schools Association, "Charter Schools—Transforming Public Education," azchar ters.org/impact.

174 **had a deficit of $44 million:** Brenna Bailey, "Acclaimed BASIS Charter Schools Nearly $44 Million in the Red, Audit Shows," *Arizona Daily Star*, March 20, 2019, tucson.com.

175 **make a $1.68 million down payment:** Craig Harris, "At BASIS Charter Schools, Another Way to Boost Teachers' Pay: Parent Donations," *Arizona*

Republic, May 7, 2018, www.azcentral.com/story/news/local/arizona
-education/2018/05/07/basis-charter-schools-seek-big-donations-parents
-subsidize-low-teacher-pay/473963002.

175 **receiving letters asking them to donate:** Ibid.

175 **"The Blocks have put their heart and soul":** Ibid.

175 **"National recognition like this is what attracts":** Jessica Boehm, "5 of
the Nation's Top 10 High Schools Are Arizona Charter Schools," *Arizona
Republic*, April 25, 2017, www.azcentral.com/story/news/local/arizona
-education/2017/04/26/top-high-school-country-arizona/306463001.

176 **"Does that statement trigger":** David Safier, "The Games BASIS Plays,"
Tucson Weekly, May 11, 2018, www.tucsonweekly.com/TheRange/archives
/2018/05/11/the-games-basis-plays.

176 **"operate on a tournament model":** Quoted in Valerie Strauss, "What the
Public Isn't Told About High-Performing Charter Schools in Arizona,"
Washington Post, March 30, 2017.

177 **Safier obtained figures:** Safier, "The Games BASIS Plays."

177 **was 77 percent Asian:** "2021 Best Charter High Schools," *U.S. News and
World Report*, www.usnews.com/education/best-high-schools/national
-rankings/charter-school-rankings.

178 **progressives describe as success stories:** Jonathan Chait, "Charter
Schools Are Losing the Narrative but Winning the Data," *New York*, September 6, 2017.

179 **point out in their own book:** Jack Schneider and Jennifer Berkshire, *A
Wolf at the Schoolhouse Door: The Dismantling of Public Education and the
Future of School* (New York: The New Press, 2020), p. 13.

179 **"What is gaining traction":** Ibid., p. xx.

179 **"He is one of the best governors":** Mike Sunnucks, "Why Arizona Is
'Ground Zero' in Koch Brothers Education Fight and a Conservative Leader's Biggest Disappointment in GOP," *Phoenix Business Journal*, February 15, 2018, www.bizjournals.com.

180 **"starts at the top":** Fernanda Santos and Charlie Savage, "Lawsuit Says
Sheriff Discriminated Against Latinos," *New York Times*, May 10, 2012.

180 **received a key endorsement:** Yvonne Wingett Sanchez, "Arpaio Endorses
GOP Governor Candidate Doug Ducey," *Arizona Republic*, August 1,
2014, www.azcentral.com/story/news/arizona/politics/2014/08/01/arpaio
-endorses-doug-ducey-arizona-gop-governor/13468969.

181 **Arizona began a headlong push:** Yvonne Wingett Sanchez and Rob
O'Dell, "Arizona School-Voucher Expansion Afoot Despite $102K of Mis-
spent Funds in 6 Months," *Arizona Republic*, January 31, 2017, www
.azcentral.com/story/news/politics/arizona-education/2017/01/31
/arizona-school-vouchers-expansion-audit/97163702.

181 **3,200 children in the program:** Ibid.

181 **signed legislation expanding:** Yvonne Wingett Sanchez, Rob O'Dell,
and Alia Beard Rau, "Gov. Doug Ducey Signs Expansion of Arizona's

School-Voucher Program," *Arizona Republic*, April 7, 2017, www.azcen
tral.com/story/news/politics/arizona-education/2017/04/07/arizona
-gov-doug-ducey-signs-school-voucher-expansion/100159192/.

181 **based on ALEC's model legislation:** Mary Bottari, "Arizona 'Ground
Zero' for Koch Attack on Public Education," Center for Media and Democracy, February 8, 2018, www.exposedbycmd.org/2018/02/08/arizona-ground
-zero-koch-attack-public-education.

181 **"a big win for students":** Dana Goldstein, "Arizona Frees Money for Private Schools, Buoyed by Trump's Voucher Push," *New York Times*, April 7,
2017.

182 **amounting to about $100 million:** James Hohmann et al., "Koch Net-
work Laying Groundwork to Fundamentally Transform America's Education System," *Washington Post*, January 30, 2018.

182 **"We've made more progress in the last five years":** Ibid.

182 **"This is a real fight in my state":** Yvonne Wingett Sanchez, "Ducey to
Koch Network: 'I Didn't Run for Governor to Play Small Ball' on School
Vouchers," *Arizona Republic*," January 30, 2018, www.azcentral.com/story
/news/politics/arizona/2018/01/30/doug-ducey-koch-network-school
-voucher-law/1078838001.

182 **found that 75 percent of ESA funds:** Rob O'Dell and Yvonne Wingett
Sanchez, "Arizona Taxpayer-Funded Vouchers Benefiting Students in More-
Affluent Areas," *Arizona Republic*, March 30, 2017, www.azcentral.com
/story/news/politics/arizona-education/2017/03/30/arizona-taxpayer
-funded-vouchers-benefiting-students-more-affluent-areas/99707518.

182 **funded a lawsuit seeking to block Proposition 305:** Steven Greenhouse,
"Billionaires v. Teachers: The Koch Brothers Plan to Starve Public Education," *The Guardian*, September 7, 2018.

182 **continued to expand nonetheless:** EdChoice briefing on Arizona Em-
powerment Scholarship Accounts, www.edchoice.org/school-choice/pro
grams/arizona-empowerment-scholarship-accounts.

183 **Michael Block and BASIS board member Don Budinger:** Craig Harris
et al., "The Rise of Big Charters in Arizona Was Fueled by Powerful
Friends," *Arizona Republic*, December 16, 2018, www.azcentral.com/story
/news/local/arizona-education/2018/12/16/arizona-rise-big-charter
-schools-fueled-powerful-friends/1822430002.

183 **BASIS.ed itself gave:** National Institute on Money in Politics, www
.followthemoney.org/entity-details?eid=47939913; Howard Fischer, "With
Outside Help, Ducey Spends Big to Keep GOP Senate Majority," *Arizona Capitol Times*, November 7, 2016, azcapitoltimes.com/news/2016
/11/07/with-outside-help-ducey-spends-big-to-keep-gop-senate
-majority.

183 **reported on other ties between the governor:** Harris et al., "The Rise of
Big Charters in Arizona Was Fueled by Powerful Friends."

184 **"the clear winners in Ducey's plans":** Ibid.

184 **"moral and wholesome environment":** Craig Harris, "Arizona Charter School Founder Makes Millions Building His Own Schools," *Arizona Republic*, July 11, 2018, www.azcentral.com/story/news/local/arizona-edu cation/2018/07/11/american-leadership-academy-charter-school-founder -glenn-way-nets-millions/664210002.

185 **made $37 million in profits:** Ibid.

185 **big payoff came:** Ibid.

185 **"The law is silent":** Ibid.

185 **personally contributed more than $145,000:** National Institute on Money in Politics, www.followthemoney.org/search-results/SearchForm ?Search=Glenn+Way.

185 **can't claim to offer:** Craig Harris, "Primavera Charter CEO Gets $8.8 Million Despite Having Arizona's Third-Highest Dropout Rate," *Arizona Republic*, August 22, 2018, www.azcentral.com/story/news/local/arizona -education/2018/08/22/primavera-online-charter-school-ceo-damian -creamer/839045002.

186 **paid himself an $8.8 million shareholder distribution:** Ibid.

186 **"I'm not concerned about the CEO":** Ibid.

186 **charter school board approved:** Alden Woods, "State Approves New Charter School Tied to Controversial Primavera CEO," *Arizona Republic*, December 11, 2018, www.azcentral.com/story/news/local/arizona-educat ion/2018/12/11/arizona-charter-school-board-approves-new-school-tied -primavera-ceo-damian-creamer/2272187002.

186 **he would sell the campuses:** Craig Harris, "Lawmaker Eddie Farnsworth Nets $13.9 Million in Charter-School Sale, Keeps Getting Paid," *Arizona Republic*, November 28, 2018, www.azcentral.com/story/news/local /arizona-education/2018/11/28/farnsworth-net-13-9-million-benjamin -franklin-charter-school-sale/2126183002.

187 **12 percent were investigated:** Craig Harris, "At Arizona Charter Schools, Parents with Complaints or Objections Find Nowhere to Turn," *Arizona Republic*, March 5, 2019, www.azcentral.com/in-depth/news/local/arizona -investigations/2019/03/05/arizona-charter-schools-parents-complaints -objections-find-nowhere-turn-american-leadership-academy/2871812002.

187 **were in some kind of financial distress:** Agnel Philip, "Analysis: 1 in 4 Charters Shows Significant Financial Red Flags," *Arizona Republic*, May 9, 2018, www.azcentral.com/story/news/local/arizona-education/2018/05 /09/one-four-charters-show-significant-financial-red-flags-state-data/54 2132002.

187 **"Charter schools were not designed":** Harris, "Arizona Charter School Founder Makes Millions Building His Own Schools."

187 **the industry's lobbyist helped write it:** E.J. Montini, "Crime Still Legal for Charter School Operators Under Arizona 'Reform' Bill," *Arizona Republic*, March 17, 2019, www.azcentral.com/story/opinion/op-ed/ej-mon tini/2019/03/17/charter-school-arizona-senate-house/3199565002.

188   **shot up by 32 percent:** Federal Reserve Bank of St. Louis, FRED Economic Data, fred.stlouisfed.org/series/AZRQGSP.

188   **cut taxes *every year*:** Arizona Center for Economic Progress, "Are State Lawmakers Working for a Fairer Tax Code for All Arizonans?," April 3, 2019, azeconcenter.org/are-state-lawmakers-working-for-a-fairer-tax-code -for-all-arizonans.

188   **"While our tax code is filled with loopholes":** Ibid.

188   **slashed its K-12 funding:** Michael Leachman, Kathleen Masterson, and Eric Figueroa, "A Punishing Decade for School Funding," Center on Budget and Policy Priorities, November 29, 2017, www.cbpp.org/research/state -budget-and-tax/a-punishing-decade-for-school-funding.

189   **"one of the leading states in the nation":** Agnel Philip, "Fact Check: Doug Ducey Claim on Education Funding Unsupported," *Arizona Republic*, October 12, 2015, www.azcentral.com/story/news/politics/fact-check /2015/10/12/doug-ducey-arizona-education-funding-fact-check/727 40022.

189   **Arizona was spending $900 less per pupil:** Craig Harris, "As Doug Ducey Faces Anger from Teachers, Supporters Spend $1 Million on Education Ads," *Arizona Republic*, March 13, 2018, www.azcentral.com/story/news /politics/arizona-education/2018/03/13/gov-ducey-faces-anger-teachers -supporters-spend-1-m-education-ads/420738002.

189   **the worst in the nation:** Dan Hunting et al., *Finding & Keeping Educators for Arizona's Classrooms*, Arizona State University, Morrison Institute for Public Policy, May 2017, files.eric.ed.gov/fulltext/ED574452.pdf.

189   **tens of thousands of teachers:** Dana Goldstein, "Arizona Teachers Vote in Favor of Statewide Walkout," *New York Times*, April 20, 2018.

189   **19 percent pay raise:** "Striking Arizona Teachers Win 19% Raise, End Walkout," *Los Angeles Times* via Associated Press, May 3, 2018.

189   **866 public school teachers had quit:** Laurie Roberts, "866 Arizona Teachers Have Already Quit This Year," *Arizona Republic*, December 19, 2017, www.azcentral.com/story/opinion/op-ed/laurieroberts/2017/12/19 /roberts-866-teachers-have-already-quit-year-some/967075001.

190   **42 percent of teachers hired:** Hunting et al., *Finding & Keeping Educators for Arizona's Classrooms*.

190   **had taken to posting photographs:** Griselda Zetino, "Arizona Teachers Share Photos of 'Disturbing' Classroom Conditions," KTAR News, April 11, 2018, ktar.com/story/2017614/teachers-share-photos-of-disturb ing-classroom-conditions.

190   **poor monitoring, chronic project delays:** Lindsey A. Perry, Arizona Auditor General, *A Special Audit of the Arizona School Facilities Board— Building Renewal Grant Fund*, June 2019, www.azauditor.gov/sites/default /files/19-105_Report.pdf.

190   **$1 million for an advertising blitz:** Harris, "As Doug Ducey Faces Anger from Teachers."

190 **Arizona still had the third-lowest:** Melanie Hanson, "U.S. Public Education Spending Statistics," Education Data Initiative, educationdata.org /public-education-spending-statistics#arizona.

191 **would generate $827 million:** Bob Christie, "Education Tax Measure Certified for November Arizona Ballot," Associated Press, August 21, 2020.

191 **"gigantic gamble with Arizona's economy":** Robert Robb, "Prop. 208, the Invest in Ed Initiative, Is a Huge Economic Gamble for Arizona," *Arizona Republic*, September 13, 2020, www.azcentral.com/story/opinion/op -ed/robertrobb/2020/09/13/prop-208-invest-ed-initiative-economic -gamble-income-tax-rates/3462904001.

191 **surplus of more than $1 billion:** Arizona Center for Economic Progress, "The Flat Tax Falls Flat for Most Arizonans," June 23, 2021, azeconcenter .org/the-flat-tax-falls-flat-for-most-arizonans.

192 **"largest tax cut in state history":** Office of the Governor Doug Ducey, "Governor Ducey Cuts Taxes for Arizona Small Businesses," press release, July 9, 2021, azgovernor.gov/governor/news/2021/07/governor-ducey-cuts -taxes-arizona-small-businesses.

192 **75 percent of the tax law's benefits:** Arizona Center for Economic Progress, "2021 Legislative Session and Budget Recap," July 1, 2021, azeconcenter.org/2021-legislative-session-budget-recap.

192 **cut the $827 million in annual school funding:** Laura Gómez, "Invest in Arizona Campaign to Overturn Tax Cuts with Voter Referendums Not Dampened by Lawsuit," *Arizona Mirror*, July 25, 2021, www.azmirror.com /2021/07/25/invest-in-arizona-campaign-to-overturn-tax-cuts-with -voter-referendums-not-dampened-by-lawsuit.

192 **"tax cut will keep Arizona competitive":** Office of the Governor Doug Ducey, "Governor Ducey Cuts Taxes."

192 **"Don't let the bill's title mislead you":** Arizona Center for Economic Progress, "SB1783 Is a Tax Cut for the Rich and Does Nothing to Help Small Businesses," February 24, 2021, azeconcenter.org/sb1783-is-a-tax-cut-for -the-rich-and-does-nothing-to-help-small-businesses.

193 **collected enough signatures for a measure:** Gómez, "Invest in Arizona Campaign to Overturn Tax Cuts."

193 **predicted that Ducey's tax cuts:** Henry Olsen, "Arizona Republicans Are Gambling They Can Win Back Their State with Tax Cuts. It Might Just Work," *Washington Post*, June 25, 2021.

7. CLEARING THE WATERS

198 **"In the forty years I lived there":** Interview with Steve Zaidman, August 21, 2020.

198 **"Wollaston Beach was a joke":** Interview with Bill Penwarden, August 21, 2020.

199   **porpoises have returned:** Lauren Sommer, "60 Years After Leaving, Porpoises Again Play in SF Bay," NPR, December 28, 2011.

200   **begun offering free lunch:** Priya Fielding-Singh, "Free School Meal Programs Don't Just Feed Hungry Kids—They're a Major Win for Moms," *Washington Post*, August 13, 2021.

200   **"Baby Bonds" initiative:** Patrick Skahill, "CT Makes Case for National 'Baby Bond' Investments," *CT Mirror*, October 5, 2021, ctmirror.org/2021 /10/05/ct-makes-case-for-national-baby-bond-investments.

200   **no longer allows admissions preferences:** Scott Jaschik, "Legacy Admissions Banned in Colorado," *Inside Higher Ed*, June 1, 2021, www.insidehigh ered.com/admissions/article/2021/06/01/colorado-bars-public-colleges -using-legacy-admissions.

200   **championed campaign finance reform:** Denis C. Theriault, "Campaign Finance Reform: Kate Brown Urges Lawmakers to Pass Donation Limits," *The Oregonian*, January 9, 2019, www.oregonlive.com/politics/2015/04 /campaign_finance_reform_kate_b.html.

200   **died without a floor vote:** Dirk VanderHart, "Good Government Groups Are Pushing Campaign Finance Limits in Oregon. They Might Have Competition," Oregon Public Broadcasting, December 7, 2021, www.opb.org /article/2021/12/07/oregon-campaign-finance-limits-funding-regu lations-labor-unions-government-groups.

200   **first in the nation to offer a "public option":** Dylan Scott, "The Public Option Is Now a Reality in 3 States," *Vox*, June 17, 2021, www.vox.com /policy-and-politics/22535267/public-option-health-insurance-nevada -colorado-washington.

200   **Career Connect Washington:** "Spread the Word on State's Programs for Alternate Career and Apprenticeship Pathways," *Seattle Times*, November 4, 2021, www.seattletimes.com/opinion/editorials/spread-the-word-on -states-programs-for-alternate-career-and-apprenticeship-pathways.

200   **guaranteed long-term care benefit:** Ron Lieber, "New Tax Will Help Washington Residents Pay for Long-Term Care," *New York Times*, May 13, 2019.

201   **second highest growth in GDP:** Andrew DePietro, "2021 U.S. States by GDP and Which States Have Experienced the Biggest Growth," *Forbes*, August 4, 2021.

201   **visited prisons twenty-six times:** Clarice Silber, "Malloy Leaves Office as National Leader on Criminal Justice Reform," *CT Mirror*, January 4, 2019, ctmirror.org/2019/01/04/malloy-leaves-office-national-leader-criminal -justice-reform.

201   **people can be tried as adults:** Ibid.

201   **20 percent decrease in its violent crime rate:** Ibid.

201   **requiring prosecutors to collect data:** "Connecticut Officials Say State to Become First to Collect Prosecutor Data," CBS News, June 6, 2019, www .cbsnews.com/news/connecticut-officials-say-state-to-become-first-to-col lect-prosecutor-data.

201   **free tuition:** Jesse McKinley, "Cuomo Proposes Free Tuition at New York State Colleges for Eligible Students," *New York Times*, January 3, 2017.

202   **plagued by delays:** Ralph Vartabedian, "Cost Overruns Hit California Bullet Train Again amid a New Financial Crunch," *Los Angeles Times*, October 8, 2021.

202   **Governor Abbott won't support it:** Ben Wear, "Why Plans for Texas Bullet Trains Are Still Mostly a Dream," *Austin American-Statesman*, November 16, 2017, www.statesman.com/story/news/local/2017/11/17/wear-why -plans-for-texas-bullet-trains-are-still-mostly-a-dream/10418578007.

203   **"As I realized what I stepped in":** Eric Jay Dolin, *Political Waters: The Long, Dirty, Contentious, Incredibly Expensive but Eventually Triumphant History of Boston Harbor* (Boston: University of Massachusetts Press, 2004), p. 99.

203   **"What do you want to do about it?":** Ibid.

204   **thousands of acres of marshes:** *U.S. v. MDC et al.*, pp. 1–2; cited in Dolin, *Political Waters*, p. 133.

204   **"flounder capital of the world":** Michael Moore, "Tumor-Free Flounder Are Just 1 Dividend from the Boston Harbor Cleanup," The Conversation, January 10, 2019, theconversation.com/tumor-free-flounder-are-just-1 -dividend-from-the-cleanup-of-boston-harbor-109217.

204   **releasing it untreated into the harbor:** Paul F. Levy and Michael S. Connor, "The Boston Harbor Cleanup," *New England Journal of Public Policy*, Vol. 8, Issue 2, September 1992, scholarworks.umb.edu/nejpp/vol8/iss2/7.

204   **never able to secure sufficient funding:** Ibid.

205   **A 1968 study by the federal government:** David Doneski, "Cleaning Up Boston Harbor: Fact or Fiction," *Boston College Environmental Law Review*, Vol. 12, Issue 3, May 1985, lawdigitalcommons.bc.edu/ealr /vol12/iss3/6.

205   **The treatment system was so antiquated:** Dolin, *Political Waters*, p. 115.

205   **served on President Nixon's Advisory Council:** Brian McGrory, "Zealot or Idealist, Golden Earns Senate Reputation as Direct, Hard Worker; from an Environmental Base, He Sets Sights on Becoming Lieutenant Governor," *Boston Globe*, June 25, 1989.

205   **"The easiest way to achieve control":** Dudley Clendinen, "About Boston," *New York Times*, October 2, 1984.

206   **"Garrity was laughing at us":** Gavin McCormick, "Closing Time for Sewage Treatment Plant; Ceremony Is Monday on Nut Island," *Patriot Ledger*, October 3, 1998.

206   **"I remember how quick he talked":** McGrory, "Zealot or Idealist."

206   **"This is what Quincy kids are forced to swim in":** McCormick, "Closing Time for Sewage Treatment Plant."

206   **feared the federal courts would be gun-shy:** Ibid.

206   **They waited until Paul Garrity rotated:** Dolin, *Political Waters*, p. 101.

207   **"He was really taking the pulse":** Ibid., p. 113.

208   **U.S. District Judge David Mazzone issued an order:** *U.S. v. MDC et al.*, pp. 1–2; cited in Dolin, *Political Waters*, p. 140.

208   **"rip the bark off the little bastard":** Rick Perlstein, "Lee Atwater's Infamous 1981 Interview on the Southern Strategy," *The Nation*, November 13, 2012.

208   **"rich political theater":** Robin Toner, "Bush, in Enemy Waters, Says Rival Hindered Cleanup of Boston Harbor," *New York Times*, September 2, 1988.

208   **near quintupling of residents' water and sewer bills:** Dolin, *Political Waters*, pp. 155–56.

209   **bacterial counts had declined by two-thirds:** Brian Fitzgerald, "Learning About the Boston Harbor Cleanup from the Waterway's Eyes, Ears, and Mouthpiece," *B.U. Bridge*, September 3, 2004, www.bu.edu/bridge/archive /2004/09-03/harbor.html.

209   **Boston Harbor flounder had been tumor-free:** "Flounder Now Tumor Free in Boston Harbor," Woods Hole Oceanographic Institution website, November 28, 2018, www.whoi.edu/press-room/news-release/flounder -now-tumor-free-in-cleaned-up-boston-harbor.

209   **commercial development in the region:** Di Jin et al., "Evaluating Boston Harbor Cleanup: An Ecosystem Valuation Approach," *Frontiers in Marine Science*, 2018, www.frontiersin.org/articles/10.3389/fmars.2018.004 78/full.

210   **"The oil gushes from a pipe":** Robert H. Boyle, *The Hudson River: A Natural and Unnatural History* (New York: W.W. Norton, 1969), p. 98.

211   **350 million gallons of raw sewage:** Arnold H. Lubasch, "U.S. Is Suing Cities on Harbor Filth," *New York Times*, July 19, 1972.

211   **145 million gallons of daily raw sewage:** Associated Press, "Hudson Sewage Plant Enters Full Operation, *New York Times*, April 22, 1986.

211   **a billion fish, eggs, and larvae were killed:** Joseph De Avila, "New York State, Indian Point Plant Operator Clash over Fate of Fish," *Wall Street Journal*, September 16, 2014.

211   **Dissolved oxygen levels have increased:** Jeff Inglis et al., *Waterways Restored: The Clean Water Act's Impact on 15 American Rivers, Lakes and Bays*, Frontier Group and Environment America Research and Policy Center, October 2014, environmentamerica.org/sites/environment/files/EA_water ways_scrn.pdf.

211   **450 Atlantic sturgeon:** Oliver Milman, "Hudson River Shows Signs of Rebound After Decades as New York's Sewer," *The Guardian*, March 28, 2019.

211   **A humpback whale was spotted:** "Humpback Whale Spotted Spouting Off in the Hudson River in Manhattan," ABC7 New York, December 8, 2020, abc7ny.com/humpback-whale-hudson-river-new-york-city-in/8612878.

211   **460 combined sewer overflow outfalls:** Nathan Kensinger, "New York Has a Plan to Clean Its Sewage-Filled Waterways. Does It Go Far Enough?,"

Curbed New York, February 20, 2020, ny.curbed.com/2020/2/20/2114 4943/new-york-water-combined-sewer-overflow-dep-plan.

212 **discharged an estimated 1.3 million pounds:** U.S. Environmental Protection Agency, "Hudson River PCBs Superfund Site: Hudson River Cleanup," www.epa.gov/hudsonriverpcbs/hudson-river-cleanup.

212 **New York State officials protested:** Jesse McKinley, "G.E. Spent Years Cleaning Up the Hudson. Was It Enough?," *New York Times*, September 18, 2016.

213 **sullied by toxic chemicals:** U.S. Department of Justice, "Houston, Texas, Agrees to Implement Comprehensive Measures Aimed at Eliminating Sanitary Sewer Overflows and Illegal Discharges from Wastewater Treatment Plants," press release, August 27, 2019, www.justice.gov/opa/pr/houston -texas-agrees-implement-comprehensive-measures-aimed-eliminating-sani tary-sewer-0.

213 **prevent Indiana from weakening:** Michael Hawthorne, "Midwest EPA Chief's Job Won't Be an Easy One; Biden Pick Will Face Slew of Challenges Across Region," *Chicago Tribune*, August 29, 2021.

213 **thousands of dead fish:** Ibid.

213 **"It was an arrogant and angering thing to do":** Shane Goldmacher, "How Andrew Cuomo's Exit Tarnished a Legacy and Dimmed a Dynasty," *New York Times*, August 14, 2021.

214 **closed down a commission:** William K. Rashbaum and Susanne Craig, "U.S. Attorney Criticizes Cuomo's Closing of Panel," *New York Times*, April 9, 2014.

214 **flush with dark money:** Andy Kroll, "All the Governors' Dark-Money Funds," *Mother Jones*, January 9, 2014.

214 **hid the true number of nursing home residents:** Jesse McKinley and Luis Ferré-Sadurní, "New Allegations of Cover-Up by Cuomo over Nursing Home Virus Toll," *New York Times*, February 12, 2021.

214 **to help in the writing:** Eric Lach, "Andrew Cuomo's Downfall Began with a Book Deal," *New Yorker*, November 23, 2021.

214 **accused by eleven women:** Office of New York State Attorney General Letitia James, *Report of Investigation into Allegations of Sexual Harassment by Governor Andrew M. Cuomo*, August 3, 2021, ag.ny.gov/sites/default /files/2021.08.03_nyag_-_investigative_report.pdf.

215 **reject $2.4 billion in federal money:** Timothy Williams, "Florida's Governor Rejects High-Speed Rail Line, Fearing Cost to Taxpayers," *New York Times*, February 16, 2011.

215 **convinced the legislature to trim:** Ginia Bellfante, "New York, Finally, Taxes the Rich," *New York Times*, April 9, 2021.

215 **He kept a lid on taxes:** Luis Ferré-Sadurní and Jesse McKinley, "Tax the Ultrarich? Cuomo Resists, Even with a $14 Billion Budget Cap," *New York Times*, September 7, 2020; Janelle Cammenga, "State Corporate Income Tax Rates and Brackets for 2021," Tax Foundation, February 3, 2021,

taxfoundation.org/publications/state-corporate-income-tax-rates-and
-brackets.

215   **"It may be hard for someone":** Nick Paumgarten, "Andrew Cuomo, the
King of New York," *New Yorker*, October 12, 2020.

215   **all with Cuomo's encouragement:** Ibid.

215   **the governor reluctantly supported:** Karen DeWitt, "Cuomo Has Res-
ervations About His Own Proposal to Tax the Rich," WXXI News, January 21, 2021, www.wxxinews.org/post/cuomo-has-reservations-about-his
-own-proposal-tax-rich.

215   **surpassing California's rate:** Karen Langley, "New York State's Tax Increase: What High Earners Need to Know," *Wall Street Journal*, April 8,
2021.

216   **record $29.5 billion for schools:** Ginia Bellfante, "New York, Finally,
Taxes the Rich," *New York Times*, April 9, 2021.

216   **Paumgarten wrote:** Paumgarten, "Andrew Cuomo, the King of New
York." Emphasis added.

217   **"become relatively moot":** Dan Goldberg, "The 2020 Dem Who May Actually Know How to Fix Health Care," *Politico*, July 28, 2019.

217   **were forbidden to use the term:** Tristram Korten, "In Florida, Officials
Ban Term 'Climate Change,'" Florida Center for Investigative Reporting
via *Miami Herald*, March 11, 2015, www.miamiherald.com/news/state
/florida/article12983720.html.

8. WHICH MODEL—CALIFORNIA OR TEXAS?

218   **"The California Dream Is Dying":** Conor Friedersdorf, "The California
Dream Is Dying," *The Atlantic*, July 21, 2021.

218   **"California Doom":** Adam Beam, "California Doom: Staggering $54 Bil-
lion Budget Deficit Looms," Associated Press, May 7, 2020.

219   **"California Burns for Better Leaders":** Holman W. Jenkins Jr., "California Burns for Better Leaders," *Wall Street Journal*, January 15, 2019.

219   **"California has become a warming, burning":** Heather Kelly et al.,
"Warmer. Burning. Epidemic-Challenged. Expensive. The California
Dream Has Become the California Compromise," *Washington Post*, Sep-
tember 12, 2020.

219   **"just take a look at California":** Carla Marinucci, "Republicans See California as Perfect Foil as Fall Campaign Begins," *Politico*, August 30, 2020.

220   **"California is now unable to perform":** Lexi Lonas, "Texas Lawmaker's
Tweets Mocking California Power Outages Resurface amid Winter Storm,"
The Hill, February 16, 2021.

220   **"Remember those high taxes":** Derek Thompson, "Why Texas Doesn't
Want Any More Californians," *The Atlantic*, January 31, 2020.

220 **"You can make a case":** David Leonhardt, "The Future of Texas," *New York Times*, February 22, 2021.

220 **a study by the Urban Institute:** Kristin Blagg et al., "America's Grade Book: How Does Your State Stack Up," Urban Institute, October 2019, apps.urban.org/features/naep.

220 **below that of most other states:** "Map: A-F Grades, Rankings for States on School Quality," *Education Week*, September 1, 2020, www.edweek.org /policy-politics/map-a-f-grades-rankings-for-states-on-school-quality /2020/09.

221 **An estimated 35 percent:** Brandon Mulder, "Fact Check: Is the Texas Oil and Gas Industry 35% of the State Economy?," *Austin American-Statesman*, December 22, 2020, www.statesman.com/story/news/politics/politifact /2020/12/22/fact-check-texas-oil-and-gas-industry-35-state-economy /4009134001.

222 **largest producer of wind energy:** U.S. Energy Information Administration, "The United States Installed More Wind Turbine Capacity in 2020 Than in Any Other Year," *Today in Energy*, March 3, 2021, www.eia.gov /todayinenergy/detail.php?id=46976.

222 **accept millions in campaign contributions:** National Institute on Money in Politics, www.followthemoney.org/show-me?dt=1&f-fc=1,2,3&c-t-eid =11281947#[{1|gro=d-cci; J.T. Stepleton, "Oil and Gas Money Gave Rick Perry the Energy to Win in Texas," FollowtheMoney.Org, January 9, 2017.

223 **"perhaps the most successful politician":** Todd S. Purdum, "Jerry Brown's Greatest Legacy Is Proving California Is Governable," *The Atlantic*, December 26, 2018.

223 **"At the end of the Brown years":** Jim Newton, *Man of Tomorrow: The Relentless Life of Jerry Brown* (New York: Little, Brown, 2020), p. 364.

223 **Census data also showed:** Hans Johnson, "Who's Leaving California— and Who's Moving In?," Public Policy Institute of California, May 6, 2021, www.ppic.org/blog/whos-leaving-california-and-whos-moving-in.

223 **The people migrating to the state:** Ibid.

224 **more than fifty thousand excess deaths:** Shawn Hubler, "A New Demographic Surprise for California: Population Loss," *New York Times*, May 7, 2021.

224 **added 1.3 million people:** Federal Reserve Bank of St. Louis, fredstlouis fed.org.

224 **Its total personal income surged:** U.S. Department of Commerce, Bureau of Economic Analysis, "Personal Income by State," www.bea.gov/data /income-saving/personal-income-by-state.

224 **real gross domestic product grew by 21 percent:** Federal Reserve Bank of St. Louis, fredstlouisfed.org.

224 **"sturdy economic growth engine":** David Byler, "Texas Population and Political Power Are Growing. Here's Why," *Washington Post*, May 3, 2021.

224   **"the latest data readout showing the Golden State"**: Matthew A. Winkler, "California Defies Doom with No. 1 U.S. Economy," *Bloomberg*, June 14, 2021.

225   **placed California dead last**: "Up for Grabs: The Best and Worst States for Business 2021," *Chief Executive*, April 28, 2021, chiefexecutive.net/up-for-grabs-the-best-worst-states-for-business.

225   **heavily favor the Republican Party**: Alma Cohen et al., "The Politics of CEOs," National Bureau of Economic Research, May 2019, www.nber.org/system/files/working_papers/w25815/w25815.pdf.

225   **"How can we reconcile"**: Michael Hiltzik, "If California Is Such an Anti-business State, Then Why Is Its Economy Booming?," *Los Angeles Times*, May 10, 2021.

225   **California had 395,608 regulations**: Kofi Ampaabeng et al., "A Policymaker's Guide to State RegData 2.0," George Mason University, Mercatus Center, policy brief, October 2020, www.mercatus.org/publications/regulation/policymaker%E2%80%99s-guide-state-regdata-20.

226   **benefits of regulation far outweigh**: "Government Regulation: Costs Lower, Benefits Greater Than Industry Estimates," Pew Charitable Trusts fact sheet, May 26, 2015, www.pewtrusts.org/en/research-and-analysis/fact-sheets/2015/05/government-regulation-costs-lower-benefits-greater-than-industry-estimates.

226   **"Without this sustained tradition"**: Richard Hofstadter, *The Age of Reform: From Bryan to F.D.R.* (New York: Vintage Books, 1955), p. 18.

227   **his son's idea of relaxation**: Miriam Pawel, *The Browns of California: The Family Dynasty That Transformed a State and Shaped a Nation* (New York: Bloomsbury Publishing, 2018), p. 214.

227   **canceling the inaugural ball**: Ibid., p. 212.

228   **"psychic income"**: George Skelton, "Gov. Jerry Brown Has Plenty of Weapons to Fight UC's Janet Napolitano," *Los Angeles Times*, November 23, 2014.

228   **appointing hundreds of women**: Pawel, *The Browns of California*, pp. 221–22.

228   **accumulating a budget surplus**: Newton, *Man of Tomorrow*, p. 182.

228   **slashed by 53 percent**: California Budget Project, "Proposition 13: Its Impact on California and Implications," April 1997, calbudgetcenter.org/wp-content/uploads/2018/09/Issue-Brief_Proposition-13-Its-Impact-on-California-and-Implications_04.1997.pdf.

229   **"consumer fraud, a rip-off"**: Lou Cannon, "With Week to Go, California Gov. Brown Is Showing His Heels," *Washington Post*, November 1, 1978.

229   **"born-again tax cutter"**: Ibid.

229   **use $4 billion of its surplus**: Pawel, *The Browns of California*, p. 271.

229   **"property tax must be sharply curtailed"**: Ibid., p. 271.

229 **"knew Gov. Brown was the man":** Cannon, "With Week to Go, California Gov. Brown Is Showing His Heels."

230 **"a decade of living under Proposition 13":** Pawel, *The Browns of California*, p. 322.

230 **ranked forty-first in the nation:** Jonathan Kaplan, "Improving but Still Behind: California's Support for K-12 Education," California Budget and Policy Center, January 2017, calbudgetcenter.org/resources/improving-but -still-behind-californias-support-for-k-12-education.

230 **schools had eliminated the sixth period:** David Savage, "The Unintended Impact of Proposition 13," *Education Leadership*, January 1982, files.ascd .org/staticfiles/ascd/pdf/journals/ed_lead/el_198201_savage.pdf.

230 **researched a puzzling drop:** Ibid.

230 **average class size for high schools:** National Center for Education Statistics, National Principal and Teacher Survey, "Average Class Size in Public Schools, by Class Type and State: 2017–18," nces.ed.gov/surveys/ntps /tables/ntps1718_fltable06_t1s.asp.

231 **paying only $227,000 an acre:** Liam Dillon, "Proposition 13 Has Strictly Limited Property Tax Increases Since 1978. Voters Could Get a Chance to Change That," *Los Angeles Times*, October 17, 2018.

231 **"it makes no sense":** Joseph T. Hallinan, "Schwarzenegger Adviser Buffett Hints Property Tax Is Too Low," *Wall Street Journal*, April 15, 2003.

232 **prisons and local jails more than doubled:** Vera Institute of Justice, "Incarceration Trends in California," fact sheet, www.vera.org/downloads /pdfdownloads/state-incarceration-trends-california.pdf.

232 **"an outlier in this country":** Plaintiffs' Second Amended Complaint, *George Ruiz et al. v. Edmund G. Brown, Jr., Governor of the State of California et al.*, United States District Court, Northern District of California, Oakland Division, 4:09-cv-05796-CW, ccrjustice.org/files/Ruiz -Amended-Complaint-May-31-2012.pdf.

232 **stealing a slice of pepperoni pizza:** Eric Slater, "Pizza Thief Receives 25 Years to Life in Prison," *Los Angeles Times*, March 3, 1995.

233 **a figure lower than it was in 1972:** Miyako Iwata, "A Look Back at Diversity in UC Berkeley Admissions," *Daily Californian*, October 30, 2021, www.dailycal.org/2018/03/22/look-back-diversity-uc-berkeley-admis sions.

233 **"By aligning himself with the immigration issue":** Frank del Olmo, "A Dissenting Vote on the Endorsement of Pete Wilson," *Los Angeles Times*, October 31, 1994.

233 **had picked up nearly 50 percent:** Alex Nowrasteh, "Proposition 187 Turned California Blue," Cato Institute, July 20, 2016, www.cato.org/blog /proposition-187-turned-california-blue.

234 **misgivings about some of the conservative positions:** Newton, *Man of Tomorrow*, p. 304.

234 **boasted in 1982 that nineteen thousand people:** Pawel, *The Browns of California*, p. 378.

234 **prison-building tab rose to $3 billion:** Ibid., pp. 378–79.

234 **prison population grew more than sevenfold:** Magnus Lofstrom, Mia Bird, and Brandon Martin, *California's Historic Corrections Reforms*, Public Policy Institute of California, September 2016, www.ppic.org/wp-content/uploads/content/pubs/report/R_916MLR.pdf.

234 **forced to triple-bunk:** Anat Rubin, "California's Jail-Building Boom," Marshall Project, July 2, 2015, www.themarshallproject.org/2015/07/02/california-s-jail-building-boom; *Brown v. Plata*, 563 U.S. 493 (2011), www.supremecourt.gov/opinions/10pdf/09-1233.pdf.

235 **ineffective in controlling crime:** "The Prison Paradox: More Incarceration Will Not Make Us Safer," Vera Institute of Justice, July 2017, www.vera.org/publications/for-the-record-prison-paradox-incarceration-not-safer.

235 **"What [did] we do to them":** Newton, *Man of Tomorrow*, p. 307.

235 **this time in the form of county jails:** Rubin, "California's Jail-Building Boom."

236 **"We are all sinners":** Sara Libby, "Brown Hits San Diego; Falconer Hits Sacramento," Voice of San Diego, September 1, 2017, www.voiceofsandiego.org/topics/government/sacramento-report-brown-in-san-diego-falconer-in-sacramento.

236 **California's number went below 100,000:** Heather Harris, "California's Prison Population Drops Sharply, but Overcrowding Still Threatens Prisoner Health," Public Policy Institute of California, March 2, 2021, www.ppic.org/blog/californias-prison-population-drops-sharply-but-overcrowding-still-threatens-prisoner-health.

237 **"California Is Doomed":** Charles Hugh Smith, "California Is Doomed," *Business Insider*, March 10, 2010.

238 **point to a host of other accomplishments:** Pawel, *The Browns of California*, p. 386.

238 **recognized for providing affordable education:** Ibid., p. 393.

239 **"Human civilization is on the chopping block":** Eric Kirschbaum, "California Gov. Jerry Brown Delivers a Blunt Climate Change Message in Germany," *Los Angeles Times*, November 8, 2017.

239 **"If Trump turns off the satellites":** Alex Johnson, "'California Will Launch Its Own Damn Satellites,' Governor Brown Tells Trump," NBC News, December 15, 2016, www.nbcnews.com/news/us-news/california-will-launch-its-own-damn-satellites-governor-brown-tells-n696771.

239 **filed more than a hundred lawsuits:** Rhonda Lyons, "California's Bill for Fighting Trump in Court? $41 Million So Far," CalMatters, January 22, 2021, calmatters.org/justice/2021/01/california-cost-trump-lawsuits.

239 **One of the reasons:** Lauren Sommer, "Five Big Things Governor Brown Did on Climate Change," WQED Public Media, January 3, 2019, www

.kqed.org/science/1936279/five-big-things-governor-brown-did-on
-climate-change.

240 **favors for key legislators:** Newton, *Man of Tomorrow*, p. 341.

240 **"When I look out here":** Ibid., p. 342.

240 **pegged the median sale price:** California Association of Realtors, "California Housing Market Continues to Normalize As Home Sales and Prices Curb in July, C.A.R. Reports," news release, August 17, 2021, www.prnewswire.com/news-releases/california-housing-market-continues-to-normalize-as-home-sales-and-prices-curb-in-july-car-reports-301357086.html.

241 **251-square-foot home facing a highway:** John R. Ellement, "One Room, Six Figures. This House Epitomizes Boston Area's Wild Real Estate Market," *Boston Globe*, September 30, 2021.

241 **supplemental poverty measure:** U.S. Census Bureau, "The Supplemental Poverty Measure: 2019," www.census.gov/library/publications/2020/demo/p60-272.html.

241 **more than half of the low-income occupants:** Sara Kimberlin, "What Should Be the State's Role in Rent Control? State-Level Tenant Protections Can Be One of the Tools to Address California's Housing Affordability Crisis," California Budget and Policy Center, April 2019, calbudgetcenter.org/resources/what-should-be-the-states-role-in-rent-control-state-level-tenant-protections-can-be-one-of-the-tools-to-address-californias-housing-affordability-crisis/.

242 **have set up special zones:** "San Jose Opens New Safe Parking Site for Homeless Residents Living in RVs," NBC Bay Area, September 6, 2021, www.nbcbayarea.com/news/local/south-bay/san-jose-opens-new-safe-parking-site-for-homeless-residents-living-in-rvs/2648562.

242 **more than 150,000:** Greg Rosalsky, "How California Homelessness Became a Crisis," NPR, June 8, 2021.

242 **Zillow found that communities:** Chris Glynn and Alexander Casey, "Priced Out: Homelessness Rises Faster Where Rent Exceeds a Third of Income," Zillow Research, December 11, 2018, www.zillow.com/research/homelessness-rent-affordability-22247.

242 **"California is a rich state":** Amy Graff, "United Nations Report: SF Homeless Problem Is 'Violation of Human Rights,'" SFGate, October 31, 2018, www.sfgate.com/bayarea/article/rapporteur-United-Nations-San-Francisco-homeless-13351509.php.

243 **"Housing politics in California":** Matt Levin, "Five Things I've Learned Covering California's Housing Crisis That You Should Know," CalMatters, January 12, 2021, calmatters.org/housing/2021/01/california-housing-crisis-lessons.

243 **When a Democratic state senator:** Conor Dougherty and Brad Plumer, "A Bold, Divisive Plan to Wean Californians from Cars," *New York Times*, March 16, 2018.

244   **after attacks from a coalition:** Marisa Kendall, "Inside Livable California's Fight for Single-Family Neighborhoods," *Mercury News*, January 26, 2020, www.mercurynews.com/2020/01/26/inside-livable-californias-fight -for-single-family-neighborhoods.

244   **"We learned that 50 percent of California's households":** Jonathan Woetzel et al., *A Tool Kit to Close California's Housing Gap: 3.5 Million Homes by 2025*, McKinsey Global Institute, October 2016, www.mckinsey .com/featured-insights/urbanization/closing-californias-housing-gap.

244   **a "stretch goal":** Liam Dillon, "Newsom Says He's Done a Good Job Fixing California's Housing Crisis. Facts Say Otherwise," *Los Angeles Times*, October 21, 2019.

244   **join the politically perilous debate:** Conor Dougherty, "California Housing Is a Crisis Newsom Can Take into His Own Hands," *New York Times*, September 16, 2021.

245   **often at below-market rates:** Elizabeth Hansburg and Cassius Rutherford, "Sweeping New Laws Will Provide the Gift of 'Granny Flats,'" *Los Angeles Times*, January 3, 2020.

245   **almost never been enforced:** Liam Dillon, "California Lawmakers Have Tried for 50 Years to Fix the State's Housing Crisis. Here's Why They've Failed," *Los Angeles Times*, June 29, 2017.

245   **followed up with hundreds of letters:** Dougherty, "California Housing Is a Crisis Newsom Can Take into His Own Hands."

245   **"a pretty meaningful failure":** Dillon, "Newsom Says He's Done a Good Job Fixing California's Housing Crisis."

246   **Hundreds of bills piled up:** Conor Dougherty, "Ahead of Recall, Newsom Lets a Polarizing Housing Bill Sit on His Desk," *New York Times*, September 14, 2021.

246   **put the number at eighty-nine thousand:** Avery Hartmans, "As Many as 89,000 Households Have Left San Francisco Since March, the Latest Sign of an Exodus Spurred by the Pandemic," *Business Insider*, December 1, 2020.

246   **many were temporary relocations:** Roland Li and Susie Neilson, "This Data Makes It Official: The San Francisco Exodus Is Over," *San Francisco Chronicle*, July 22, 2021.

247   **outlawed single-family zoning statewide:** California Legislative Information, Senate Bill No. 9, leginfo.legislature.ca.gov/faces/billNavClient .xhtml?bill_id=202120220SB9.

247   **easily rezone neighborhoods:** California Legislative Information, Senate Bill No. 10, leginfo.legislature.ca.gov/faces/billNavClient.xhtml?bill _id=202120220SB10.

247   **allowed cities to override zoning laws:** Hannah Wiley, "New California Housing Law Challenged in Court by Los Angeles Nonprofit," *Sacramento Bee*, September 23, 2021, www.sacbee.com/news/politics-government /capitol-alert/article254476462.html.

247 **"It's a birthday present to the developers":** Ibid.
248 **"there are no safeguards":** Los Angeles Conservancy, "SB 9 and SB 10," www.laconservancy.org/issues/sb-9-and-sb-10.
248 **began collecting signatures:** Alexandra Applegate, "Fight Isn't Over for Many Opponents of S.B. 9 and 10," USC Annenberg Media, www.uscannenbergmedia.com/2021/09/23/fight-isnt-over-for-many-opponents-of-sb-9-and-10.
248 **"This isn't just a California problem":** "To Save California, Sacrifice Single-Family Zoning," editorial, *Los Angeles Times*, August 22, 2021.
249 **California cities issued more than 26,000:** "The Three Facts of California's ADU Boom," Accessory Dwellings, accessorydwellings.org/2021/06/10/the-three-facts-of-californias-adu-boom.
249 **every GOP candidate:** Thomas Elias, "Proposed Housing Bills Could Cause Radical Changes in California," *Desert Sun*, August 2, 2021, www.desertsun.com/story/opinion/columnists/2021/08/02/proposed-housing-bills-could-cause-radical-changes-california/5455563001.
250 **Rents are rising fast:** Juan Pablo Garnham, "In San Antonio, Rents Are Rising but Wages Aren't," *Texas Tribune*, January 16, 2020, www.texastribune.org/2020/01/16/san-antonio-rent-rising-wages-arent/; Brandon Formby, Darla Cameron, and Chris Essig, "As Texas Grows, an Affordable Housing Crisis Looms," *Texas Tribune*, October 5, 2018, www.texastribune.org/2018/10/05/affordable-housing-texas-things-know.
250 **three abandoned children:** Nicole Hensley et al., "Abandoned Kids Lived for Weeks with No Power, Relied on Neighbor for Food and Phone Charging," *Houston Chronicle*, October 24, 2021, www.houstonchronicle.com/news/houston-texas/crime/article/Skeletal-remains-three-children-found-in-Harris-16559130.php.
250 **"disjointed and dangerous child-protection system":** Emma Platoff, "Years After a Judge Ordered Fixes, Texas' Child Welfare System Continues to Expose Children to Harm, Federal Monitors Say," *Texas Tribune*, June 16, 2020, www.texastribune.org/2020/06/16/texas-child-welfare-harm-federal-monitors.
251 **mental health system was severely overburdened:** Alex Stuckey, "How Texas Fails the Mentally Ill," *Houston Chronicle*, February 25, 2021, www.houstonchronicle.com/news/investigations/article/In-Crisis-How-Texas-cuts-fails-mentally-ill-Texans-15966617.php.
251 **the industry was doing little:** James Osborne, "Texas Natural Gas Industry Showing Limited Progress in Winter Storm Prep, Experts Say," *Houston Chronicle*, October 19, 2021, www.houstonchronicle.com/business/energy/article/Texas-natural-gas-industry-winter-storm-prep-16543874.php.
251 **help complete his border wall:** Uriel J. Garcia, "Five Firms Being Considered for Design and Construction of Texas-Mexico Border Wall That Gov. Greg Abbott Promised," *Texas Tribune*, October 26, 2021, www

.texastribune.org/2021/10/26/texas-mexico-border-wall-contract-greg
-abbott.

251   **legally questionable state trespassing charges**: Jolie McCullough, "Texas
Prosecutor Drops Charges After Migrants Claimed They Were Marched
to Private Property, Then Arrested for Trespassing," *Texas Tribune*, October 5, 2021, www.texastribune.org/2021/10/05/texas-migrants-arrest
-charges-dropped.

251   **short forty thousand qualified employees**: David S. Andrews et al., "The
Talent Well Has Run Dry," Accenture Strategy, 2017, www.accenture.com
/t20170630T025458__w__/us-en/_acnmedia/PDF-55/Accenture
-Strategy-Talent-Well-Oil-Gas.pdf.

252   **Innumerable immigration experts**: David J. Bier, "Why the Wall Won't
Work," *Reason*, April 10, 2017, www.cato.org/publications/commentary
/why-wall-wont-work.

252   **child welfare agency website**: Patrick Svitek, "GOP Primary Foe Don
Huffines Sees Impact as Gov. Greg Abbott Pushes Rightward," *Texas Tribune*, October 14, 2021, www.texastribune.org/2021/10/14/greg-abbott
-2022-don-huffines.

253   **not even adopted a strategy**: David Schechter and Chance Horner, "Texans Face Greater Risk of Heat, Drought and Hurricanes, but Abbott Administration Has No Plans to Tackle Future Threats of Climate Change,"
WFAA website, November 7, 2021, www.wfaa.com/article/tech/science
/climate-change/texas-climate-change-risks-gov-abbott-un-summit
-scotland/287-75b20337-0f82-4f83-a214-09b2f07309be.

253   **I am in Midland**: Patrick Svitek, "Governor Greg Abbott Says He'll Fight
Joe Biden's Energy and Climate Agenda," *Texas Tribune*, January 28, 2021,
www.texastribune.org/2021/01/28/abbott-biden-energy.

9. PROGRESSIVE FEDERALISM

255   **enjoyed wide public support**: Monmouth University Poll, "National:
Biden Impact on Rich, Poor, and Middle Class," news release, July 29, 2021,
www.monmouth.edu/polling-institute/documents/monmouthpoll_us
_072921.pdf.

257   **64 percent of the nation's economic output**: Mark Muro and Sifan Liu,
"Another Clinton-Trump Divide: High-Output America vs Low-Output
America," Brookings Institution, November 29, 2016, www.brookings.edu
/blog/the-avenue/2016/11/29/another-clinton-trump-divide-high
-output-america-vs-low-output-america.

257   **52 percent of the nation's GDP**: Richard C. Schragger, "Federalism, Metropolitanism, and the Problem of the States," *Virginia Law Review*, December 2019, Vol. 105, Issue 8, pp. 1537–1604, www.jstor.org/stable/10
.2307/26891056.

257   **with the help of model legislation**: Ibid.

258 **discriminating against any source of energy:** Erin Douglas, "Texas Gov. Greg Abbott Signs Law to Bar City Climate Plans from Banning Natural Gas as Fuel Source," *Texas Tribune*, May 18, 2021, www.texastribune.org /2021/05/18/texas-natural-gas-bans-climate-plans.

258 **overturning the regulation:** Priscilla Aguirre, "Gov. Greg Abbott Says Austin's New Dine-in Restrictions Are Not Allowed. Period," *Houston Chronicle*, December 30, 2020, www.chron.com/news/local/article/Austin -dine-in-greg-abbot-15836296.php?IPID=Chron-HP-CP-Spotlight.

258 **twenty-six states that had passed laws:** Economic Policy Institute, "Workers' Rights Preemption in the U.S.," August 2019, www.epi.org/preemption-map.

258 **"Preemption moves government action away":** Alan Stonecipher and Ben Wilcox, *Preemption Strategy 2.0*, Integrity Florida, February 2021, www.integrityflorida.org/wp-content/uploads/2021/02/Preemption-2.0 -Report_FINAL.pdf.

259 **2.1 million civilian employees:** Congressional Research Service, "Federal Workforce Statistics Sources: OPM and OMB," June 24, 2021, sgp.fas.org /crs/misc/R43590.pdf.

259 **state and local payrolls of nearly 20 million:** Elizabeth Dippold et al., "Annual Survey of Public Employment and Payroll Summary Report: 2019," U.S. Census Bureau, www.census.gov/content/dam/Census/library /publications/2020/econ/2019_summary.pdf.

259 **"Washington can't go it alone":** Heather K. Gerken et al., "Progressive Federalism: A User's Guide," *Democracy Journal*, Spring 2017, democracy journal.org/magazine/44/progressive-federalism-a-users-guide.

260 **gas-powered lawn equipment:** Sebastian Blanco, "California Enacts Ban on Gas-Powered Lawn Mowers," *Car and Driver*, October 19, 2021, www .caranddriver.com/news/a38004981/california-ban-gas-powered-lawn -equipment.

260 **brought suit against tax preparers:** Gerken et al., "Progressive Federalism."

261 **cooperated in setting standards:** Council of State Governments, "What Are Interstate Compacts?," compacts.csg.org/compacts.

262 **have eclipsed political parties:** Raymond J. La Raja and Jonathan Rauch, "Want to Reduce the Influence of Super PACs? Strengthen State Parties," Brookings Institution, March 24, 2016, www.brookings.edu/blog/fixgov /2016/03/24/want-to-reduce-the-influence-of-super-pacs-strengthen -state-parties.

262 **reneged on its promise:** Matt Friedman, "Dark Money Disclosure Effort Went Dark During Pandemic," *Politico*, February 4, 2021.

262 **California has a law:** J.T. Stepleton, "When State Laws Are Away, Federal PACs Will Play," FollowTheMoney.org, January 8, 2018.

263 **fifty national companies signed a letter:** Joseph Choi, "More Than 50 Companies Sign Letter Opposing Texas Abortion Law," *The Hill*, September 21, 2021.

263 **paid for television and digital ads:** Corporate Accountability Action, "Corporate Accountability Action Launches #OfftheBANWagon

Campaign to Hold Financial Backers of Texas Abortion Ban Accountable," news release, September 23, 2021, www.prnewswire.com/news-releases /corporate-accountability-action-launches-offthebanwagon-campaign-to -hold-financial-backers-of-texas-abortion-ban-accountable-301383994 .html.

263   **passed laws or issued executive orders:** Human Rights Watch, "States Use Anti-boycott Laws to Punish Responsible Businesses," April 23, 2019, www.hrw.org/news/2019/04/23/us-states-use-anti-boycott-laws-punish -responsible-businesses.

264   **"specialized knowledge is transmitted easily":** Richard C. Schragger, "Federalism, Metropolitanism, and the Problem of the States," *Virginia Law Review*, December 2019, Vol. 105, Issue 8, pp. 1537–1604, www.jstor .org/stable/10.2307/26891056.

265   **"As the justices are well aware":** "To Protect Abortion Rights, Turn to Elections," *New York Times*, November 27, 2021.

Index

About the Author

William Kleinknecht is a longtime newspaper reporter who covered politics, government, criminal justice, and the environment for the *Detroit Free Press, New York Daily News,* and *Newark Star-Ledger.* The author of *The Man Who Sold the World: Ronald Reagan and the Betrayal of Main Street America* and *The New Ethnic Mobs: The Changing Face of Organized Crime in America,* he lives in Ridgewood, New Jersey.

Publishing in the Public Interest

Thank you for reading this book published by The New Press. The New Press is a nonprofit, public interest publisher. New Press books and authors play a crucial role in sparking conversations about the key political and social issues of our day.

We hope you enjoyed this book and that you will stay in touch with The New Press. Here are a few ways to stay up to date with our books, events, and the issues we cover:

- Sign up at www.thenewpress.com/subscribe to receive updates on New Press authors and issues and to be notified about local events

- www.facebook.com/newpressbooks

- www.twitter.com/thenewpress

- www.instagram.com/thenewpress

Please consider buying New Press books for yourself; for friends and family; or to donate to schools, libraries, community centers, prison libraries, and other organizations involved with the issues our authors write about.

The New Press is a 501(c)(3) nonprofit organization. You can also support our work with a tax-deductible gift by visiting www.thenewpress.com/donate.